W9-AWN-514

Shakespeare in American Life

Shakespeare in American Life

Compiled and edited by
Virginia Mason Vaughan and Alden T. Vaughan

Folger Shakespeare Library
Washington, DC 2007

This volume has been published in conjunction with the exhibition
Shakespeare in American Life presented at the Folger Shakespeare
Library, Washington, DC, from 8 March through 18 August 2007,
in celebration of the Library's 75th anniversary.

Gail Kern Paster, Director
Richard Kuhta, Eric Weinmann Librarian
Rachel Doggett, Andew W. Mellon Curator of Books Emerita

The exhibition and this catalogue accompanying it have been
funded by the Winton and Carolyn Blount Exhibition Fund and the
Andrew W. Mellon Publication Fund of Folger Shakespeare Library.

Copyright ©2007
by Folger Shakespeare Library.
All rights reserved.

Printed in the United States.

Distributed by University of Washington Press,
Seattle and London
ISBN 10: 0-295-98715-4
ISBN 13: 978-0-295-98715-6

Photographs by Julie Ainsworth and Tom Wachs.

Frontispiece:
Detail from "Mr. Ira Aldridge as Aaron" (CAT. NO. 84)

75 Years | FolgerSHAKESPEARE
LIBRARY
Advancing knowledge & the arts

Contents

Foreword
Gail Kern Paster

There is no more eloquent expression of the centrality of Shakespeare to American life than the beautiful white marble building, two blocks from the U.S. Capitol, which houses the ashes of Henry Clay Folger and Emily Jordan Folger and the unique collection they gave to the American people. This catalogue honors the Folger Shakespeare Library's seventy-fifth anniversary by celebrating this centrality. The Folgers' passion for Shakespeare was rooted in a quintessentially American belief that England's National Poet, properly understood, was a spokesman for republican values and a symbol, in his life's remarkable history and achievement, of the American commonplace that extraordinary talents might have unexceptional origins.

As this catalogue demonstrates, American society harbored an ambivalent attitude towards theatrical performance from its inception, yet embraced the words of Shakespeare with a fervor equal to that of Shakespeare's own compatriots. Shakespeare was a part of this country's colonial heritage that was easiest to assimilate, and the story of his absorption by and effect upon American culture encompasses virtually all aspects of American life. He is found on the frontier where an edition of Shakespeare and a copy of the Bible were cherished possessions in the humblest home; his works are travestied and parodied by blackface minstrel shows; he becomes the battleground for American and British theatrical rivalries and performance styles; and he emerges as an instrument of assimilation for immigrant children.

A seventy-fifth-anniversary Folger exhibition on Shakespeare and American life was the inspiration of Rachel Doggett, Andrew W. Mellon Curator of Books and Exhibitions Emerita, and it was our collective good fortune to enlist the uniquely qualified team of Virginia Mason Vaughan and Alden T. Vaughan to serve as guest curators. Their wonderfully sympathetic working relationship with Rachel and the entire Folger library staff made work on this exhibition a special pleasure for all involved. Rachel and the Vaughans together assembled a distinguished array of scholarly experts on the many aspects of this broad topic. Their masterful essays—contained herein—branch far beyond the physical limits of the Folger's Great Hall to suggest Shakespeare's deep involvement with American history from the nation's inception and to document his deep influence on all American popular art forms to the present day.

This exhibition, like all others, has benefited greatly from the generosity of lenders. We are deeply grateful to the Bermuda Maritime Museum; the American Antiquarian Society; the Nantucket Historical Association Museum; the Performing Arts Reading Room, Music Division, Library of Congress; and Robert and Hildegard Armstrong. Folger staff, especially Curator of Art and Special Collections Erin Blake and Curator of Manuscripts Heather Wolfe, contributed their special expertise, and Leigh Anne Palmer was the inspired organizer of the "American Scrapbooks" interlude.

For Rachel, who retired in October 2006 after forty years of service to the Folger, this exhibition and catalogue consummate a brilliant career that has seen a period of steady growth in the Folger collection and a remarkable transformation in the scope, authority, and graphic elegance of Folger exhibitions. As a capstone to such a career, this exhibition and catalogue are simply stunners: together, they express the breadth and depth of the Folger's American Shakespeare holdings and demonstrate Shakespeare's central place in the rich canvas of the American cultural landscape.

Introduction

Virginia Mason Vaughan and Alden T. Vaughan

William Shakespeare would surely be pleased, and probably surprised, at how thoroughly Americans have embraced his plays and poems. At his death in 1616, English-speaking toeholds in America were few (Virginia since 1607, Bermuda since 1609, and Newfoundland since 1610) and barely viable; probably no settlement contained a single Shakespeare publication. But as this catalogue and its companion exhibition graphically demonstrate, by the eve of the American Revolution, Shakespeare had become a major component of American culture and remains so to this day.

The library established by Henry Clay Folger and his wife, Emily Jordan Folger, the foremost American collectors of writings by and about Shakespeare, has played a vital, ongoing role in that cultural symbiosis. When planning their library in the late 1920s, the Folgers were concerned primarily with a safe and accessible home for their lifelong gathering of Shakespeare books and manuscripts, especially the rare Quartos and First Folios. Mr. Folger assumed that only four or five readers would use the library at a time, enjoying the atmosphere of an elegant private home and kept warm in winter by the huge reading-room fireplace; visiting scholars would be his personal guests. The founding father did not live to carry out that plan, but his expectation of only a few readers initially proved accurate. Fewer than one hundred scholars availed themselves of the library's resources in the year after its dedication on Shakespeare's birthday in 1932. But over time the collection grew, as the Folgers intended, through additions to the writings of Shakespeare (early and modern editions) and acquisitions in Tudor-Stuart history and literature and theater history from Shakespeare's day to the present, including audio and film recordings.

The Folger's holdings also expanded geographically. Under director Louis B. Wright (1948–68), an authority on the cultural life of the British colonies in America, as well as Elizabethan England, the numbers of volumes on early

America—Spanish, French, Dutch, and English—grew immeasurably, and succeeding directors expanded continental European holdings. Inevitably, the Folger Library's enlarged resources attracted scholars of several academic disciplines other than that of Shakespearean literature, many from nationalities other than American and British, so that the Folger Shakespeare Library is now more diverse and influential than the founders could have predicted. It serves hundreds of readers a month in two Reading Rooms and several carrels, scores of professors and graduate students a year in a lively program of seminars and workshops, and the public at large, including countless schoolchildren, through its outreach programs and web site.

"Shakespeare in American Life" celebrates the extraordinary English poet's influence on American culture—whether high-, low-, or middlebrow—to mark the 150th anniversary of Henry Folger's birth and the 75th anniversary of the great library he and Emily Folger created for Shakespearean scholarship. A sampler of such scholarship is presented here in nine essays that offer contexts for the multitude of images and objects on display in the Folger Library's Great Hall during the spring and summer of 2007, many of them—and a few additional images—reproduced in this catalogue.

The nine authors are themselves a reflection of the Folger Library's ever-expanding resources and intellectual vitality. Although we are of widely disparate ages, backgrounds, ethnicities, institutional affiliations, and specific interests, we share a fascination with Shakespeare's impact on America and firsthand experience using the Folger Library's incomparable resources. The youngest of us has used the library for a few years, the oldest for several decades. One is a former member of the Folger's redoubtable staff, and another still is. The essays—most of them researched and several written at the Folger—explore Shakespeare's influence on America's cultural history from a variety of perspectives. Chronologically, they range from the colonial period to the adoption of Shakespeare as an "American genius" in the nineteenth century; to twentieth-century musical comedy, film, and theater; and finally to Shakespeare as we know him in twenty-first-century America. Culturally, the essays range from the academic (editors and scholars), to the theatrical (Shakespeare's continuous presence on the American stage), to the popular (the appropriation of Shakespeare as a familiar icon in advertising, folk art, and kitsch).

It is a special honor for us to serve as guest curators for *Shakespeare in American Life* and to help celebrate the Folger Shakespeare Library's 75th anniversary by coediting this catalogue. Thirty years ago, we met over coffee in the Founders' Room when Alden, an American historian, was mining the Folger's texts on England's early footholds in North America, while Virginia was writing a Shakespeare monograph. Since then, we have collaborated on several projects, most of them researched and written within the Folger's welcoming walls. To the scholars who use its matchless facilities, the Folger is an intellectual home away from home. Although there are no fires in the Old Reading Room fireplace, Folger readers find comfort and inspiration in the stained-glass windows, tapestries, and elegant décor. With the support of its remarkable staff, access to an incredible storehouse of materials, and the encouragement of an international community of fellow researchers, Folger readers are the most fortunate scholars we know. We are lucky to be among them.

Both the exhibition and the catalogue on *Shakespeare in American Life* draw on materials from the Folger Library's collections, except where we borrowed items from other institutions to illustrate particular points. For lending us treasures in their possession, we are deeply grateful to the American Antiquarian Society, Robert and Hildegard Armstrong, the Bermuda Maritime Museum, the Nantucket

Historical Association, and the Library of Congress. For the financial support that made it all possible, we are grateful to the Winton and Carolyn Blount Exhibition Fund and the Andrew W. Mellon Publication Fund of the Folger Shakespeare Library.

Many hands have helped to mount the exhibition and prepare the catalogue. Rachel Doggett, Andrew W. Mellon Curator of Books Emerita, whose wealth of experience in the supervision of exhibits and catalogues has been invaluable, directed this project from start to finish with her unmatched combination of knowledge, patience, and efficiency. During the early stages, we benefited from the work of Leigh Anne Palmer, who culled uncatalogued collections and scrapbooks to find some of the most intriguing and unusual items in our display. We are also grateful to Louis B. Thalheimer Head of Reference Georgianna Ziegler, Curator of Manuscripts Heather Wolfe, and Curator of Art and Special Collections Erin Blake for providing information on a host of topics. Betsy Walsh and the Reading Room staff were always patient and encouraging, no matter how often they had to locate uncatalogued items or move huge scrapbooks. Head of Conservation J. Franklin Mowery and his staff took care that the many fragile items on display were properly preserved and displayed. Finally, throughout the preparation of this exhibition, Gail Kern Paster, Folger Director, and Richard Kuhta, Eric Weinmann Librarian, provided encouragement and support. To all, we extend our heartfelt thanks. To Rachel Doggett, we dedicate the catalogue.

W. H. Harrington. *Wreck of Sea Venture*. Painting, 1981.
Courtesy of the Bermuda Maritime Museum.
CAT. NO. 7

Shakespeare Discovers America: America Discovers Shakespeare

Alden T. Vaughan

When three shiploads of Englishmen launched their nation's first permanent American outpost at Jamestown, Virginia, in May 1607, Shakespeare must have been far from their thoughts. Some early immigrants probably saw a Shakespeare play in London (he had already written thirty or more), and a few literate colonists may have read a Shakespeare play or poem (many had been printed), but the fledgling Americans had no time for theater and little taste for books, save manuals of practical advice. America's discovery of Shakespeare—in the Renaissance meaning of discover, to reveal or make known—was far in the future.

Meanwhile, Shakespeare discovered America, although not as quickly or prominently as many other playwrights and poets. George Chapman, Ben Jonson, and John Marston's *Eastward Ho* (1605), for example, spoofed the presumed survivors of the "Lost Colony" at Roanoke and urged further ventures to "Virginia [which] longs till we share the rest of her maiden-head." Englishmen in America, boasted Captain Seagull, have "no more law then conscience, and not too much of eyther." Michael Drayton's "Ode to the Virginian Voyage" urged the expedition that founded Jamestown "To get the pearle and gold, / And ours to hold, / VIRGINIA,/ Earth's only Paradise." A few years later, a character in Jonson's *Epicœne* claimed to have drawn a portrait of Nomentack, an American Indian who visited London in 1608. Shakespeare, except for a few passing references to Spanish America and the West Indies, ignored the New World and its denizens until a furious storm, an improbable landfall, and poignant reports by several participants inspired him to draw on English America in his final plays, especially the last one he wrote by himself.

The story of the *Sea Venture*'s wreck on the Bermuda Islands has often been told, but it bears a brief summary here because it opened Shakespeare's works to the influences of English colonization and, perhaps more importantly, because it undergirds the theory—espoused intermittently since the late nineteenth century—that Shakespeare set *The Tempest* on Bermuda and intended the characters to reflect early American persons and events. Bermuda, to this day, reminds visitors of its reputed *Tempest* connections with venues like Prospero's Cave (a night club), Caliban's Bar, and the Ariel Sands Beach Club.

The five hundred potential colonists in nine ships that departed England in early June 1609 expected to sail north of Bermuda on their westward route from the Canary Islands to Virginia. When they were several days short of their destination, a massive hurricane scattered the fleet. One vessel sank; seven ships straggled into Jamestown, weeks overdue. The flagship *Sea Venture*, carrying the fleet's admiral, Sir George Somers, and Virginia's new governor, Sir Thomas Gates, never arrived at Jamestown and was presumed to have been lost.

News of the tragedy reached England when the surviving ships headed home from Jamestown, "laden with nothing but bad reports and letters of discouragement." England's only American colony, readers learned, was beset by Indians, ravaged by sickness, verging of starvation, and shorn of legitimate leadership. Its "headless and unbridled multitude," lamented the Virginia Company of London (the colony's supervisory body), had succumbed to "disorder and riot." Company spokesmen blamed everything, directly or indirectly, on "the Tempest."[1]

Against all expectations, the *Sea Venture* had weathered the storm—barely. Among the survivors, William Strachey described the experience most vividly in a very long letter (twenty-two folio pages when finally printed), written in Virginia to an unnamed lady in England.[2] For three days and four nights, Strachey remembered, all hands—crew and passengers, noblemen and commoners—pumped, bailed, cast trunks and barrels overboard, and jettisoned much of the ship's rigging, while sailors, lighting their way with candles (see cat. no. 2, a candlestick from the *Sea Venture*), stuffed the leaking hull with whatever came to hand, even beef from the ship's larder. Many distraught souls, resigned to a watery death, bid their friends farewell or took refuge in drink. But "it pleased God," another survivor gratefully recalled, to push the *Sea Venture* within three-quarters of a mile of Bermuda, where it "fast lodged and locked" between coral boulders.[3] All 150 passengers and crew rode the ship's boats to land.

No humans, European or aboriginal, inhabited the Bermuda archipelago when the *Sea Venture* fortuitously arrived. In the previous century, ships of many nations had crashed on its reefs, and a few survivors had lived to describe the "Isle of Devils," but the most tangible signs of those accidental visits were the wild hogs whose ancestors had swum ashore from shipwrecked vessels. Yet Bermuda was, as the *Sea Venture*'s passengers quickly realized, an island paradise strategically located for transatlantic commerce or piracy and free for the taking. Instead of the reputed devils and malicious spirits, the English encountered docile and abundant birds, fish, tortoises, and the immigrant hogs; fruits and berries were ubiquitous. The climate was salubrious, the environment healthy. During the next nine months, Admiral Somers supervised the construction of two seaworthy vessels from Bermuda cedar and the *Sea Venture*'s salvageable timbers and tackle.

Not everyone pitched in. Some men preferred a life of ease on Bermuda to the imagined perils of Virginia and refused to build the ships. Other men objected to cutting and carrying cedar logs, still others resented Gates and Somers's firm authority, and a few cast covetous eyes on the survivors' valuable goods. Strachey's letter bristles with charges of "conspiracy," "Mutinie," "Rebellion," and "bloudy issues and mischiefes." By the time the *Sea Venture*'s passengers and crew sailed to Jamestown in the newly completed *Deliverance* and *Patience* in May 1610, one man had been executed, one (maybe two) had been murdered,

and two men who hid from harsh punishment were left behind.

The Virginia colony, Strachey discovered on arrival, was comparably chaotic. "[W]e found the Pallisadoes torne downe, . . . the Gates from off the hinges, and emptie houses . . . burnt" for firewood. Outside the fort, "the *Indian[s]* killed as fast . . . if our men stirred but beyond the bounds of their blockhouse, as Famine and Pestilence did within." With only sixty men and women surviving from the several hundred who had reached Jamestown since 1607, Gates and the disheveled remnant abandoned the colony; only the unexpected arrival of fresh settlers and supplies under a new governor, Francis West, Lord De La Warr, saved the day. With order largely restored, Sir Thomas Gates left for England in early September 1610, carrying Strachey's letter. It was too candid for the Virginia Company of London to permit publication, but the manuscript fascinated many readers, including William Shakespeare. *The Tempest* (completed in late 1610 or early 1611) borrowed some of Strachey's words, phrases, and themes, as well as touches from Silvester Jourdain's less revealing pamphlet (1610) and many other—mostly non-American—texts and ideas.[4] In 1613, Shakespeare and John Fletcher would take a leaf from Ben Jonson's *Epicœne* by invoking an Indian from England's colonial sphere. A muscular captive named Epenow, displayed frequently in London "as a wonder," almost surely inspired *Henry VIII*'s porter to smirk, "have wee some strange Indian with the great *Toole*, come to Court, the women so besiege us?" (5.3). English America had entered Shakespeare's literary source book.

The barriers to launching Shakespeare's influence in America were more formidable. Even after sheer survival had largely been accomplished, social stability and economic viability came slowly to the English colonies—Virginia,

Plymouth, Massachusetts, Maryland, and the rest—each carved from a rugged and often hostile environment. The demand was insatiable for craftsmen and laborers of almost every kind but not for actors or, for similar reasons, for portrait or landscape painters or musicians, except drummers and buglers. Colonizing companies discouraged the migration of entertainers, who were widely perceived as useless and distracting, a policy that would prevail throughout British America in the seventeenth century and well into the eighteenth, especially in New England and, almost as virulently, Pennsylvania. Works by Shakespeare or any other playwright were viewed with suspicion by church and state.

Verbal assaults on the theater emanated from both sides of the Atlantic. Less than three years after the founding of the Virginia outpost, the Reverend William Crashaw reminded its parent company in London that actors, being "Idle persons," were unwelcome in the colony; the company advertised repeatedly for "honest and good artificers," which implicitly excluded players and playwrights.[5] The founders of other English colonies followed suit, insisting on diligent, productive workers.

The puritanical mood that forced England to close its theaters in 1642, not to reopen them until the Stuart Restoration of 1660, dominated New England. In 1687, the eminent Congregational clergyman Increase Mather castigated "pernicious" stage plays for wasting time and money and for undermining piety: "Persons who have been Corrupted by *Stage-Plays*, are seldom, and with much difficulty Reclaimed." Twenty-seven years later, Judge Samuel Sewall refused to allow plays in Boston's Town House: "Let not Christian Boston goe beyond Heathen Rome in the practice of shameful Vanities." As late as 1750, the Massachusetts General Court tried to prevent "the many and great mischiefs which arise from publick stage-plays" by authorizing fines of twenty pounds on the venue's proprietor and five pounds on every actor and spectator, "one half to his majesty . . . the other half to him or them that shall inform."[6] That deterrent sufficed; Massachusetts had no "Synagogues of Satan," nor did its neighboring colonies. Rhode Island's prohibition of the theater was even stricter.[7]

The Quakers of Pennsylvania, later joined by Baptists, Presbyterians, and Lutherans, were similarly hostile to the theater. William Penn's laws of 1682 authorized severe punishment for "stage plays, cards, dice, . . . masques, revels, bull-baitings, cock-fightings, bear-baitings, and the like, which excite the people to rudeness, cruelty, looseness, and irreligion."[8] Eighty years later, a Pennsylvania writer urged, satirically, that American parents send their children to the theater to learn "the genuine airs, manners, and insincerity of a court; . . . all the lasciviousness of a stew; . . . [and] every species of fraud and iniquity." Not until the third quarter of the eighteenth century, when the Quakers and their allies no longer dominated Pennsylvania's political and social mores, did the government relent.

To counter the critics' charges that stage plays undercut morality and encouraged idleness, supporters countered that plays taught valuable moral lessons. In New England especially, the earliest Shakespeare productions were readings rather than performances. At Newport, Rhode Island, in 1761, for example, *Othello* was advertised and subsequently presented as "Moral Dialogues, in Five Parts," which would enlighten its auditors to "the evil effects of Jealousy and other Bad Passions." Touring companies sometimes generated public sympathy by dedicating the profits of one or more shows to charitable causes—the proceeds from one performance in Newport went to buy corn for the poor.[9] It was an ongoing contest in which the theater's friends made slow and uneven progress.

Pronouncements against actors and theaters did not prevent colonists from acquiring Shakespeare's texts. A few immigrants surely brought Shakespeare's plays and poems in their baggage. American booksellers, recognizing an emerging market for Shakespeare, imported individual plays and complete sets, while colonists returning from trips abroad for study or business included plays or poems by Shakespeare among the volumes they carried home. A prominent Virginia planter, William Byrd of Westover, owned a copy of the Fourth Folio, presumably acquired while he was in England from 1684 to 1696. A copy of *Macbeth* was mentioned in a Virginia will of 1700, and another Virginia will, written in 1718, lists Shakespeare's complete works, probably Nicholas Rowe's edition of 1709 or 1714, rather than one of the four bulky and expensive folio versions. The Virginia Colony had enough copies of Shakespeare's plays by 1771 for Thomas Jefferson to include Edward Capell's recent edition in a list of essential volumes for a friend's private library. "[A] lively and lasting sense of filial duty," Jefferson explained, "is more effectually impressed on the mind of a son or daughter by reading King Lear, than by all the dry volumes of ethics and divinity that ever were written."[10]

Literate Pennsylvanians were not far behind the Virginians. Colonial secretary James Logan owned a set of Rowe's eight-volume edition of 1714, and Benjamin Franklin caused the Library Company of Philadelphia in 1746 to purchase Thomas Hanmer's six-volume set of 1744. A visiting Scottish physician, Alexander Hamilton, spent the morning of 18 September 1744 reading *Timon of Athens*, which, he opined, abounded "with inimitable beauties peculiar to this excellent author." Hamilton neglected to say whether he had brought the volume with him or borrowed it in Philadelphia. A decade later, Hamilton's facetious history of an Annapolis, Maryland, gentlemen's club frequently cited the plays and poems of "the Celebrated Shakespeare."[11]

Despite New England's long-standing contempt for the theater, many of its citizens read, and some owned, Shakespeare's plays. In 1722 the library of Boston's *New-England Courant*, published by Benjamin Franklin's elder brother James, owned the complete works. At about the same time, Harvard College purchased a set, and Yale soon received one by gift. Those two college holdings suggest that many New England students were at least dabbling in the dramas. Perhaps young John Adams (class of 1755) first encountered them at Harvard; in any case, the diaries he kept as a schoolteacher and student of the law reveal his fascination with the writer he called "great Shakespeare." Adams's diary entries for the 1750s and 1760s attest to his familiarity with *King Lear, Romeo and Juliet, Henry VIII,* and *Timon of Athens,* and it is likely that he had read most of the other plays as well. In 1772, Adams praised "Shakespeare, that great Master of every Affection of the Heart and every Sentiment of the Mind as well as all the Powers of Expres-sion." Nor was Adams's veneration of Shakespeare unusual in eighteenth-century New England, at least among Harvard graduates. His cousin by marriage, Josiah Quincy, Jr. (class of 1763), copied his favorite Shakespeare passages into a commonplace book exclusively for that purpose (he had another for excerpts from political writers, ancient and modern) and peppered his own writings with Shake-speare quotations and allusions. The Adams-Quincy clan, in fact, was almost addicted to the Bard. John Quincy Adams, born in 1767 (Harvard class of 1787), would later boast that he had been, "man and boy, a reader of Shakespeare. . . . A pocket edition of him was among the books on my mother's nursery table, and at ten years of age I was as familiarly acquainted with his lovers and his clowns, as with Robin-son Crusoe, the Pilgrim's Progress, and the Bible."[12]

The edition on Abigail Adams's table was necessarily an English import, as were all versions of Shakespeare's

Advertisement in *New-York Mercury.* New York, 1761.
Courtesy of the American Antiquarian Society.
CAT. NO. 5

complete works before 1795. By midcentury, American buyers could choose between a substantial array of English editions: the folios of 1623, 1632, 1663, and 1685 (expensive and hard to find); Nicholas Rowe's two editions of 1709 (six volumes) and a third in 1714 (eight volumes), Alexander Pope's of 1723–25 (six volumes), Lewis Theobald's of 1733 (seven volumes) and 1740 (eight volumes), Thomas Hanmer's of 1744 (six volumes), and William Warburton's of 1747 (eight volumes). The enthusiasm for Shakespeare in England after midcentury, highlighted by the Stratford Jubilee of 1769, spawned several editions in ten volumes, such as Samuel Johnson's in 1766, Edwin Capell's in 1767–68, and Samuel Johnson and George Steevens's in 1773. A generous choice for the colonial buyer, indeed, but all from the mother country.

Although no complete edition of Shakespeare's plays was published in the western hemisphere before the final decade of the eighteenth century, two plays were printed separately. On 20 July 1761, Hugh Gaine, a New York printer, bookseller, and stationer, announced in the *New-York Mercury* that he had published that day a considerable assortment of comedies and tragedies, including *The Tempest* (how fitting!) and *King Lear.* Gaine's newspaper advertisement is the only surviving evidence (no copies of the plays have been found), but presumably the first American printing of *King Lear* reproduced Nahum Tate's seventeenth-century version of Shakespeare's text, while *The Tempest* probably appeared in the John Dryden-William Davenant adaptation that largely displaced Shakespeare's version between the Restoration and the early nineteenth century.[13] Presumably, Gaine also printed the two Shakespeare plays—along with works by Ben Jonson, Nicholas Rowe, John Vanbrugh, Ambrose Philips, and others—because he could sell enough copies to make a profit. A century and a half after the founding of Jamestown, American customers could finally buy American editions

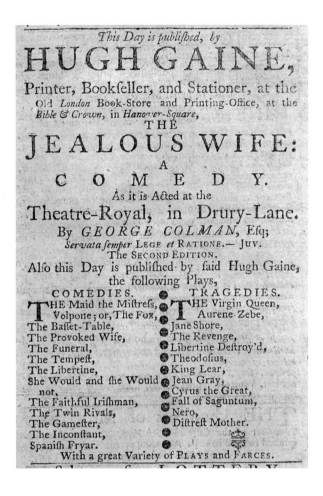

of two Shakespeare standbys, although those editions had almost certainly been edited—and perhaps drastically revised—in England.

In the eighteenth century, as now, reading Shakespeare's plays was one thing, while seeing them performed was quite another. Many avid readers of Shakespeare, the elder Adams among them, may have enjoyed published versions of the plays for years, perhaps decades, before they witnessed a performance. That was especially the case in New England but, broadly speaking, it was true throughout British America during the colonial and Revolutionary eras.

New York, not Virginia, hosted the first known performance of a Shakespeare play. Touring British acting companies had appeared as early as the second decade of the eighteenth century in Williamsburg, Virginia and soon after in other eastern communities, but no evidence survives of Shakespeare productions until 1730. In early March of that year, Dr. Joachimus Bertrand advertised a forthcoming performance of *Romeo and Juliet* in which he would, appropriately, play the apothecary. According to the *New-York Gazette*, Shakespeare's play would be "the first to be acted at the Revenge Meeting House, which is fitted up for that purpose."[14] Nothing is now known about the quality of the performance or its faithfulness to Shakespeare's text—or, indeed, whether it actually occurred, although it is assumed that Dr. Bertrand, having quoted extensively from Shakespeare in his newspaper advertisement and having secured and prepared the venue, must have staged at least one performance. The absence of further records (the *Gazette* for that period is lost) permits no conclusions about the size and composition of the audience or additional performances of the play.[15]

Twenty years passed before the next documented Shakespeare performance. In 1749, Walter Murray and Thomas Keen formed a theatrical company that staged a variety of plays at Plumstead's Warehouse in Philadelphia until the city council clamped down. Joseph Addison's *Cato* is the only title preserved in the records, but among the unknown works may have been one or more by Shakespeare. In any case, in early 1750 Murray and Keen moved to New York, where they obtained an appropriate space on Nassau Street. There, in March 1750, they opened their season with Colley Cibber's mangled version of *Richard III*. It was popular enough to be repeated twice, although plays by more recent writers soon took over. But the Murray-Keen company was on the move again, this time to Williamsburg, Virginia, where they built a primitive theater and again offered *Richard III* and several modern plays. Their Virginia Company of Comedians lasted twenty years and often toured the small towns. The records of its performances are meager.[16]

In 1752, a company of English actors with experience at Bartholomew Fair and elsewhere in London arrived in Williamsburg. This "London Company of Comedians" featured Lewis Hallam as principal factotum and second-tier actor, his wife as the female lead, and several of their sons and daughters in supporting roles. After purchasing and improving the Murray-Keen theater, in September 1752 the Hallams staged an adaptation of *The Merchant of Venice*, with singing and instrumental accompaniment. A month later, the audience for *Othello* included several prominent Cherokees who were in town to renew a treaty of friendship with the Virginia government, and a large audience of gawkers more attracted by the Indians, apparently, than the play. Despite the good box office occasioned by the Cherokees and Williamsburg's periodic influx of legislators, merchants, students, and colonial dignitaries, the Virginia capital's year-round population did not satisfy the London Company. After a year of erratic support, the Hallams moved, with somewhat better success, to New

York City and later to Philadelphia; Charleston, South Carolina; and finally Jamaica. Shakespearean plays in their extensive repertoire included *Henry IV* and *The Merry Wives of Windsor,* as well as the old standby, *Richard III.*[17]

Four years later, a revamped company, now under the direction of David Douglass, another Englishman living in Jamaica, again toured North American cities. This troupe included several of the original actors (including Mrs. Hallam, who had married Douglass after Lewis Hallam's death); like its predecessor, its key actors were English. For nearly twenty years thereafter (1758–74), Douglass's "London Company of Comedians"—renamed "The American Com-pany of Comedians" in 1763 in an appeal to British America's emerging identity —performed in eastern seaboard cities and towns from South Carolina to Rhode Island. Despite financial and artistic struggles, Douglass's company persisted. In 1767, it built a new theater on John Street in New York, near Broadway, with space for perhaps nine hundred spectators in the boxes, gallery, and pit. Once again, as at Williamsburg in 1752, visiting Cherokees proved a boon to the box office and attracted widespread attention to a nascent American theater. A week after the new venue opened, the eminent Attakullakulla— who in 1730 had witnessed professional shows in London— and nine of his tribesmen saw *Richard III,* and after a subsequent show (not by Shakespeare) they performed a war dance on the stage.[18] On such occasions, the house was full, but Douglass's company, like its predecessors, encountered much apathy and occasional hostility, both official and popular. Profits were disappointing. The tide, however, was slowly turning; supporters gradually out-numbered detractors.

Most of the Douglass company's numerous imported plays were light comedies or musicals: John Gay's *Beggar's Opera,* George Farquhar's *Recruiting Officer* and *Beaux' Stratagem,* and, in a more serious vein, George Lillo's *History of George Barnwell* and Addison's *Cato.* But Shakespeare was the single most popular author, even if the audience sometimes had difficulty recognizing his handiwork. Only *Othello* and *Hamlet,* and perhaps *The Merchant of Venice* and *Cymbeline,* were performed more or less as he wrote them, although usually with substantial cuts. The most popular Shakespeare play in the American colonies, *Romeo and Juliet,* was usually the version contrived by David Garrick and others; *Richard III* was Colley Cibber's greatly altered script; and *The Taming of the Shrew* came in the guise of David Garrick's farcical *Catharine and Petruchio,* often presented as an afterpiece to a longer play. *Macbeth* was customarily performed in the operatic version by William Davenant and Henry Purcell; *Antony and Cleopatra* appeared as John Dryden's *All for Love; King Lear* was Nahum Tate's revamped *King Lear and His Three Daughters.* George Granville, Lord Lansdowne, had greatly modified *The Jew of Venice, or the Female Lawyer,* although by the mid-eighteenth century his version had fallen from favor in England and probably in America. *The Tempest* was barely recognizable in the musical version by Dryden and Davenant, often known by its added subtitle, *The Enchanted Island.*[19] These adaptations were not aimed primarily at American audiences; the same versions played regularly in London.

Although Shakespeare was genuinely popular, both in print and on stage, the media were out of sync: the multi-volume editions for sale in Britain and America bore little substantive resemblance to the play books used in theatrical performances on either side of the Atlantic. Scholarly editions were generally faithful to the Bard's originals, as edited by English specialists, while the theater sought enter-tainment, pure and simple. If that meant rewriting the plot, bowdlerizing the text, and adding music and dance or even new characters and dialogue, so be it. Directors, actors, scenic designers, and musical accompanists wanted

Charles Willson Peale. *Nancy Hallam as Imogen.* Oil on canvas, 1771.
The Colonial Williamsburg Foundation.

to fill the house and believed they knew best how to do it. American productions of *The Tempest* in 1773–74 are a case in point. Besides several characters added by John Dryden in the 1660s, these productions featured song, dance, and "elegant" stage machinery.[20] In an age of theatrical innovation, William Shakespeare's work was as vulnerable to adaptation as any playwright's.

By late 1774, when the first Continental Congress urged American colonists to shun the theater, along with other entertainments and luxuries, Shakespeare had made impressive inroads into American culture. In the quarter-century since the initial documented performance of 1750, at least 181 performances had been staged, and the actual total, if the missing evidence could be retrieved, might be 500 or more. Of the fifteen Shakespeare plays known to have been produced in that span, *Romeo and Juliet* headed the list (as it did in London) with at least thirty-five performances, closely followed by *Richard III* with thirty-three, *Hamlet* with twenty-four, and Garrick's version of *The Taming of the Shrew (Catharine and Petruchio)* with twenty-two. At least six other plays had reached double figures: *Othello*, *Cymbeline*, *Macbeth*, *The Merchant of Venice*, the Nahum Tate version of *King Lear*, and the Dryden-Davenant *Tempest*. A few performances are documented of *1 Henry IV*, *King John*, and *Julius Caesar* and only one of *The Merry Wives of Windsor*. Philadelphia, now British America's largest city, with a population of 40,000 by 1776, had overcome its earlier antipathetic policies to become the favorite theatrical venue; New York, with bigger theaters but fewer people, was a close second. Much smaller Charleston, South Carolina, and Annapolis, Maryland, shared a distant third place, but several even smaller communities had hosted a few Shakespeare productions by touring companies.[21] In each of these communities,

Shakespeare shared the boards with the era's favorite British dramatists.

The Continental Congress's crusade against the theater was not entirely effective, as new resolutions against plays and players in 1778 implicitly admit. Even the American army put on shows, most notably Addison's *Cato* at Valley Forge in April 1778. Congressional disapproval was nonetheless inhibiting enough to drive Douglass's American Company of Comedians to Jamaica for the duration. From 1774 to 1783, most Americans who flouted Congress's prohibition were loyalists who joined with theatrically minded British officers in occupied Boston, New York, or Philadelphia. The same Hugh Gaine who had printed the earliest Shakespeare volumes now sided with the Tories and actively promoted performances in New York; in Boston, General John Burgoyne organized plays in Faneuil Hall. In such venues, Shakespeare remained popular, with perhaps a dozen of his plays performed at least once. Not surprisingly, for nearly a decade during and immediately after the war, the taint of loyalism linked Shakespeare's plays with America's enemies: Shakespeare, for a time, was "their" author, not "ours."[22]

But given the importance of Shakespeare to the early American stage, wartime antagonism could not last. The emergent American culture not only embraced and Americanized the English language but did much the same to that language's most distinguished writer. In 1782 John Henry, one of the American Company's leading actors, returned from his self-imposed exile in Jamaica to perform one-man shows, including an elegy entitled "Shadows of Shakespeare, or Shakespeare's Characters paying Homage to Garrick." By the mid-1780s, full-scale performances of Shakespeare's plays reappeared on public stages and soon regained their prewar popularity. Emblematic of this resurgence was the attendance of George Washington— during a respite from presiding over the Constitutional

Convention of 1787—at a performance of *The Tempest* (the Dryden-Davenant adaptation) at Philadelphia's Southwark opera house. Less than a decade later, the new United States had their own edition of Shakespeare's works, also produced in Philadelphia. More American printings would follow of both individual plays and collected editions, as would American actors, American theater companies, and American literary and theatrical critics.[23] After a brief wartime hiatus, America had again discovered Shakespeare.

1. Various documents concerning the Virginia colony, the relief expedition, and the *Sea Venture*'s fate are printed in Alexander Brown, *The Genesis of the United States: . . . A Series of Historical Manuscripts Now First Printed*, 2 vols. (Boston: Houghton, Mifflin, 1890). Quotations here are from 1:333, 347, 348.

2. Soon after his arrival in Virginia in May 1610, Strachey composed "*A true reportory of the wracke, and redemption of Sir* Thomas Gates *Knight; upon, and from the Ilands of the* Bermudas; *his comming to* Virginia, *and the estate of the Colonie then. . . .*" Strachey dated the letter 15 July but composed it over several days or weeks before it accompanied Sir Thomas Gates to England. The letter circulated there in one or more manuscript copies before Samuel Purchas published it in *Hakluytus Posthumus, or Purchas His Pilgrimes*, 4 vols. (London: for Henry Fetherston, 1625), 4:1734–56. A modernized and annotated version is in *A Voyage to Virginia in 1609*, ed. Louis B. Wright (Charlottesville: University of Virginia Press, 1964).

3. Silvester Jourdain's slim pamphlet, *A Discovery of the Barmudas, otherwise called the Ile of Divels* (London: for Roger Barnes, 1610), complements Strachey's longer account but without the latter's exposé of conspiracies in Bermuda and deplorable conditions in Virginia. *A Discovery of the Barmudas* is reprinted, with modern spelling, in Wright (no. 2). A new charter for the Virginia colony, issued in 1612, put Bermuda within its boundaries, although the islands soon became a separate jurisdiction in the English empire.

4. Purchas, 4:1749; S. G. Culliford, *William Strachey, 1572–1621* (Charlottesville: University of Virginia Press, 1965), 151–58. Robert Ralston Cawley, "Shakspere's Use of the Voyagers in *The Tempest*," *PMLA* 41 (1926): 688–726, compares Strachey's (and other) narratives to *The Tempest*.

5. Brown, 1:367.

6. Increase Mather, *A Testimony against several prophane and superstitious customs, now practised by some in New-England* (London, 1687), sig. A3; Sewall is quoted in Odai Johnson and William J. Burling, *The Colonial American Stage, 1665–1774: A Documentary Calendar* (Cranbury, NJ: Associated University Presses, 2001), 98–99; *Acts and Resolves, Public and Private, of the Province of the Massachusetts Bay*, 3 (Boston: Printed for the Commonwealth, 1878), 500–501.

7. Kenneth Silverman, *A Cultural History of the American Revolution: Painting, Music, Literature, and the Theatre* (New York: Thomas Y. Crowell, 1976), 67.

8. *William Penn and the Founding of Pennsylvania, 1680–1684: A Documentary History*, ed. Jean R. Soderlund (Philadelphia: University of Pennsylvania Press, 1983), 132; Silverman, 108.

9. Silverman, 66–67.

10. Alfred Van Rensselaer Westfall, *American Shakespeare Criticism, 1607–1865* (New York: H. W. Wilson Co., 1939), 32–34; *The Papers of Thomas Jefferson*, ed. Julian P. Boyd, 31 vols. (Princeton, NJ: Princeton University Press, 1950), 1:77.

11. *Gentleman's Progress: The Itinerarium of Dr. Alexander Hamilton, 1744*, ed. Carl Bridenbaugh (Chapel Hill: University of North Carolina Press, 1948), 191; Alexander Hamilton, *The History of the Ancient and Honorable Tuesday Club*, ed. Robert Micklus, 3 vols. (Chapel Hill: University of North Carolina Press, 1990), 1:201, 247; 2:21, 26, 28, 139, 145, 393.

12. *Diary and Autobiography of John Adams*, ed. L.H. Butterfield, et al., 4 vols. (New York: Atheneum, 1964), 1:61; 2:53; *Portrait of a Patriot: The Major Political and Legal Papers of Joseph Quincy Junior*, ed. Daniel R. Coquilette and Neil Longley York (Boston: Colonial Society of Massachusetts, 2005), 81, 88; Westfall, 34–38.

13. *New-York Mercury*, no. 468, repeated verbatim in the next issue of the weekly newspaper, 27 July 1761 (no. 469).

14. Quoted in Hugh F. Rankin, *The Theater in Colonial America* (Chapel Hill, NC, 1960), 23. Other helpful publications on the early American stage are Esther Cloudman Dunn, *Shakespeare in America* (New York: Macmillan, 1939); Brooks McNamara, *The American Playhouse in the Eighteenth Century* (Cambridge, MA: Harvard University Press, 1969); Charles H. Shattuck, *Shakespeare on the American Stage: From the Hallams to Edwin Booth* (Washington, DC: Folger Shakespeare Library, 1976); Michael Dobson, "Fairly Brave New World: Shakespeare, the American Colonies, and the American Revolution," *Renaissance Drama* 23 (1992): 189–207; Christopher D. Felker, "Print History of *The Tempest* in Early America, 1623–1787," in *The Tempest: Critical Essays*, ed. Patrick M. Murphy (New York: Routledge, 2001), 482–508; and Frances Teague,

Shakespeare and the American Popular Stage (Cambridge: Cambridge University Press, 2006).

15. Westfall, 44–45; Rankin, 23–24.

16. Rankin, 30–32; Westfall, 47; *The Cambridge History of American Theatre*, vol. 1, *Beginnings to 1870*, ed. Don B. Wilmeth and Christopher Bigsby (Cambridge: Cambridge University Press, 1998), 36; Johnson and Burling, 66–67.

17. Rankin, 54–57.

18. Silverman, 134–37.

19. Shattuck, 9, presents compelling evidence that American audiences probably saw Shakespeare's, rather than Lord Lansdowne's, version of *The Merchant of Venice*.

20. Johnson and Burling, 40; Rankin, 137.

21. A chronological list of the performances and summaries by title, year, and location are in Westfall, 50–55. Since the publication of that book in 1939, other performances have been uncovered, which accounts for the discrepancies between Westfall's figures and the generalizations in this essay. See Johnson and Burling, especially the table, 66–67, which does not include *Catharine and Petruchio* in their numerical summaries of Shakespearean productions or *Coriolanus*; both appear in Westfall.

22. On stage productions during the war, see Jared Brown, *The Theatre in America during the Revolution* (Cambridge: Cambridge University Press, 1995), esp. 31–32 where Hugh Gaines is discussed, and Wilmeth and Bigsby, 42.

23. Brown, 162, 186; Silverman, 571; Kim C. Sturgess, *Shakespeare and the American Nation* (Cambridge: Cambridge University Press, 2004), 15–52.

Thomas Sully. *Charlotte Cushman.* Oil on canvas, 1843.
CAT. NO. 19

Making Shakespeare American:
Shakespeare's Dissemination in Nineteenth-Century America[1]
Virginia Mason Vaughan

Although Shakespeare was performed off and on in the years leading up to the American Revolution in Williamsburg, Annapolis, Charleston, Philadelphia, and New York, not until the war ended did the theater gradually emerge as a staple of American culture. Entrepreneurs in New York, Philadelphia, and even Boston built theaters and lured down-and-out actors from England with promises of fame and fortune. Shakespeare was particularly adaptable for the star system that emerged in early nineteenth-century America. As historian Lawrence Levine observes, "Only the existence of a small repertory of well known plays, in which Shakespeare's were central, made it feasible for the towering stars of England and America to travel throughout the United States acting with resident stock companies wherever they went."[2]

And travel they did. George Frederick Cooke (1756–1812) was the first to take the celebrity tour to North America. Known for his command of Shakespeare's villainous roles—especially Richard III, Iago, and Shylock—Cooke had attained great fame in England, but his penchant for drink left him penniless. His first season in America (1810–11) took him to New York, Boston, and Philadelphia. Sometimes he performed effectively; more often his impersonations were ruined by inebriation. The second season was, not surprisingly, a failure, and on 26 September 1812, he died in New York of alcoholism.

Among the most notable English actors who traveled to America to make their fortune was Edmund Kean (1787–1833). The leading actor of his day, Kean was best known for Othello and Richard III, parts he performed with such incredible emotional intensity that audiences went wild. His first tour began in 1820 in New York and then continued to Philadelphia, Boston, and Baltimore. After great success in those venues, Kean returned to Boston late in the spring of 1821. Despite advice that there would be small audiences for theater at that time of year, the actor insisted on

performing. Scheduled to enact Richard III on 25 May, Kean saw only twenty people in the audience and left the theater. He had, the press reported, "insulted Boston."[3]

Back in Boston four years later, Kean encountered a hostile press and a volatile audience. Early-nineteenth-century American audiences took their theater seriously and often divided into camps in favor of one actor or another, much the way we might support a sports team against its opponent. The result for Kean was disastrous. When he tried to apologize for his earlier behavior, the audience yelled so loudly that he could not be heard. Anti-Kean forces rioted and tore the theater apart. Kean fared better in Canada, where he was made an honorary chieftain in the Huron tribe. Even so, he must have been relieved to return to England. His last appearance was in London, where he collapsed during a performance of *Othello* and died in 1833.

Kean was followed by William Charles Macready (1793–1873), who made three tours to the United States. Macready was respected in London for his efforts to make the English theater respectable and to restore Shakespeare's original texts to the theater. His first visit to America (September 1826 to June 1827) was well received. In New York, Macready performed his standard repertoire of roles, including Othello and Macbeth, to great acclaim. But Macready's early triumph was not to be repeated, as he became embroiled in a public contest with the American actor Edwin Forrest.

Forrest (1806–1872), born in Philadelphia, began his acting career at age eighteen. By the time he began his rivalry with Macready, Forrest was a star. Well-built and athletic, he was known for a melodious voice that could resonate with passion. In 1834, he sailed to Europe, where he visited France, Italy, and Russia; he then landed in London for a debut at Drury Lane. Macready attended Forrest's performances more than once and admired his native abilities, but he thought the American actor needed more discipline. When Macready's friend and associate, the journalist John Forster, wrote a scathing review in the *London Examiner* of the American actor's Othello, Forrest assumed the negative criticism came from Macready (although in this he was mistaken).[4] A bitter conflict ensued.

Macready's second journey to the United States, from October 1843 to September 1844, took him away from the urban playhouses of the East Coast to the hinterlands of the South, from Charleston to Mobile, New Orleans, and St. Louis. When Macready returned to New York, Forrest was already there and had appropriated the English actor's favorite roles. This seemed ungentlemanly to Macready. He did not understand that Forrest's action signified more than a personal feud between a British actor and an American rival. Riding upon a tide of nativist sentiment, Forrest deliberately created a competition with the English actor, proclaiming that Shakespeare should be performed in America by those who understood the common people as Shakespeare had understood them—by Americans like himself.

The transatlantic contest continued when Forrest visited England in 1845. After performing Macbeth in London to negative reviews, he again blamed the bad press on Macready. Sometime later he attended a performance of Macready's Hamlet and loudly hissed his rival, an act he justified in a letter to the *London Times*. When Macready toured the United States in 1848–49, the competition between the two actors reached its climax. Forrest was the darling of working-class people in New York's Bowery, whereas to many upper-class New Yorkers Macready was a distinguished and welcome visitor from England. Forrest's fans were more volatile. As theater historian Alan Downer observes, "To a great mass of Americans, chiefly urban laborers, Macready had become not merely the English

actor who contested the superiority of their idol, but the Foreigner, symbol of the constant threat to what was even then described as the American Way of Life."[5] On 10 May, 1849, an angry mob of Forrest's followers interrupted Macready's presentation of Macbeth at New York's Astor-Place Theatre and threw rocks through the theater's windows. The militia arrived and killed twenty-three people in its efforts to control the crowd. Macready escaped to Boston and then back to England. He never returned to the United States.

Other English actors fared better. Junius Brutus Booth (1796–1852), tired of working in Edmund Kean's shadow, emigrated to America in 1821 to seek his fortune. He spent his life moving from city to city and, in his last years, traveled as far as the Gold Rush country outside San Francisco. In theater venues across the country, he starred in *Richard III*, *The Merchant of Venice*, *Othello*, *Macbeth*, *King Lear*, and *Hamlet*. But his most interesting role, at least in hindsight, was Cassius, leader of the conspiracy to assassinate Julius Caesar. Perhaps this impersonation inspired his youngest son, John Wilkes Booth.

The senior Booth settled his growing family at a farm near Baltimore, and three of his children—Junius, Edwin, and John Wilkes—followed in his footsteps on the stage and traveled with him to California. Their father died on the return trip, but the three Booths continued in the family tradition, appearing together in 1864 in a production of *Julius Caesar* at New York's Winter Garden Theatre. By this time, Edwin had become a prominent actor, but after his younger brother assassinated President Lincoln in 1865, he temporarily retired from the stage and vowed never to perform in Washington again.

While Junius Brutus Booth and sons were presenting Shakespeare's plays in the West, other American-born actors, their craft honed in American theaters, crossed the Atlantic and attained success on London's stages. James

Riot at the Astor-Place Opera-House, New York. Engraving, 1849.
CAT. NO. 12

RIOT AT THE ASTOR-PLACE OPERA-HOUSE, NEW YORK.—(SEE PAGE 372.)

[COUNTRY EDITION.]

Playbill, *Julius Caesar*. New York, 1864.
CAT. NO. 21

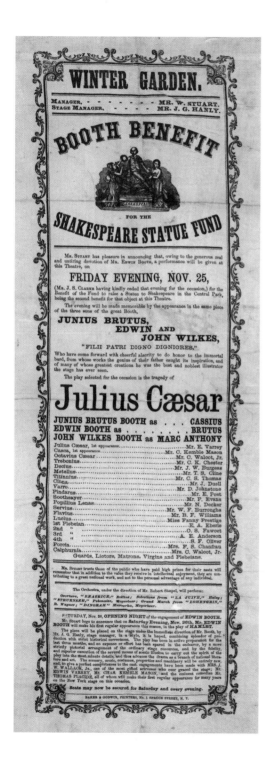

Henry Hackett (1800–71), a successful comedian, known for his impersonations of "Yankee" characters, began his career with what was by now a routine tour of theaters across the country, from Boston to New Orleans, west to San Francisco, and back to New York. Hackett excelled as Falstaff and frequently performed the role in England during the 1840s and 1850s. Hackett was, as Charles Shattuck opines, the "first important American actor to reverse the westward stream of talent by carrying American stage art to England and winning a sort of acceptance there."[6]

Charlotte Cushman (1816–76), another notable American actor, was born in Boston to middle-class parents. Living under straitened circumstances, she sought financial independence through a singing career. She made her opera debut in Boston in 1835, and then moved to New Orleans to be an apprentice at the St. Charles Theatre. The training she received there ruined her singing voice, and a fellow performer advised her to quit the opera and become an actress. She debuted in 1836 as Lady Macbeth, a role she perfected. When William Charles Macready came to New York in 1843, he asked Cushman to be his Lady Macbeth and paid the expenses to bring her from New York to Boston to enact the role there as well. Macready was now her mentor and encouraged her to go to England, where she triumphed, not only as Lady Macbeth but in traditionally male roles such as Romeo and Hamlet. For the rest of her life, Cushman made extensive tours of both the United States and England and was widely recognized as the greatest American-born actress of the nineteenth century. Toward the end of her career, Cushman returned to America and, after a brief run at Edwin Booth's Theatre in New York, made her farewell to the stage as Lady Macbeth on 7 November 1874.

While Cushman reigned as America's leading actress, Edwin Booth's only competitor for the title of best American actor was the aging Edwin Forrest (for whom he was named). When Forrest died in 1872, Booth's claim to that title was uncontested. Despite financial setbacks and the closing of his New York theater, Booth was celebrated at home and abroad. In 1880 he journeyed to England, where he performed with Britain's most acclaimed actor, Henry Irving, in Shakespeare's *Othello*; on successive evenings the leading British and American actors alternated between Othello and Iago so that audiences could compare them in both roles. Reviews suggest that Booth outshone his British competitor.

Booth may have been the most talented homegrown Shakespearean actor of the nineteenth century, but he was not alone. Almost every corner of the sprawling country hosted touring American actors who performed for enthusiastic audiences. Alternating with popular melodramas and burlesques, Shakespeare was a staple in every itinerant actor's repertoire. Actors carried their favorite roles with them, rigged up productions wherever they went, and spoke the lines with an American inflection. By the last half of the nineteenth century, in theaters of the United States Shakespeare had become American.

Audiences who loved Shakespeare on stage wanted to read him at home. As American theater spread across the country, the demand for copies of his work increased. In England, the editing of Shakespeare's plays had already become something of an industry; "editions of Shakespeare grew organically, like the English constitution," in "a prolonged and collaborative process of accumulation and inclusion," observes Gary Taylor.[7] Each editor built upon what previous editors had done, so that subsequent editions grew heftier and heftier. By the time Samuel Johnson and George Steevens completed *The Plays of William Shakespeare* in 1773—the edition most cited by the earliest American editors—notes took up a substantial portion of the page.

The first complete American edition of Shakespeare was published in Philadelphia in 1795, but its claim to be American is based simply on the place it was printed. The text was "Corrected from the latest and best London editions, with notes by Samuel Johnson,"[8] although the copy text was actually the 1791 Dublin *Royal Edition*, edited by Samuel Ayscough.[9] John Hopkinson, a prominent Philadelphia lawyer, put the edition together, so in one sense he was the first American editor if, in a larger sense, he was not.

Appropriating the work of eighteenth-century English scholars was the easiest and fastest way to produce a reasonably priced Shakespeare edition for a growing middle-class market. Philadelphia remained a linchpin in the Shakespeare industry throughout the nineteenth century and into the twentieth, but Boston and New York were not far behind in producing editions geared to their local readers. The first Boston edition is typical. Completed in 1807 and sold by subscription, it was based on a British version and included Johnson's *Preface*.[10]

As the century progressed, the need emerged for an American scholar to edit Shakespeare's text. In 1804 Joseph Dennie, another Philadelphia lawyer, announced plans for a variorum edition—that is, one incorporating the entire history of critical opinion for each line. The goal of such an edition was to provide the reader with sufficient information to make his or her own interpretation. But Dennie did not complete his work until 1809. Dennie wanted to add to the researches of English scholars and make independent judgments about Shakespeare's texts, but he was hampered by not having the necessary primary sources.[11] He, too, was forced to rely on British commentators.

As Alfred Van Rensselaer Westfall notes, "Early American printers copied illustrations as shamelessly as they borrowed notes and text."[12] By the 1840s, publishers sensed a demand for a pictorial edition of the plays, similar to Charles

Knight's English edition. Another lawyer, this one from New York, was selected to prepare such a text. Gulian Crommelin Verplanck (1786–1870) produced the first fully illustrated American edition of Shakespeare in three volumes, published between 1844 and 1847. Verplanck was cognizant of the work British scholars had done on textual matters, but he was not afraid to interject his own opinion and his notes indicate some original research. Verplanck was also the first American editor to try to determine the order in which the plays were written, but because he did not have adequate access to primary sources, once again, he remained dependent on the work of English scholars.[13]

Verplanck was succeeded as America's leading Shakespeare editor by Henry Norman Hudson (1814–86), a schoolteacher from New England. Hudson began his Shakespeare career by delivering lectures on the dramatist's works, lectures that were published in 1848. Following their success, Hudson turned to editing *The Works of Shakespeare*, which appeared in eleven volumes (1851–58). Hudson claimed that his texts were fully annotated, and he drew freely from outside sources, adding many of his own opinions to the notes. He also included introductions for each play with material taken from his lectures. Although Hudson's edition was popular with general readers, America had yet to produce a truly scholarly edition.

That void was filled between 1857 and 1861, when Richard Grant White (1822–85) compiled a new edition. A New Yorker to the core, White had studied law and medicine but made his living as a journalist. He began his career as a Shakespeare scholar in 1853 by discrediting the work of the English editor and forger John Payne Collier. White's version of the plays soon followed, and for the first time, an American editor worked directly with primary sources and edited the plays without relying on his British predecessors. In a major shift from previous editions, White provided sparse but clear annotations, a tactic consistent with his advice to the first-time reader of Shakespeare:

> [T]he first rule—and it is absolute and without exception . . .—is to read him only. Throw the commentators and the editors to the dogs. Don't read any man's notes, or essays, or introductions, aesthetical, historical, philosophical, or philological. Don't read mine. Read the plays themselves. . . . [K]eep your mind entirely free from the influence of what this or that eminent critic has said about them.[14]

In his efforts to produce a clear and accurate text, White included dozens of his own emendations, many of which are retained by today's editors, although at the time of publication White's straightforward edition did not appeal to the general public. Dismayed by poor sales, White went back to journalism.

Whatever their failures and successes, Hudson and White made it clear that American editors needed the same primary materials as British scholars had if they were to build an editing tradition of their own. English scholars had access to Oxford's Bodleian Library, to Cambridge's University Library, and to the British Museum. Where would American editors find such a wealth of material? This challenge fell to Horace Howard Furness, another Philadelphia lawyer. Born in 1833, Furness was inspired to a love of Shakespeare by his friendship with the actress Fanny Kemble, who traveled the country giving public readings of Shakespeare's texts. In 1860, Furness joined the Shakspeare Society of Philadelphia (composed mainly of lawyers), a club devoted to the careful analysis of Shakespeare and his sources.

With the backing of J. P. Lippincott Publishers, Furness collated all of the important editions of each play to produce a variorum edition. Lippincott issued *Romeo and*

Juliet in 1871; after that, the production of complete, variorum editions of each play became Furness's life work. He completed thirteen more volumes before his death; *Cymbeline* was published posthumously in 1913.

Furness also gathered a Shakespeare library to undergird his variorum volumes; his extensive collection is now housed at the University of Pennsylvania. The Furness Library contains a complete run of the early printings of Shakespeare's plays, copies of all subsequent editions, commentaries and criticism, and the writings of Shakespeare's contemporaries, as well as promptbooks and other theatrical materials.[15] By the end of the nineteenth century, Furness was America's most important Shakespeare scholar. With access to critical materials, editions, and primary sources, Furness could draw his own conclusions about Shakespeare's texts, independently of what other American, British, or German scholars, had to say. To this day, Shakespeare scholars look to Furness's variorum editions when they want the complete history of critical opinion up until the date of Furness's publication.

Thanks to the efforts of American printers and publishers, popular editions of Shakespeare's plays were readily available by the 1850s. Karl Knortz, a German visitor to America, observed in 1882 that

> *there is no land on the whole earth in which Shakespeare and the Bible are held in such high esteem . . . ; should one enter a blockhouse situated in the far west, and should the dweller there exhibit very definitely evidences of backwoods life, yet has he nearly always furnished a small room in which to spend his few leisure hours, in which the Bible and in most cases a cheap edition of the works of the poet Shakespeare are nearly always found.*[16]

And once editions were available to be read and pondered, Americans were free to interpret Shakespeare for themselves.

American small cities and frontier towns during the early nineteenth century hungered for entertainment and information; they found both in the lectures of traveling preachers, teachers, and public intellectuals. With printed books and newspapers comparatively scarce, Americans were steeped in the oral traditions of religious and political oratory. American Shakespeare criticism accordingly began on the lecture circuit. After a successful tour, itinerant speakers often polished their lectures for publication; their ideas about Shakespeare circulated widely, first orally and later in print.

Henry Norman Hudson traveled and taught for four years before preparing his *Lectures on Shakespeare*, published in 1848. Hudson's first objective was to convince his audience that Shakespeare was not the immoral playwright he had been painted to be by their puritan forebears. No, indeed—the highest moral principles could be found in Shakespeare's work. Like John Quincy Adams, who proclaimed that Shakespeare was the best "*teacher of morals*,"[17] Hudson believed that "Morality comes from him as from nature, not in abstract propositions, to set our logic-mills a-going, but in a living form of beauty, to inspire us with love and noble passion." Hudson admitted that "there are passages in Shakespeare's works, as indeed there are in the Bible itself, which, taken by themselves, may produce a bad effect; but there cannot be found a whole play, scarcely even a whole scene in them, whose integral impression is not altogether good."[18]

After establishing Shakespeare's morality and utility, Hudson offered meticulous discussions of the plays, especially the dramatist's characters. Although the treatment of dramatis personae as real people may strike a modern reader as old-fashioned, Hudson's analyses reflected nineteenth-century interest in human psychology. The people who inhabited the plays, akin to characters in nineteenth-century novels, exhibited human traits and qualities; it seemed important to understand what made them tick. Hudson's analysis of Iago is a good case in point. Reacting to Samuel Taylor Coleridge's charge that Shakespeare's villain was a study in "motiveless malignity," Hudson argued that "his actuating principle seems to be a lust and pride of intellect and will, which finds its dearest gratification in the annulling or reversing of moral distinctions." In such cases, "the mind comes to act, not for any outward ends or objects, but merely for the sake of acting." In Iago, we have "a dry, frigid, prurient intellectuality, . . . which frequently and naturally manifests itself in a fanaticism of intrigue, an enthusiasm for mischief, a sort of hungering and thirsting after unrighteousness."[19] Hudson continues in this vein for several more pages and then devotes the next lecture to a similarly detailed analysis of Othello and Desdemona. A skilled orator trained to preach, as Hudson was, could thus provide a host of general observations about human nature drawn from the particularities of Shakespeare's major characters.

This quality—the ability to reveal human nature in all its complexity—also fascinated the most famous speaker on the 1840s lecture circuit, Ralph Waldo Emerson (1803–82). Born in Boston, Emerson was the son of a Congregational minister who died in 1811, leaving a wife and eight children in genteel poverty. Emerson worked his way through Harvard, spent four years as a teacher, then returned to Harvard for a degree in divinity. After six years as a minister, he resigned over a fundamental disagreement with his church's teaching regarding communion. From then on, Emerson made his living as a man of letters—lecturer, essayist, and sage.

During the last half of the 1840s, Emerson delivered a series of lectures on the theme of genius, published in 1850 under the title *Representative Men*. Described as "winter evening entertainments," the lectures focused on men of genius whose thinking and writing transcended their particular biographies. Audiences jammed the Odeon Theatre in Boston—and venues in England during Emerson's tour of 1846–48—to hear the sage of Concord wax eloquent on such worthies as Plato, Swedenborg, Montaigne, Napoleon, Goethe, and most important, Shakespeare.

Although Emerson refers to the English Shakspeare Society's recent discoveries concerning Shakespeare's life and sources, his interest is clearly not biographical. Emerson's concern is the dramatist's representations of human nature, portraits which allow the reader to understand himself and his neighbor. Emerson begins by defending Shakespeare from detractors who sneer at his lack of originality: "The greatest genius is the most indebted man."[20] Like Homer and Chaucer before him, Shakespeare "knew that tradition supplies a better fable than any invention can." It doesn't matter whether his ideas come from translations of other works, tradition, travel to distant countries, or inspiration.[21] What does matter is the poet's ability to make new matter out of old. In this sense, Shakespeare is American. Like native writers struggling to find their own voices in the early republic, Shakespeare inherited a rich tradition but inflected it with new resonances.

Shakespeare is also American in his optimism or, as Emerson puts it, his cheerfulness. "He loves virtue, not for its obligation, but for its grace: he delights in the world in man, in woman, for the lovely light which sparkles from them. Beauty, the spirit of joy and hilarity, he sheds over the universe."[22] Shakespeare, it would seem, was a transcendentalist, his characters embodying truths that emanated from Nature itself, a Nature that was basically benign if one had the wit to perceive it.

Like Hudson before him, Emerson found Shakespeare's essence in his characters, but he described them in terms far more general: Shakespeare "wrote the text of modern life; the text of manners: he drew the man of England and Europe; the father of the man in America: he drew the man, and described the day, and what is done in it: he read the hearts of men and women, their probity, and their second thought and wiles; the wiles of innocence, and the transitions by which virtues and vices slide into their contraries." In sum, Shakespeare "clothed the creatures of his legend with form and sentiments, as if they were people who had lived under his roof, and few real men have left such distinct characters as these fictions."[23] Shakespeare's understanding of common humanity, irrespective of caste or class, made him a true democrat. Or, as Emerson opined in his remarks at the celebration of the Bard's three-hundredth birthday in 1864, "what a great heart of equity is he! How good and sound and inviolable his innocency, that is never to seek, and never wrong, but speaks the pure sense of humanity on each occasion."[24]

Like the other men of genius in Emerson's pantheon, Shakespeare was not perfect. The Bard's fatal flaw, Emerson concludes, was that he devoted his genius to entertainment. Never a priest or a prophet, "He was a master of the revels to mankind." The best poet of the English language, Shakespeare "led an obscure and profane life, using his genius for the public amusement." Yet, like all great men, Shakespeare existed so that other great men to follow could build upon the foundations he had laid. "The world," Emerson opines, "still wants its poet-priest."[25]

Emerson's uneasiness with Shakespeare's profession of playwright was shared by another speaker on the lecture circuit, Delia Bacon (1811–59). Born in a log cabin in frontier Ohio, Bacon was raised, after the death of her father, in Hartford, Connecticut, where she briefly attended Catherine Beecher's school for young ladies. Although her brother Leonard became a prosperous clergyman, Delia lived from hand to mouth most of her life. She tried to establish several schools of her own in the late 1820s, then turned to writing and teaching; she finally found a niche in lecturing, where her discussions of English history and literature impressed audiences with their enthusiasm and insight.

Sometime in the late 1840s, Bacon became convinced that the player from Stratford could not possibly have written such transcendent works of literature. She speculated that the plays were compiled by an aristocratic literary coterie, spearheaded by Sir Walter Ralegh, Francis Bacon, and Edmund Spenser. She promoted her ideas around New England's literary circles, impressing Emerson and others with her enthusiasm, if not her mastery of facts. In 1853, with a letter of introduction from Emerson to Thomas Carlyle, Bacon sailed to England. Carlyle was a generous host, but his suggestion that she use the archives at the British Museum and other scholarly repositories fell on deaf ears. Instead, Bacon retreated into an inner life, re-reading Shakespeare's plays and working out her theories by sheer power of the imagination. She published an essay outlining her argument in *Putnam's Monthly* (January 1856) and, with the support of Nathaniel Hawthorne (the American consul at Liverpool), published a book, *Philosophy of the Plays of Shakspere Unfolded*, in 1857. By the time the book appeared, Bacon had become so mentally unstable she needed to be institutionalized. In 1858, her nephew George Bacon took her back to the United States where she soon died.[26]

Neither Hudson, Emerson, nor Bacon can be seen as a forerunner of American Shakespeare criticism today, at least as it is practiced in colleges and universities in the United States. But they do indicate continuing threads in nonacademic criticism. The enduring appeal of Hudson's kind of character study is reflected in Harold Bloom's anthologies for Shakespeare's major characters. Emerson's single essay on Shakespeare's genius reemerges in the bardolatry of many Shakespeare societies and perhaps in Bloom's claim that Shakespeare invented our notions of what it means to be human.[27] And, in a tacit nod to Delia Bacon, the greatest boosters of the anti-Stratfordian movement—-whether in favor of Sir Francis Bacon or the earl of Oxford—have been Americans.[28]

By the second half of the nineteenth century, America had thoroughly appropriated Shakespeare. Portrayed as a lover of mankind in all its infinite variety, the Bard of Avon was now considered a closet democrat. Walt Whitman, America's preeminent poet of the common man, spoke for many in his essay, "What Lurks behind Shakespeare's Historical Plays?" (*The Critic,* 1884), when he claimed that underlying the history plays was a subversive interest in displaying "the morbid accumulations," "politics and sociology" of the medieval world. Readers of the future, he opined, would be able to see in Shakespeare's historical works the "inauguration of modern democracy."[29] Shakespeare was as American as Uncle Sam himself— and so he remains.

1. This essay is deeply indebted to Charles H. Shattuck's *Shakespeare on the American Stage: From the Hallams to Edwin Booth* (Washington, DC: Folger Shakespeare Library, 1976), and to Alfred Van Rensselaer Westfall's *American Shakespeare Criticism, 1604–1865* (New York: H. W. Wilson, 1939).

2. Lawrence W. Levine, *Highbrow / Lowbrow: The Emergence of Cultural Hierarchy in America* (Cambridge, MA: Harvard University Press, 1988), 45.

3. Shattuck, 42.

4. Shattuck, 73–77.

5. Alan Downer, *The Eminent Tragedian: William Charles Macready* (Cambridge, MA: Harvard University Press, 1966), 296–97.

6. Shattuck, 59.

7. Gary Taylor, *Reinventing Shakespeare: A Cultural History from the Restoration to the Present* (Oxford: Oxford University Press, 1991), 130.

8. Westfall, 84.

9. Westfall, 86.

10. Westfall, 98.

11. Westfall, 107.

12. Westfall, 128.

13. Westfall, 131–32.

14. Richard Grant White, *Studies in Shakespeare* (Boston and New York: Houghton, Mifflin, 1896), 3.

15. See Michael Bristol, *Shakespeare's America, America's Shakespeare* (London and New York: Routledge, 1990), 64–70.

16. Karl Knorts, *Shakespeare in Amerika* (Berlin: Theodor Hoffmann, 1882), quoted in Westfall, 60.

17. Westfall, 197–98.

18. Henry Norman Hudson, *Lectures on Shakespeare*, 2 vols. (New York: Baker and Scribner, 1848), 1:80 and 1:76.

19. Hudson, 2:296.

20. Ralph Waldo Emerson, *Representative Men: Seven Lectures,* ed. Andrew Delbanco (Cambridge, MA: Harvard University Press, 1996), 109.

21. Emerson, 113.

22. Emerson, 123.

23. Emerson, 121.

24. *The Complete Works of Ralph Waldo Emerson,* online at www.rwe.org.

25. *Complete Works*, 124–25.

26. For a brief account of Delia Bacon's life, see Samuel Schoenbaum, *Shakespeare's Lives*, 2nd ed. (Oxford: Clarendon Press, 1991), 385–94. For more extensive treatment, see Vivian C. Hopkins, *Prodigal Puritan: A Life of Delia Bacon* (Cambridge, MA: Belknap Press of Harvard University, 1959); and Theodore Bacon, *Delia Bacon: A Biographical Sketch* (Cambridge, MA: Riverside Press, 1888).

27. Harold Bloom, *Shakespeare: The Invention of the Human* (New York: Riverhead Books, 1998).

28. The most prominent American Oxfordian is perhaps the late Charlton Ogburn. See *The Mysterious William Shakespeare: The Myth and the Reality* (New York: Dodd and Mead, 1984).

29. From the original manuscript, Folger S.b.89.

Desdemonum: An Ethiopian Burlesque. New York, 1874.
CAT. NO. 26

Playing with (a) Difference:
Early Black Shakespearean Actors, Blackface and Whiteface

Francesca T. Royster

It is early August 2005. I've come to visit Washington, DC, to read the Folger's holdings on the black presence in Shakespeare studies. It is drippingly humid. One of the free newspapers that I pick up near the Metro tells me that Washington is "abandoned" at this time of year: the Senate is in recess, and many Washingtonians will be on vacation or hiding out in their air-conditioned houses and apartments. Perhaps with the absence of senators and interns and some office workers and tourists, there *are* fewer people hanging out at cafes and bars near the South Capitol area. But every day, as I move in a rhythm of study and food, entertainment and rest, and then study again, I see many faces that grow increasingly familiar as the week passes. Many of those faces are brown or black, like mine: maintenance workers clipping the hedges around the Library of Congress, the baristas at the Firehook Bakery who were up much earlier than I, the security guards who view my Reading Room card with a chuckle, street vendors selling batik and beads and knit caps; joggers, smokers, office workers in linen, silk, and cotton. According to my *Lonely Planet* guidebook, Washington has a 60% African-American population. I have come to the Folger at other times of the year, but for the first time as I move around in its neighborhood, I slip unnoticed into a population of people of color: African-Americans, Ethiopians, Salvadorans, Pakistanis.

The dynamic changes as I walk up the Folger's white marble steps and into the cool, dark interior. I am much more conspicuous inside the Library than out. While this may be awkward, it should not be much of a shock—it is still a reality that most of the people who study, write about, and perform Shakespeare are white. As I think and write about the black presence in Shakespeare studies, I can't help but feel my own.

I spend the first half of my week pointedly avoiding the Folger's substantial collection of Shakespeare minstrel-show scripts and illustrations. I look with wonder at the red, cracked leather promptbook from a 1930s production of *Othello* starring Paul Robeson, read every entry in the Ira Aldridge clippings file, leaf happily through James Earl Jones's autobiographical analysis of *Othello*. Jones, who at the age of thirty-three won an Obie award for his 1964 portrayal of Othello in Joseph Papp's Shakespeare in Central Park production, opens his book with this confession: "I have always taken *Othello* personally—perhaps too personally—and I am not alone."[1] These artifacts seem alive with real voices, with stories of labor and creative transformation. I find photos and stagebills from performances by Earle Hyman, William Marshall, Moses Gunn, Sydney Hibbert, Thomas Winfield, Brenda Thomas—black actors, sometimes one of a handful at a particular historical moment, who played Shakespearean roles in festivals around the country.

But one day, as I return from lunch, I am summoned to the reading room's front desk. *They* are waiting for me: Othello with wide-lipped jelly-jar smile and corncob pipe on the cover of *Desdemonum* (1874); Othello with banjo and spurs in *Othello, a Burlesque* (ca. 1870). These minstrel-show parodies were often the first way that many Americans in the nineteenth century and at the turn of the twentieth century saw and ingested Shakespeare. (By comparison, very few Americans ever had the chance to watch African-American Ira Aldridge, whose career was predominantly in Europe.) So I take the stack of books, find an empty chair and reading lamp, and assume the position of study. I slog through them with a sense of duty; they are like the bad-dream monster who must be beheaded before I can wake up. As you view these minstrel-show Shakespearean parodies on display, you too may wonder how many fingers leafed through these books, who owned them before they became part of the collection, and how they ended up here. Or you may just want to avoid them, let your eyes slide right over them like jelly sliding off a plate in search of something brighter, cleaner, less familiar. Because yes, these are familiar images. We have all seen them before in some form. They are very American. Perhaps you saw something like *The Ethiopian Burlesque's* goggle-eyed Othello or foolish Desdemona in that antique mall off I-80 you stopped in one crisp October day. Or maybe you remember watching cartoons like this with your grandpa. He waited until your mother left, because she was newfangled and didn't approve. The black children seemed harmless, even cute, and as they bubbled up in the big black cauldron, their wide smiles only grew. Both you and your grandpa nearly jumped out of your skin (just like Buckwheat) when you heard your mother's car coming up the gravel driveway. These images continue to be reproduced and circulated in American culture, linking an unfortunate past to the present. Unlike the celebrities of racial uplift—James Earl Jones, Ira Aldridge, or Paul Robeson, or even the lesser-known black actors who you see here—these minstrel shows are part of our vague, weary, everyday fabric of racism. The linking of their tired images of black buffoonery with Shakespeare cannot elevate them beyond this banal level of evil.

We might think of the minstrel-show artifacts as both racial kitsch and Shakespeare kitsch. Racial kitsch—Aunt Jemima and Uncle Remus salt-and-pepper shakers, hitching posts, advertisements, songs, and slogans—are objects and images that use the racialized body (here, the black body) as object. These objects have become the material aspects of our most intimate actions (eating, laboring, cleaning, and entertaining), and yet they function to make the people represented by these bodies distanced from "us." Shakespeare kitsch can include parodies, appropriations, and especially products circulated and mass-produced, which seem to be increasingly distanced from an idealized "original" state or performance (however flawed this notion

of originality might be). The production of Shakespeare kitsch can be dated to the creation of a more bifurcated American culture viewed as highbrow and lowbrow. Minstrel-show performances arrive precisely at that moment. Readily available, easily consumable, they sometimes seem to serve as comment on the elevation of Shakespeare beyond our everyday lives and problems. More recent examples of Shakespeare kitsch include Shakespeare figurines and bobbleheads, chocolates, mints, Star Trek salutes, and Shakespeare-themed pornography.

Perhaps the best response to Shakespeare minstrel shows, a form of racial kitsch, is laughter. While laughter may help us to reassert our dignity, in many ways laughing at these objects echoes the original response intended by their creators. Cultural critic Tavia Nyong'o writes that

to well-meaning people today, and especially to those of us racialized as "others," the only pleasurable response to [racist kitsch] is the pleasure of mastering the urge to laugh with the joke. Through disgust, we assert our dignity and attain distance from the pleasure that the stereotype urges upon us. This oppositional distance places the racist object in a new frame, one in which the object is re-signified. From a token of mundane enjoyment, it becomes a totem of our racial survival.[2]

Nyong'o suggests that the object of racial kitsch cannot easily escape the ritual of scapegoating because as we laugh at these representations of black bodies, the body is reinscribed as an object of hatred and scorn. We onlookers, in turn, are redrawn again into the orbit of suffering and contempt.

Another urge might be to destroy the physical object, removing it from circulation completely. For some critics, racial kitsch, as it takes up the space and attention that could be given to other, more human images, acts as a form of "visual terrorism," in Robin Chandler's words.[3] Critic Michael Harris agrees, suggesting that because such imagery "is linked to, and a product of, white imagination, the attempt to invert and reconstruct another's dream inevitably keeps one tied to and preoccupied with that other rather than the self."[4]

A third strategy might be to curate or display the artifact in a way that encourages critical laughter and engagement, rather than looking away. It is in this spirit, I would argue, that we engage the minstrel parodies' place in this exhibition. We gain power from confronting the objects, dismantling the disgust that we feel as projections of disgust that others see and feel in response to the black body. Nyong'o suggests that by remaining mindful of the shame and abjection that we feel in response to the racist object, we create a point of departure: "At bottom, the shame of racist kitsch resides in the idea that 'I am thought of as less than human.' And yet, the very shame that floods through at that thought, a shame that were we not human, we would have no capacity to feel, is our best internal evidence that the thought is wrong and vulgar: I feel (shame), therefore I am (human)."[5]

As I'd like to illustrate further in this essay, by displaying and juxtaposing the minstrel-show parodies with artifacts from the lives of black actors as they negotiate predominantly white space and produce creative responses, this exhibition can foster an "oppositional gaze." Here, I call on bell hooks's notion of the oppositional gaze, as a critical form of looking that takes agency and pleasure in reading against the grain of structures of domination.[6] By looking oppositionally at such artifacts we cannot maintain our distance. We are forced to take their presence personally. This isn't easy. But the gift is that we see more clearly the web of ideas that links us to these earlier moments and to the struggles of those whose lives are unknown or even forcibly forgotten.

To begin our analysis of these structures of domination, it is useful to think about the dynamics of blackface and whiteface as forms of racialized performance negotiated by black American Shakespeare actors.

From the nineteenth century onward, blackface minstrel-show productions have integrated Shakespeare characters, plots, and language with plays that negotiate interracial and interethnic relations in American life. As cultural historians David Roediger and Eric Lott have suggested, for white immigrants coming to the United States in the middle decades of the nineteenth century, performing the minstrel show's artificial codes of blackness was a way of both becoming American and becoming white. Irish, Jewish, and other contingently white immigrants participated in the American social structure by finding work in minstrel theaters.[7]

Shakespeare and other cultural links to the Old World, like morris dances or Irish folk songs, were combined with approximations of African American music, dance, and dialect. These shows, then, Robert Toll argues, were "products of and responses to the way common Americans transformed old cultural institutions" like Shakespeare "to meet their new needs and desires."[8] Since the pleasures and dangers of political and intimate interaction between blacks and whites constitute the subject of Shakespeare's *Othello*, it makes some sense that this play has been the subject of several minstrel burlesques, including the Christy's Minstrels' *Othello*, an *Otello* by T. D. Rice, and two anonymous burlesques, *Dar's de Money* (ca. 1880) and *Desdemonum* (1874).

The birth of minstrelsy in the United States came out of a postslavery cultural moment, where the slave trade had enabled a whole technology of reproduction blackness under white control. In putting on blackface, we see a liberty to play with the reproduction of blackness that has been born of the institutionalized breeding of the slave trade.

Dar's De Money. New York, ca. 1880.

CAT. NO. 28

JAKE. Well?

PETE. And it 'peared to me somebody round de corner was a-callin' me, and I left 'cordingly.   So I'm starvin' now.

JAKE. Are you really?   Well, I'm full! (*strikes his chest.*)

PETE. (*jumps back*) Graciousness! if *I* was to do dat I'd snap in two!

JAKE. No money?

PETE. (*shakes his head.*)

JAKE. No nuffin'?

PETE. (*shakes his head*) No nuffin'.

JAKE. Come an' join me?

PETE. (*eagerly*) I will! (*cautiously*) In what?

JAKE. Doin' nuffin'!

PETE. Good!

JAKE. I'm on a strike! (*leads* PETE *forward*) You see, I've squirrelled with my manager.

PETE. Man-a-ger?

JAKE. Yes! I'se an actor! play-actor—on de stage! (*strikes attitude and introduces imitation of some well-known actor, short, as:* "In charge of drovers entirely strong, the cattle-pen am mightier dan de sword!")

PETE. (*starts*) Ky! so am I! Dis is my wardrobe! (*holds up bag*)

JAKE. You! dat your wardrobe? Ain't it rader scant?

PETE. Oh, no! I plays de lovers—and de fervency of my emotions covers all my defishingcies.

JAKE. Lovers (*lifts up* PETE'S *coat tail and turns him round*) Here's a shape for lovers! Why, look a-here, dat's *my* line!

PETE. No!

JAKE. Yes!

PETE. No!

JAKE. Yes! Hamlet! "get thee to a mummery!" "Oh, Juli-et! oh, Juli-et!" I forget what it was she eat! Yes, I'm lover.   I've broke wid my manager, 'cause he gave me too much to do.   I'm tired ob dese fellers.

PETE. So 'm I.

In the minstrel tradition, blackness is more than a blacking up of the face. Each time an actor puts on blackface, he rewrites the narrative of black racial origins—putting himself at the center. The black-faced minstrel works within a narrow vocabulary of black identity, of what black is and black ain't (in Ralph Ellison's words). He controls the signification of blackness, so that black difference is narrowed down to one shade of skin; widened, reddened lips; or a few other fetishized body parts. Eric Lott writes that in minstrelsy, "Black performance itself, first of all, was precisely 'performative,' a cultural invention, not some precious essence installed in black bodies; and for better or worse it was often a product of self-commodification, a way of getting along in a constricted world."9 By reconstructing blackness, the minstrel tradition continually negotiates and performs the question of national and racial origins.

In minstrelsy, there is both fear and desire to become what one portrays on stage, to extend the boundaries of the imagination. For example, white American actor George Thatcher writes of his boyhood dreams of becoming a minstrel: "I found myself dreaming of minstrels. I would awake with an imaginary tambourine in my hand, and rub my face with my hands to see if it was blacked up."10 Minstrel actors labor to capture the essence of black difference while at the same time self-consciously distancing themselves from these roles. Toll mentions a joke included in the Ethiopian Serenaders' 1846 English tour: "'Why am I like a young widow?' a comedian asked. After the line was slowly repeated, he fired back, 'Because I do not stay long in black.'"11 The blackface tradition then dramatizes the crossing of borders from other to self, the desire to see oneself in the other, even while burlesquing one's difference from the other. Through burlesque, and its categorization of high and low, racial boundaries are protected.

Throughout most of the nineteenth century and into the twentieth, blackface minstrel performances dominated American theater, as well as other forms of entertainment. These performances were most often by white actors. Eventually, by the end of the nineteenth century, some skilled black actors such as Earnest Hogan, Bert Williams, and George Walker were able to create a space for themselves as "coons"—blackface entertainers who capitalized on their "authenticity" in shows like *The Two Real Coons* (ca. 1896–99) or *All Coons Look Alike to Me* (1896). While these shows seem like accommodation to racism, cultural historian David Krasner suggests that we think of them as also creating a space for critique "below the radar." For black actors, Krasner suggests, blackface could provide a kind of critical mask to critique white power through parody: black actors were "forced to adopt traditional Western poetic forms as 'masks' to get a hearing and then, presumably unbeknownst to the 'master,' they deformed and remade the white conventions with a difference, exemplifying one of the classic strategies of the black vernacular trickster hero."12 It is in this "difference"—what may look like a mere gesture or turn of phrase, a shift in posture, or new rhythm—that we can see the possibilities for resistance and for a development of black style and artistry. Blackface performer Bert Williams conveys the possibility he sees implicit in blackface:

> I shuffle onto the stage, not as myself, but as a lazy, slow going negro . . . the real Bert Williams is crouched deep inside the coon who sings and tells stories. . . . I'd like a piece that would give me the opportunity to express the whole of the negro's character. The laughter I have caused is only on the surface. Now I'd like to go much deeper and to show our depths that few understand, yet. . . .[I]f I could interpret in the theatre [an] underlying tragedy of the race, I feel that we would be better known and better understood. Perhaps the time will come when that dream will come true.13

Despite blackface's tremendous hold on the American public imagination, we do see some ways that black actors fought also to forge new creative spaces, sometimes through the performance of Shakespeare. As early as 1820, African-American William Brown created the African Grove Theater, housed first in a tea garden and then in an old hospital in Manhattan. Said to be America's first black theater company, the African Grove Theater—sometimes also known as the African Company—performed *Richard III* and *Othello*, as well as ballets, pantomimes, and plays written by its own company. This company became the launching pad for some of America's first black Shakespeare actors, including James Hewlett, Charles Taft, and Ira Aldridge. Other examples of early African-American theater companies that performed Shakespeare include the Astor Place Company of Colored Tragedians, founded in New York in 1878 by Benjamin Ford and J. A. Arneux; Our Boys Dramatic Club of Baltimore, an amateur theatrical troupe, active by 1888; and Chicago's Colored Professional Stock Company, founded in 1896 by stage actor, director, and educator Charles Winter Wood.[14]

Theater historian Marvin McAllister suggests that we think of these early black actors'—and their black audience's—use of Shakespeare roles and Shakespearean authority as a form of whiteface. This in turn might be viewed as a response to the stranglehold that the artificial blackness of "blackface" had on the culture. By "whiteface," McAllister means both performing "stage Europeans"—roles that perform white identity and that were conceived as being played by white actors, like Richard III or Shylock—*and* the act of performing white social positions: inhabiting white spaces, or spaces once designated as white in a segregated city; dressing "white" or in a way designated as fashion reserved for whites; using "white" speech patterns and gestures; or taking part in institutions socially constructed as white, including theaters, universities, and even families.

For example, when the African Grove Theater was founded, McAllister notes that newspapers published letters from alarmed New York citizens who feared the growing public presence of black people. Extratheatrical entertainments and rituals, like going for a promenade down Broadway on a Sunday, were now being invaded, mocked, and, perhaps most significantly, reshaped by black "dandies" and "dandizettes." These men and women dressed in outfits that recalled white fashions but had their own special "turn" or difference, often read as vulgar or gaudy by white viewers.[15] One letter to the *New York Evening Post* gives a nervous description of an increased black presence on Broadway:

Two gentlemen, on Sunday afternoon last had the curiosity to count the number of Negroes, male and females, that passed a house in Broadway, near Washington Hall. In about two hours they amounted to fourteen hundred and eighty. Several hundred passed in the course of the evening. It was observed that these people were all well dressed, and very much better than the whites. The men almost without exception, wore broadcloth coats, very many of them boots, fashionable Cossack pantaloons, and white hats; watches and canes. The latter article was observed to be flourished with inimitable grace, to the annoyance of all the passengers.[16]

Newspaper editor M. M. Noah, in an early article on the African Grove, described the clothing and bearing of the theater's patrons in a kind of detail that reveals close watching: he describes a black man wearing

a blue coat fashionably cut; red ribbon and a bunch of pinchback seals; wide pantaloons; shining boots, gloves and a tippy rattan and a colored lady sporting her pink kid slippers, her fine Leghorn, cambric dress, with open work; corsets well fitted; reticule, hanging on her arm. . . .

Ira Aldridge. Autograph note, signed. Manuscript, 1853.
CAT. NO. 85

[T]hese black fashionables saunter up and down the garden, in all the pride of liberty and unconsciousness of want. In their address; salutations; familiar phrases; and compliments; their imitative faculties are best exhibited.[17]

McAllister comments that "Ever the astute editor, Noah recognized the self-consciousness or artificiality of these 'free' attitudes and recognized the thoroughly performative nature of this 'imitative' whiteface show, fertile ground for a 'becoming' identity process."[18]

For early black actors, performing Shakespeare was a way of tapping into a proven popular market with recognizable characters and stories; it was a way, too, of gaining cultural power—of being taken seriously. Perhaps most significantly, Shakespeare provided a text and a tradition against which an African American aesthetic style— a "difference"—could be forged. James Hewlett, a West Indian immigrant to New York, recognized as the first black actor to perform professionally on a U.S. stage, was the African Grove Theater's first celebrity, and he starred in many of its central productions, drawing praise from the theater's black and white patrons. A portrait of Hewlett as Richard III in the African Grove production is the first graphic depiction of a black performer in a dramatic production in the United States. After a tussle with British actor Charles Matthews, who burlesqued him and other black Shakespeare actors in his *A Trip to America*, Hewlett turned the tables on Matthews, performing burlesque imitations of popular (white) English and American Shakespeare actors such as Matthews, Edmund Kean, and others. Hewlett's career as an actor sustained itself even after Brown's African Company was shut down for "disturbing the peace," and he often advertised himself as "Shakespeare's proud representative" until his death in the 1840s.[19]

Performing Shakespeare meant, to some extent, not merely imitating but also commenting on that position. Often, this commentary was performed through a break in highbrow style, what Brenda Dixon Gottschild identifies in her study of Africanist aesthetics as high-affect juxtaposition (the hot and the cool):

Mood, attitude, or movement breaks that omit the transitions and connective links valued in the European academic aesthetics are a key note of this principle. For example, a driving mood may overlap and coexist with a light and humorous tone, or imitative and abstract movements may be juxtaposed. The result may be surprise, irony, comedy, innuendo, double entendre, and finally, exhilaration.[20]

We can see this use of hot-and-cool affect in African Grove Theater actor Charles Taft's "improvement" of *Richard III*, described by Marvin McAllister:

Noah's September 1821 review of the premier Richard III *production recalled how the dapper waiter immediately played to his crowd, especially the fawning "black ladies" waving handkerchiefs on his entrance. To romance his public, Taft allegedly spoke these revised lines: "Now is the vinter of our discontent/ made glorious summer by de son of New York." Noah then noted, "Considerable applause ensued, although it was evident that the actor had not followed strictly the text of the author."* . . . *By calling himself a "son of New York," Taft highlighted the fact that he was a native New Yorker performing a much heralded role dominated by British imports. Taft's native status would have endeared him to New Yorkers, black or white, male and female, and elicited "considerable applause." Also one can read his textual alteration as an extreme act of hubris in that this "son of New York," not* the "sun of York," transformed a discontented winter into summer through his glorious presence in Brown's makeshift theater.[21]

As Shakespeare scholar Peter Erickson has documented, black artists' complex and often critical engagement with Shakespeare is a tradition that continues into the twentieth and twenty-first centuries and includes poets Maya Angelou, Rita Dove, George Lamming, and Derek Walcott; novelist Ishmael Reed; and visual artist Fred Wilson.[22]

In contrast to the relatively long and full career of James Hewlett, the careers of many early black Shakespeare performers and directors were vulnerable to shifts in fortunes and politics. Racial segregation, poverty, competition with white theater companies, a fickle and sometimes violent audience cut short many careers. Charles Taft, an ex-slave, after starring in the African Grove's first *Richard III* production, was imprisoned for stealing one hundred dollars' worth of clothing—rumored to be his costume for the role of Richard.[23] After the African Grove closed, there is no further evidence of the career of S. Welsh, the African-American actor and former chambermaid who performed male and female roles for the company, including a spirited Lady Anne to Hewlett's Richard III. William Brown's theater became the subject of vicious lampoons by M. M. Noah's *National Advocate*, which misrepresented productions as farcical minstrel shows. This, combined with audience riots, police surveillance, political assault, and the growing influence of blackface minstrelsy on the marketplace, contributed to the theater's eventual closure in 1822.[24] Other black actors and directors adjusted and adapted. Most famously, Ira Aldridge, who began his career in the African Grove Theater, eventually emigrated to Europe and was able to build a career performing Shakespeare in England, Germany, and Russia.

In the "Memoir of Mr. Aldridge," from the *Theatrical Times*, dated 15 April 1848 and part of the Folger's collection, we witness Aldridge's public voice, one that is carefully constructed around an image of noble descent, learning, and a hint of adventure and danger:

The progenitors of the African Roscius down to his grandfather, were Princes of the Foolah tribe, whose dominions were situated in Senegal, on the banks of the river of that name. Mr. Aldridge's father was sent for his education to Schenectady College, near New York, and he had hardly quitted his native land, before an insurrection broke out amongst the tribe, in consequence of their King expressing a desire to exchange the prisoners taken in battle, in lieu of following the usual barbarous practice of selling them to slavery. The Prince's humanity however, interfered with a long established perquisite enjoyed by some of the principal officers of his court, and their jealousy being aroused, he fell a victim through their interested policy, to the inflamed passions of his mutinous subjects. Thus [was he] deprived of the means of asserting his birthright and claims, and to a certain extent cast upon society as a clergyman, and officiates at the present time at New York. Mr. Aldridge was intended for the same profession, but the sock and the buskin presenting stronger charms to his fancy than the study of divinity, he quitted the paternal roof, and sought the shores of Old England.[25]

In this memoir, there is no mention of his links with the African Grove Theater or of the experience of racism or segregation in the United States. Instead, Aldridge seems to take on a mixture of nobility and adventure somewhat akin to Othello's own tales of "most disastrous chances, / Of moving accidents by flood and field, / Of hair-breadth scapes" (1.3). Perhaps most significantly, this story emphasizes that Aldridge was born a free man.

While Aldridge sometimes melded the role of Othello into his own autobiography, the mantle of Shakespeare was often not sufficient protection against racism and class bias. The Folger's clipping file on Ira Aldridge includes an 1833 letter to the editor of *The Omnibus*, in which Aldridge insistently corrects a false claim that he has traveled to London as a servant, rather than as an actor and a free man: "I had the pleasure of Mr. Wallack's friendship whist he performed in Chatham Street Theatre, New York, but I never was his servant—nor the servant of any man. My respected father's circumstances, have, thank Providence, been all times too good to admit that any of his family to be in a state of servitude." Even more revealing is the letter's postscript, where Aldridge says "I beg leave to add that the Editor of the publication alluded to, not content with loading me with the most scurrilous abuse, has accused me of insulting females on the Surrey Establishment, which I declare to be a most infamous falsehood."[26]

Aldridge came to Europe to escape the segregated theaters of the United States, but he still met critics and sometimes even hostility in Europe. As Shakespeare scholar Joyce Green MacDonald points out, Aldridge's performances were perceived in the context of shifting notions of "acting black," informed by conflicting Emancipation movements in London and the British colonies, as well as a cultural appetite for minstrelsy entertainments.[27] London's proslave lobby cut short Aldridge's run at Covent Garden in April 1833. One English notice of his Othello performance that appeared in *The Times* complains that "owing to the shape of his lips it is utterly impossible for him to pronounce English in such a manner as to satisfy even the unfastidious ears of the gallery."[28] A more favorable review in a March 1834 issue of *The Freeholder* still expresses surprise that Aldridge matches the quality of white Shakespearean actors and minstrel shows:

> [W]e confess we never were more astonished than by the acting of this "Child of the Sun." The correctness of his diction—the melody of his voice (nothing can be more sweet)—his eye—his easy action, tout ensemble so admirable! Let him wherever he goes say he pleased a Cork audience.[29]

Given this constant comparison between Aldridge and the constructed black images that dogged his heels, it is understandable that Aldridge exploited his claim to an "authentic" blackness. Take, for example, a review of a 10 February 1837 performance at the Theatre Royal which appeared in the *Manchester Guardian*, where Aldridge's blackness was used as a selling point. The poster boasts:

> The Singular Novelty of <u>An Actor of Color</u>, Personating the routine of MOORISH AND AFRICAN CHARACTERS, has tendered the performances of the African Roscius, highly attractive in the Theaters in which he has appeared; — and the nightly plaudits with which he has uniformly been honoured by Crowded Audiences evince the estimation in which his talents are held by the Public.[30]

The posters and playbills for Aldridge's Othello drew in an audience expecting both novelty and authenticity. Aldridge's stage name, "The African Roscius," further invested him with native African authenticity. In addition, Aldridge delivered this promise by incorporating "proofs" of his blackness into his performance style. Aldridge was apparently notorious for slowly enclosing Desdemona's white hand in his dark one. This gesture is a variation of an early blackface convention used by white Othellos who blackened their hands and, then hid them in white gloves until the consummate moment of stripteasing revelation. Dame Madge Kendall, Aldridge's most famous Desdemona, recalls in her memoir:

When Othello said "Give me your hand, Desdemona,"
[3.4.33] Mr. Aldridge opened his hand and made me
place mine in it to emphasize the difference in their
colour. How he managed it, I could never make out, but
the effect he produced was so great that the audience
always rewarded it with a round of applause.[31]

Distilling his blackness to one powerful, black appendage
(and perhaps also signifying another even more dangerous
appendage kept hidden), Aldridge's hand swallows up
Kendall's whiteness, blurring their physical boundaries and
perhaps, as well, the boundaries between performance and
real life. Ultimately, Desdemona's life is taken by Othello's
hands. If the audience does not keep a watchful eye on the
stage, could the fictionality of the roles disappear as well?
Could that black man on stage really strangle the white
woman he has kissed, with whom he has lain in bed? We
see this same thrill of pleasure and danger in a still from
Paul Robeson's 1930 performance of *Othello*, where it is
unclear whether Robeson is caressing or about to strangle
Dame Peggy Ashcroft, who is kneeling docilely at his feet.
The titillation and the horror of losing control of the
theatrical fiction attached to Aldridge's performance are
reflected in this Russian review:

We find so many unusual, savage and uncontrolled
elements, entirely unknown to us until now. . . . [H]e is
a genuine tiger and one is terrified for the artists who
play Desdemona and Iago, for it seems that actually they
will come to harm.[32]

A St. Petersburg correspondent for *Le Nord* expresses a
similar sentiment in a review of Aldridge's Othello, dated
23 November 1858:

That shriek still seems to sound in my ears; it sent a
thrill of horror through all the spectators. Real tears roll
down his cheek, he foams at the mouth. . . . [A]n actor
told me that he saw the great tragedian sob for several
minutes after he came behind the scenes.[33]

For this reviewer, the effects of Aldridge's performance
extend past the boundaries of the falling curtain. If, in
Othello, Shakespeare forces us to consider the social repercussions of blackness, the social repercussions of Aldridge's
performance followed his viewers home. Certainly, too,
by watching what was probably their first authentically
black Othello kiss and kill a white Desdemona on stage,
Aldridge's viewers were watching social change take place
before their eyes. To a certain extent, Aldridge's self-
conscious reference to his own black difference on-and
offstage gained him access to a theater otherwise closed
to him.

In these reviews and artifacts, it is sometimes impossible
to distinguish between the self-image that Aldridge know-
ingly performed and the image the audience projected
onto him. For Aldridge, as well as for the other black actors
discussed in this essay, the web of fantastical blackness
was impossible to escape entirely. To fully appreciate the
complexity of the lives of early black Shakespeare actors
such as Aldridge, Hewlett, and Taft, we must keep in our
gaze the dehumanizing tradition of blackface minstrelsy.
With these images at our periphery, we more fully understand early black actors' struggles for voice, audience,
and creative freedom.

1. James Earl Jones, *Othello* (New York: Faber and Faber, 2003), 3.

2. Tavia Nyong'o, "Racial Kitsch and Black Performance," *Yale Journal of Criticism* 15 (2002):371–91.

3. Robin Chandler, quoted in Nyong'o, 372.

4. Michael Harris, quoted in Nyong'o, 372,

5. Nyong'o, 389.

6. bell hooks, *Black Looks: Race and Representation* (Boston: South End Press, 1992), 115–31.

7. See David Roediger, *The Wages of Whiteness: Race and the Making of the American Working Class* (New York: Verso, 1999), 115–31; and Eric Lott, *Love and Theft: Blackface Minstrelsy and the American Working Class* (New York: Oxford University Press, 1995), 89–107.

8. Robert Toll, *Blacking Up: The Minstrel Show in Nineteenth-Century America* (New York: Oxford University Press, 1977), 4.

9. Lott, 39.

10. Toll, 33.

11. Toll, 20.

12. David Krasner, *Resistance, Parody and Double-Consciousness in African American Theatre, 1895–1915* (New York: Palgrave, 1997), 4.

13. Bert Williams, quoted in Krasner, 10.

14. Bernard Peterson, ed., *Profiles of African American Stage Performers and Theatre People, 1816–1960* (Westport, CT: Greenwood Press, 2001), 19–46.

15. Marvin McAllister, *White People Do Not Know How to Behave at Entertainments Designed for Ladies and Gentlemen of Colour: William Brown's African and American Theatre* (Chapel Hill: University of North Carolina Press, 2003), 23.

16. McAllister, 24.

17. McAllister, 31.

18. McAllister, 31.

19. Peterson, 117.

20. Brenda Dixon Gottschild, *Digging the Africanist Presence in American Performance: Dance and other Contexts* (Westport, CT: Praeger Publishers, 1996), 15.

21. McAllister, 55.

22. See Peter Erickson's *Rewriting Shakespeare, Rewriting Ourselves* (Berkeley: University of California Press, 1994), and his *Citing Shakespeare: The Reinterpretation of Race in Contemporary Literature and Art* (New York: Palgrave McMillan Press, 2007).

23. McAllister, 42.

24. McAllister, 133–66.

25. "Memoir of Ira Aldridge." *Theatrical Times*, 15 April 1848.

26. Ira Aldridge, letter to the editor, *The Omnibus*, 15 May 1833.

27. Joyce Green MacDonald, "Acting Black: *Othello*, *Othello* Burlesques and the Performance of Blackness," *Theatre Journal* 46:2 (1994): 231–49, esp. 232.

28. Julie Hankey, ed. *Plays in Performance: "Othello"* (Bristol: Bristol Classical Press, 1987), 81.

29. *The Freeholder*, 3 March 1834, Theatre section.

30. Quoted in Ruth Cowhig, "Blacks in Renaissance Drama and the Role of Shakespeare's *Othello*," in *The Black Presence in English Literature*, ed. David Dabydeen (Manchester: Manchester University Press, 1985), 241.

31. Madge Kendall, *Dame Madge Kendall: By Herself* (London: J. Murray, 1933), 86–87.

32. Hankey, 82.

33. Hankey, 82.

Photograph of the American Vitagraph Film Company, 1915.
Billy Rose Theatre Division, The New York Public Library for the
Performing Arts, Astor, Lenox and Tilden Foundations.

Shakespeare Film in America: O Brave New World of Bardolatry!

Kenneth S. Rothwell

In one of his trademark metaphysical conceits, John Donne's fevered imagination managed to yoke sexual urgency with the Elizabethan frenzy over the discovery of America.

> Licence my roaving hands, and let them go,
> Before, behind, between, above, below.
> O my America! My new-found-land,
> My kingdome, safeliest when with one man man'd,
> My Myne of precious stones, My Emperie,
> How blest I am in this discovering thee!

"To His Mistris Going to Bed," ca. 1600

Ignore the fact that "America" here blazons forth an erotic act best left unexplicated on a family television show. Do note, however, that Donne's trope for exploration, similar to Camillo's eloquent "wild dedication . . . / To unpath'd waters, undream'd shores" in *The Winter's Tale* (4.4.567),[1] embodies humanity's craving for charismatic rebirth. Even when the American dream has seemed close to being transmogrified into a Kafka-like nightmare, this seductive fantasy has prevailed over gloomier assessments. Moreover, Marshall McLuhan's revolutionary definition of the "cool medium" and Jean Baudrillard's identification of a "media simulacrum" have underscored the growing trend of mass audiences to confuse the hyperreality of moving images with reality itself.

Donne's analogy also provides a template for the Shakespeare film in America. It would ultimately, although not at first, become the job of the roving camera to peer unflinchingly at the work of William Shakespeare, with camera angles from "before, behind, between, above, [and] below." Pioneer filming of Shakespeare's plays in America started early in 1906, both in Bay Shore, Long Island, where beaches provided a locale for the opening of *Twelfth Night*,

and in Brooklyn's Flatbush, where J. Stuart Blackton—ex-cartoonist, Edison aide, and impresario—had established a considerable physical plant solely dedicated to the manufacture of movies, usually at ten cents a foot.[2] The studio's relocation from Manhattan to Brooklyn removed it from the Broadway theater. Subsequently, when New York film companies migrated to California, filmmaking was further liberated to become an indigenous art, unlike the British films that cozily nestled in theatrical venues, such as F. R. Benson's 1913 Royal Shakespeare Company *Richard III*, or the French *film d'art* that reduced movies to recording performances of great actors, such as Jean Mounet-Sully's *Hamlet*.[3]

It must be asked: What, after all, is an *American* Shakespeare movie? In this transnational era when movies are financed in one country and filmed in another, the question becomes all the more complicated. Any Shakespeare film, however, that incorporates fundamental American values may be considered. For example, Blackton's Brooklyn Vitagraph applied Henry Ford's assembly-line technique to manufacturing a dozen one-reel Shakespeare titles that included *A Midsummer Night's Dream*, *Antony and Cleopatra*, *As You Like It*, *Henry VIII (Cardinal Wolsey)*, *Julius Caesar*, *Macbeth*, and *King Lear*. (A planned *Hamlet* with Clara Kimball Young as Ophelia never materialized.) The brevity of these ten- to-fifteen minute films gave them a jumpy, nervous look, but Vitagraph adhered to the Motion Picture Patents Company's rigid one-reel standard until 1912.[4] A surviving panoramic photograph of the Vitagraph company exposes its late Victorian world view—the women in stylish millinery and coats, the finer gentlemen in bowler hats, the stagehands in cloth caps, the boys in knickerbockers, the moguls like Blackton himself at the center in a black Chesterfield and derby and sporting a huge cigar.

From the beginning, there was a search for sound, to rescue Shakespeare on silent film from its status as a risible oxymoron;[5] thus, the movie trade journals were crammed with all kinds of panaceas for ending the terrible silence.[6] Genteel young ladies brought up to play piano for dinner guests became hot commodities as managers installed them "in a safe environment" to play movie theme music. Edison wax cylinders behind the screen cranked out sound effects, and lecturer W. Stephen Bush of Philadelphia offered theater managers advice on how to "attract the best class of people,"[7] although the Gaumont Chronophone talking picture machine was doomed by its tinny amplification.[8] At Vitagraph before World War I, the camera could not rove but, with rare exceptions, remained stationary and recorded what could be seen immediately "before" it. In the Vitagraph *Julius Caesar*, one cinematic trope occurs with the materialization of Caesar's ghost from thin air in Brutus's tent before Philippi, after the fashion of Georges Méliès's pioneering trick photography.

By 1912 the cavernous new "Palace" and "Bijou" theaters (replacing the scruffy nickelodeons) needed feature-length movies to fill seats. Adolph Zukor's importation of Sarah Bernhardt's film *Elizabeth* broke the back of the one-reel tyranny and added the mystique of the world's greatest actress to the tacky film business. The earliest feature-length American movie turned out to be an ambitious five-reel production of seventy-seven scenes from *Richard III* produced by M. B. Dudley and shot mainly in New York's Westchester County. As Gloucester, Frederick B. Warde (1851–1935),[9] a peripatetic British Shakespearean, brought a convincing miasma of evil to the role and doubtless satisfied the American fetish for "high-class" actors. Despite his stage background, Warde's costume drama is as filmic as F. R. Benson's contemporaneous British *Richard III* (1911) was stage-bound in its Stratford-upon-Avon theater. In a supercolossal, pre-DeMillian, no-expense-spared extravaganza, spear-brandishing infantry, mounted knights, and bevies of lavishly dressed ladies-in-waiting fill the mise-en-

scène. Scenarist James Keane introduced a two-masted Lancastrian warship arriving at Milford Haven. Warde, as "this bottled spider" (4.4.81), dominates the screen with his seriocomic antics, elaborately wiping his bloody sword after skewering poor mad King Henry. A 1916 *King Lear*, produced by Edwin Thanhouser and his talented actress wife, Gertrude Homen, even more graphically showed how an acrobatic camera could heighten reality. The Thanhousers' sweeping shots, in ambition nearly at the level of D. W. Griffith's *The Birth of a Nation* (1915), took the action not only "before" the audience but also "above" and "below." A hirsute Frederick B. Warde again starred, with the aura of "class" that insecure Americans thought only the British owned.

In 1916, the American Shakespeare movie launched its own public relations blitz when warring companies Metro and Fox fought over rights to commemorate the three-hundredth anniversary of Shakespeare's death by simultaneously releasing two *Romeo and Juliet*s plus an *Antony and Cleopatra*. Francis X. Bushman—a matinee idol out of central casting, with his square jaw, enviable physique, and sleazy personal life—played Romeo opposite Beverly Bayne's virginal Juliet in the now-lost $250,000 Metro film, released as "refined entertainment . . . for ladies and gentlemen." While the Metro film was highly praised for its "beautifully composed scenes of the streets of Verona" and Juliet's funeral procession,[10] the casting of "vampire" Theda Bara (née Theodosia Goodman) as Juliet opposite Harry Hilliard in the rival Fox production set up a formidable competitor. As with the Metro version, "no expense [was] spared" on design, and Theda Bara's inspired eyerolling captivated the fans, although it was admitted that perceiving her as a "sweet, innocent" Juliet was a huge leap from her famous roles as a "vamp."[11]

Theda Bara continued her career as a quasi-Shakespearan actress with an eponymous role in *Cleopatra* (1917), a role already undertaken by Helen Gardner in 1913,[12] with a splashy epic featuring the Middle Eastern ambience that appealed to popular taste after Sarah Bernhardt's nineteenth-century stage production.[13] Robert Hamilton Ball got it right when he said that *Cleopatra* was "not Shakespearean but an eye-filling recreation of glamorous pseudohistory."[14] A press book gushed that it was not merely "sumptuous" but also "luxuriant," and not just "costly" but also "expensive." The film's promoters also thought that theater lobbies should be "festooned . . . with many colored drapings . . . silhouettes of camels, sphinxes and pyramids," and that the ushers should be garbed in togas, twin obelisks raised outside the theater, the floor strewn with sand, and the manager rent a camel. In an early marriage of pedagogy and marketing, it was urged that high school students compete in an essay contest about the film. Still, killjoys like critic Richard Stokes huffed over the skimpiness of Bara's famous "costumes," and another noted that in one scene Cleopatra wore "virtually nothing but beads."[15]

The full weight of Americanism, in the grand tradition of Sinclair Lewis's immortal George Babbitt, landed squarely on Shakespeare when America's sweetheart, Mary Pickford, playing Katharina Minola, along with Douglas Fairbanks as Petruchio, coproduced the first feature-length talking Shakespeare movie, *The Taming of the Shrew* (1929). Like other enterprising young American women, such as Clara Kimball Young and Helen Gardner, Pickford showed the gumption of a Kate Minola in carving out a business career. Director Sam Taylor's notorious screen credit, "written by William Shakespeare with additional dialogue by Sam Taylor," became immortal for its hubris, but there remains doubt if the credit ever really appeared.[16] United Artists gave Taylor a unit director's independence, but he still relied on the Hollywood infrastructure of skilled unionized craftsmen.[17] The talented artistic director William Cameron Menzies, who learned the "Warner look"

from German expressionist Anton Grot, had also designed the spectacular sets for *The Thief of Bagdad* (1924) and later, for *Gone with the Wind* (1939). Swashbuckling Douglas Fairbanks, wearing his trademark expression of maddening insolence, fit the American ideal of the goal-oriented hero who knows how to stay the course, whether as Robin Hood, Zorro, the Greek, the thief of Bagdad, or Petruchio. Mary Pickford apparently was depressed by the outcome, but time has treated the re-released movie with increasing respect.[18]

The success of Max Reinhardt's Hollywood Bowl production of *Midsummer Night's Dream* (1935) inspired movie executive Jack Warner, whose company normally churned out gangster films and Busby Berkeley musicals, to gamble $1.5 million on a 38,000-square-foot sound stage, with Max Reinhardt and William Dieterle codirecting the film. German cinematography had by then become a major Hollywood staple, showing again the capacity of America to absorb from other cultures. A close-up head shot of the premier ballet dancer in the "Masque of Night" (choreographed by Branislawa Nijinska, with incidental music from Mendelssohn) combines expressionistic soft focus and the Continental Weimar style of Rembrandt portraiture. This exquisite moment may not be Shakespeare, but it is pure Reinhardt, who had been staging the play since 1905. The play's darker side—the nightmare wood of gnarled elves and unicorns—is also there, mainly thanks to William Dieterle, whose *Hunchback of Notre Dame* (1939) later testified to his impeccable taste for the grotesque.

If the spirit of Weimar Germany hovered over *Midsummer Night's Dream*, the ghost of Britannia haunted the staid 1936 *Romeo and Juliet*, whose producers lived in fear of the purists who had mocked Hollywood for putting toughguy actors like James Cagney into Shakespeare. To exorcize these demons, Irving Thalberg and George Cukor crammed the screen with a veritable waxworks of seemingly

Mary Pickford and Douglas Fairbanks in *The Taming of the Shrew*.
Photographic still, 1929.
Used with permission of the Mary Pickford Institute for Film Education.
CAT. NO. 107

Mickey Rooney as Puck and Dick Powell as Lysander.
Photographic still, 1935.
A Midsummer Night's Dream © Turner Entertainment Co.
A Warner Bros. Entertainment Company.
All Rights Reserved.
CAT. NO. 105

aristocratic British actors recruited from Hollywood's expatriate colony: Leslie Howard (Romeo), Violet Kemble-Cooper (Lady Capulet), and C. Aubrey Smith (Capulet). Thirty-five-year-old American Norma Shearer was allowed to play Juliet because she was a talented actress, but she was no more antiquated than Katherine Cornell, then playing Juliet on the Broadway stage. Forty-four-year-old Basil Rathbone was cast as the fiery Tybalt. To add an even greater aura of class, the producers selected the great John Barrymore as a scenery-chewing but nevertheless charming Mercutio. Norma Shearer's Juliet and Leslie Howard's forty-three-year-old Romeo exactly fit the middle-brow stereotype for sublime Shakespearean actors, which seventy years ago was better embodied in a dignified Sir Johnston Forbes-Robertson than in a callow Leonardo DiCaprio. All met with the academic approval of Professor William Strunk of Cornell University, the famed rhetorician and the movie's respectable front. In an aptly fitting way, the MGM style of fetishized shot, crosscutting, and camera angles neatly interfaces with the thematic implications and rhythms of Shakespeare's tragedy. The camera travels deep inside the narrative, moves upside down, sideways, and everywhere, and then allows us, godlike, to view the action from an Olympian distance. Unhappily, the film's timidity in other respects straitjackets the play in the way that the sonnet imprisons Juliet's language at the Capulet ball, until she "gallops apace" (3.2.1), so to speak, in her own uninhibited blank verse.

By 1953, when MGM released producer John Houseman and director Joseph L. Mankiewicz's $2 million *Julius Caesar*, classical Hollywood studio cinema was near collapse from the new specter of mass television. *Julius Caesar* marked a new direction for the American Shakespeare film in that it was neither purely American like the 1929 *Taming of the Shrew*, nor heavily Germanic like the 1935 *Midsummer Night's Dream*, nor faux-British like the 1936 *Romeo and Juliet*, but instead would-be New York Actors Studio with an adroit mixture of British and American stage and film actors. In *Julius Caesar*, however, Shakespeare had lacked the foresight to create a classical Hollywood hero. Except possibly for the ruthless Caesar Augustus (Douglas Watson), neither Brutus (James Mason), nor Cassius (John Gielgud), nor Caesar (Louis Calhern), nor even Marlon Brando as an inspired Antony follows a clear arc to fulfillment. These are men of stone. Ubiquitous statues of prominent citizens with their hair brushed well forward in the high Roman style expressively fill the mise-en-scène as the camera tracks Cassius and Brutus up and down and sideways through public squares and palace corridors,[19] enough statuary, I estimate, to stock the Metropolitan Museum of Art. A deeply embedded political subtext, echoing the Wellesian Mercury Theatre antifascist *Julius Caesar*, may or may not link the lamentable fate of Cinna the poet with the Red Scare of the early 1950s: "I am not Cinna the conspirator. . . . It is no matter, his name's Cinna" (3.3.32).

After the Mankiewicz film, marquees for the American Shakespeare movie went dark for nearly two decades. Pioneering television instead transmitted considerable Shakespeare when talented unknowns like Charlton Heston appeared as Petruchio in *Taming of the Shrew* on Studio One/CBS (1950) and as Macbeth on Westinghouse Studio One (1951).[20] Heston would later rededicate his Shakespearean vocation with a lavish investment in *Antony and Cleopatra* (1972), filmed in Spain, that received little exposure in the United States.

A major Shakespeare movie, *Macbeth*, finally emerged in 1970 under the American sponsorship of Hugh Hefner's *Playboy* magazine to take its place alongside Orson Welles's brilliant but confused Republic Pictures sketch of *Macbeth* (1948).[21] Only marginally American, Roman Polanski's movie was filmed in Wales, its scriptwriter (Kenneth Tynan) was British, and its great director, Polish. When Polanski's young heiress wife was murdered by the so-called Manson gang of demented young women, the film became inseparable from the notorious murder case. Even though Polanski has always denied any connection, it is impossible to watch the savage stabbing of Duncan without suspecting a roman[Polanski] à clef alluding to the gory fate of Sharon Tate and her friend Abigail Folger. When the film was released, Shakespeare, it seemed, had been decisively entangled with popular culture. Polanski's violent images of blood find precedents in Shakespeare's text, as well as in the Manson murders. His movie also belongs beside Peter Brook's *King Lear* (1971) as an outgrowth of the current fascination with Jan Kott's theory of the Grand Mechanism—history as an implacable and unending power struggle. Polanski's daring *Macbeth* foreshadowed the century's later bold remakes, like Derek Jarman's *Tempest* (1979), Michael Almereyda's *Hamlet* (2000), and Baz Luhrmann's *Romeo + Juliet* (1996), which for lack of space cannot be discussed here. The mixture of the fair and foul ("Fair is foul, and foul is fair,/ Hover through the fog and filthy air" [1.1.11]) becomes Polanski's, as well as Shakespeare's, leitmotif.[22]

Technologies of television and film have recently evolved into a closer symbiosis, making a derivative and sometimes "dumbed-down" American Shakespeare "movie" popularly available on VHS and DVD. A gaggle of spinoff Shakespeare TV movies reveals the volatile literary undercurrents beneath the plastic surface of American consumerism. Tim Blake Nelson's *O* (2001) might easily be mistaken for another high school movie like *Fast Times at Ridgemont High* (1982) except for its groveling debts to *Othello*, displacing Shakespeare's play into a prep school where the repulsive Hugo, a surrogate for Iago, soars like a hawk over friends and rivals. Like the Polanski *Macbeth*, its narrative is deeply embedded in contemporary American tabloid journalism, hinting at the unsolved homicide of O. J. Simpson's wife, as well as the massacre at Columbine High School.

It is a companion piece to Geoffrey Saxe's Masterpiece Theater *Othello* (2001), whose mature characters recast as members of the London police make their translation into high drama more plausible.

The Tempest (1998), dismissed by Caryn James in *The New York Times* as a "clunker," is one of those "paratextual" Shakespeare productions that abandons the language entirely and reinvents Shakespeare's characters as soldiers in the American Civil War, although it does retain such themes as the unanswerable political (and American) question of how best to govern the irrational. With army blue all over the mise-en-scène it would be hard to envision a more flamboyant stars-and-stripes ambiance for Shakespeare; even the casting of Peter Fonda as Gideon Prospero could not save it. Paul Mazursky's very New York film of *The Tempest* (1982), starring John Cassavetes, was also a paratext in its abandonment of Shakespeare's language, but the film shows again this skillful director's sensitivity for Shakespeare (see, for example, his *Harry and Tonto* [1974], based on *King Lear*).

In another demonstration of the Shakespearean afterlife, shards of *King Lear* are reimagined in a Turner Network *King of Texas* (2002), which takes place on a ranch shortly after the liberation of Texas from Mexico. Its opening freezes the blood when old John Lear hangs two of his daughter's ranch hands for theft. The enraged daughters—Susannah, Rebecca, and Claudia—despise their violent father, played by Patrick Stewart. At one point Rebecca accuses him of working their mother to death, which is a novel answer to the stock question about what happened to King Lear's queen. Mr. Highsmith, not content to gouge out Westover's eyes, must scorch one out with a hot poker. His wife, Rebecca, cheerfully joins in the caper by searing out the second. The outsized Texas accents of the young women and of Patrick Stewart are impressively accurate, especially when Rebecca, holding a shotgun announces to her father that "Ah own this property." This mainstream TV offering of *King Lear* deserves comparison with the excellent film of Jane Smiley's spin-off from *King Lear, A Thousand Acres* (1997), which gives a powerful and typically American feminist twist to the story of a chauvinistic old man and his three daughters.

Other entries at the turn of the century included a reworking of *The Taming of the Shrew* in *10 Things I Hate about You* (1999), a clever movie with crude sex-related humor and dialogue and alcohol- and drug-related scenes, all involving teens. On the surface, it is another high school chick flick, yet the director manages to retain the broad outlines of the play's plot, with Julia Stiles as Katerina "Kat" Stratford and Heath Ledger as Patrick "Pat" Verona creating an amusing palimpsest for Shakespeare's comedy.[23] Stiles, who successfully managed Viola in the 2002 production of *Twelfth Night* at New York's Delacorte Theater, shows versatility, especially when she delivers her speech of surrender to Pat Verona, the surrogate for Petruchio. Joseph Gordon-Levitt as Cameron (Lucentio) even manages to utter Shakespeare's words directed to Tranio on first glimpsing Bianca (Larisa Oleynik): "I burn, I pine, I perish" (*Shrew*, 1.1.155).

At the millennium, film and video makers could not seem to get enough of *Hamlet*. In 2000, youthful director Michael Almereyda steered the American Shakespeare movie right into cyberspace with a modernization that embraced the power of contemporary virtual reality over the "words, words, words" (*Hamlet*, 2.2.192) of Shakespeare's prince. Ophelia's flowers appear on screen as pictures of reality, not reality itself. Hamlet (Ethan Hawke) is the postmodern child of the fin de siècle whose grubby outfits, oversized ski caps, and generally grungy look identify him as a malcontented son of the privileged classes. Hamlet is not a poet but a film-school freak, using his low-tech Pixelvision camcorder, hypnotized by images rather than words. His "Mousetrap" is a curious montage of shots from animated depictions of the poison being dropped into the king's ear, to home-movie shots of little Hamlet with his true father (Sam Shepard) and mother, to a clip from a silent movie showing a man in terminal agony, to other clips of another indeterminate silent film based on the Roman plays. Hamlet's electronic arsenal carries the mechanical reproduction of art to a reductio ad absurdum, with camcorders, cell phones, laptops, and palm pilots becoming extensions, or diminutions, of the soul. The Ghost (Sam Shepard) materializes and disappears out of a vending machine in token of the iron grip of advertising on the consumerist commonwealth.

Ophelia (Julia Stiles), unlike predictable Ophelias modeled on Olivier's ethereal Jean Simmons, has the petulant cuteness and inner toughness of young girls from the MTV generation. Memorably, she goes mad on one of the circular ramps in the Guggenheim Museum on Fifth Avenue. On a slim budget Almereyda assembled an impressive cast and kept the play's spirit of groping toward some elusive truth inviolate.[24] On the other hand, Jonathan Penner's *Let the Devil Wear Black* (1999) turns his prince into a weird Los Angeles graduate student, who returns home to find his mother romantically involved with his uncle. In this whirling universe, a flurry of bizarre camera angles, jump cuts, and daring sound effects—fodder for just another crime thriller—bring the hero to his inevitable doom. On a more solemn note is the Campbell Scott-Hallmark *Hamlet* (2000), which continues the exploitation of the American Civil War motif in a stage-bound video treatment of the play, where literalness sometimes drains the text of significance. As the son of the charismatic George C. Scott, who incarnated General George Patton, Campbell Scott self-referentially fills the niche of a young prince in quest of his father's approval. The son's uncanny resemblance to the father flickers across the screen, as if the father's looming ghost were still there. Shreds of *Hamlet* and other plays surface elsewhere as well in Steve Martin's hilarious *L.A. Story* (1991), Arnold Schwarzenegger's surprising *Last Action Hero* (1993) that includes footage from the Olivier *Hamlet*, Danny DeVito's *Renaissance Man* (1994), Al Pacino's flippant but informative documentary *Looking for Richard* (1996), and the prize-winning *Shakespeare Behind Bars* (2005) that brought inmates of a Kentucky prison into the moral universe of *The Tempest*.[25]

Titus Andronicus, a long-standing puzzle and trial for Shakespeare critics, underwent a strong revival on the American screen, notably with Julie Taymor's brilliant film *Titus* (2000) that starred Anthony Hopkins reprising his cannibalistic proclivities as Dr. Hannibal Lecter in *The Silence of the Lambs* (1991). Taymor's aesthetic eclecticism, originating in her study of Asian dance, turned Shakespeare's rodomontade language and Senecan violence into a fine art-house movie. She crams a bewildering gallery of characters into a tiny space, partly by filtering them through the eyes of a small boy (Osheen Jones), who when the movie begins is happily smashing toy soldiers on a 1950s-style kitchen table, before moving on to the Coliseum of ancient Rome (actually Croatia). Like King Lear, Titus continues to make spectacular errors in judgment over and over again. The "Penny Arcade Nightmare" episodes scattered through Taymor's movie reprise Mutoscope peepshows that entertained the crowds at the turn of the century.[26]

John Dunne's very low-budget *Titus* cannot hope to match Taymor's achievement as a serious American Shakespeare movie, but it competes for a first prize in the category of slasher drive-in movie. Horror upon horror spills out of the screen, from the maniacal laughter generated by the flaying of Alarbus, to the grisly slaughter of the Nurse by Aaron the Moor, to the brutal slaying of Aaron's infant son, to the unspeakable Thyestean feast.

Kenneth Branagh's *Love's Labour's Lost* (2000), though only liminally of American origin, nevertheless shows the crossover effect that American Shakespeare movies exerted on European directors, in a reversal of the continental tides that once flowed into American moviemaking. In turning the recherché wit of *Love's Labors Lost* into a whimsical musical comedy, Branagh followed the path of earlier films that adapted *The Comedy of Errors* into *The Boys from Syracuse* (1940) and *The Taming of the Shrew* into *Kiss Me Kate* (1953). As an impresario, he understood the need, which the BBC series disastrously neglected, for casting American actors and exploiting American popular culture. In *Hamlet*, he earned Bronx cheers for recruiting Jack Lemmon as Marcellus, although Lemmon's performance was by no means so egregious as his critics thought. The court of Navarre was displaced to the ominous eve of World War II, when young people still danced cheek to cheek, wore Fred Astaire's trademark white tie and tails at proms, and reveled in radio's Lucky Strike Hit Parade. Broadway superstar Nathan Lane takes over the play of the Nine Worthies, leading the entire company in Irving Berlin's brassy American "There's No Business Like Show Business." All the frolics at Navarre have been but a stalling time, awaiting the arrival of the messenger of death, Monsieur Marcade, so that humanity's dark battle against time lurks just under the surface of the frivolous play. A farewell at the airport, echoing the classic scene in *Casablanca* between Ingrid Bergman and Humphrey Bogart, further inserts the movie into the American melting pot.[27]

Another crossover between America and Europe occurs with Michael Hoffman's 1999 *Midsummer Night's Dream* ("Based on the play by William Shakespeare"), which was shot on a fabulous hilltop town in Tuscany, Italy, but not exactly the Athens of Shakespeare's play. Visually the film is a masterpiece, stunningly designed and costumed. At the opening, familiar themes from Felix Mendelssohn's "Incidental Music" yield to stirring chorales from *La Traviata* that sonically enhance the citizens' light-heartedness as they promenade in the village's exhibitionistic hour. Titania (Michelle Pfeiffer) wears gowns inspired by the pre-Raphaelites, while Hippolyta (Sophie Marceau), a woman of ineffable dignity with her parasol and flowing dress, and Hermia (Anna Friel) with her epic millinery could both pose for John Singer Sargent portraits. Feistier is Calista Flockhart, star of the TV series *Ally McBeal,* as the forlorn Helena who appears astride a bicycle in a sign of the Victorian era's growing liberation of women. Kevin Kline as Bottom becomes a major character, a kind of Holy Fool, who bears the burden of an off-the-book nagging wife. The bower of Titania, a cluster of Etruscan tombs and caves, resembles a house of ill repute, while her fairy king, Rupert Everett, simultaneously looks raffish and heroic.[28]

Scotland PA (2001) came with the new century. Its surface impudence conceals a resourceful modernization that places *Macbeth* in the midst of today's cultural wars. When a powerfully attractive and persuasive Pat McBeth says to her vacillating husband, Joe "Mac" McBeth, who cannot summon up the will to kill Duncan, "We're not bad people, Mac. We're just underachievers who have to make up for lost time," she demonstrates the movie's translation of Shakespeare's heightened poetry into dumbed-down but still-effective contemporary prose. As Pat McBeth, Maura Tierney suffers a burned wrist while helping (inadvertently) to drop Duncan (James Rebhorn) into a vat of boiling grease. The festering sore, just "a little burn," becomes the surrogate for the blood on Lady Macbeth's hands that a "little water" can supposedly wash away. After the grisly and heartless murder of Duncan, Pat, in another direct echo of *Macbeth,* says to Mac (James LeGros) "You did it, Mac. You did it. It's done. It can't be undone." Her transition from a confident, nagging wife into a nervous wreck is a tour de force of acting skill, which stands outside the film's aura of black comedy. Christopher Walken as police Lieutenant Ernie McDuff, a fiercely intelligent Columbo-type detective, moves from affability to steely relentlessness as he plays a cat-and-mouse game with the wretched suspects, Pat and Mac. Duncan's two sons, Malcolm and Donald, are portrayed as ne'er-do-wells, a would-be musician and a closeted homosexual who turn over their father's hamburger-joint empire with the recurring prefix of "Mc" and "Mac" to Mac and Pat. The 1970s ambiance receives first-rate support from non-diegetic rock-and-roll theme music. Through its rhythm and continuity the film achieves the jolt of a crime thriller, with overtones from its long-gone archetype.[29]

As *Scotland PA* and many other movies show, Shakespeare's American acolytes will not willingly let him die. He goes on sometimes whole, sometimes in bits and fragments, sometimes wounded, sometimes glorified—but he goes on. *Before, behind, between, above, below.* At the frontier of the digital revolution, when the power of images has nearly overwhelmed reality, when even words on a computer screen are viewed as images, the films based on his work expand into even greater cultural landmarks. No American multiplex lives without him. He has long been America's greatest scenarist.

Filmography

A Midsummer Night's Dream, Antony and Cleopatra, As You Like It, Henry VIII (Cardinal Wolsey), Julius Caesar, Richard III, Macbeth, King Lear (United States [USA] 1905–10). Produced by J. Stuart Blackton. Silent. Vitagraph. 10 to 15 minutes.

The Life and Death of King Richard III (USA 1912). Produced by M. B. Dudley. Silent. The Richard III Film Company, Inc., with Frederick B. Warde. 5 reels.

Romeo and Juliet (USA 1916). Directed by J. Noble, with Francis X. Bushman and Beverly Bayne. Silent. Metro. 60 minutes.

Romeo and Juliet (USA 1916). Directed by J. Gordon Edwards, with Theda Bara and Harry Hilliard. Silent. Fox. 50 minutes.

Cleopatra (USA 1917). Directed by J. Gordon Edwards, with Theda Bara. Silent. Fox. Runtime not available.

The Taming of the Shrew (USA 1929). Directed by Sam Taylor, with Mary Pickford and Douglas Fairbanks. Sound, black and white (B&W). United Artists. 68 minutes.

A Midsummer Night's Dream (USA 1935). Directed by William Dieterle and Max Reinhardt. Sound, B&W. Warner Brothers. 132 minutes.

Romeo and Juliet (USA 1936). Directed by George Cukor, with Leslie Howard and Norma Shearer. Sound, B&W. MGM. 126 minutes.

The Boys from Syracuse (USA 1940). Directed by A. Edward Sutherland, with Alan Jones and Joe Penner. *The Comedy of Errors.* Universal. 73 minutes.

Macbeth (USA 1948). Directed by Orson Welles. Sound, B&W. Republic Pictures. 89 minutes.

Julius Caesar (USA 1953). Directed by Joseph Mankiewicz, with Marlon Brando. MGM. 121 minutes.

Kiss Me Kate (USA 1953). Directed by George Sidney, with Howard Keel and Kathryn Grayson. Musical of *The Taming of the Shrew.* MGM. 109 minutes.

Macbeth (United Kingdom [UK] 1971). Directed by Roman Polanski, with Jon Finch and Francesca Annis. Playboy/Columbia-Warner. 140 minutes.

Romeo + Juliet (USA 1996). Directed by Baz Luhrmann, with Leonardo DiCaprio and Claire Danes. 20th-Century Fox. 120 minutes.

A Thousand Acres (USA 1997). Directed by Jocelyn Moorhouse, with Jessica Lange. *King Lear.* Beacon. 105 minutes.

The Tempest (USA 1998). Directed by Jack Bender, with Peter Fonda and Harold Perrineau, Jr. Bonnie Raskin Productions. Run time not available. TV movie.

King Lear (UK 1998). Directed by Richard Eyre, with Ian Holm. BBC/Masterpiece Theater. 150 minutes. TV movie.

Let the Devil Wear Black (USA 1999). Directed by Jonathan Penner, with Randall Batinkoff. *Hamlet.* Trimark Pictures. 89 minutes.

A Midsummer Night's Dream (USA 1999). Directed by Michael Hoffman, with Kevin Kline and Michelle Pfeiffer. Fox Searchlight. 115 minutes.

10 Things I Hate about You (USA 1999). Directed by Gil Yunger, with Patrick Verona and Julia Stiles. *Taming of the Shrew.* Touchstone Pictures. 97 minutes.

Titus (USA 1999). Directed by Julie Taymor, with Anthony Hopkins and Jessica Lange. *Titus Andronicus.* Fox Searchlight Pictures and Clear Blue Sky Productions with Overseas Film Group. 163 minutes.

Titus Andronicus (USA 1999). Directed by Christopher Dunne, with Candy K. Sweet. Lexton Raleigh. 147 minutes. TV movie.

Hamlet (USA 2000). Directed by Michael Almereyda, with Ethan Hawke, Diane Venora, and Julia Stiles. Double A Films/Miramax. 122 minutes.

Love's Labour's Lost (UK/France/USA 2000). Directed by Kenneth Branagh, with Kenneth Branagh andNathan Lane. Arts Council of England/Miramax. 93 minutes.

Hamlet (USA 2000). Directed by Eric Simonson and Mary Francis Budig, with Scott Campbell. Hallmark Entertainment. 178 minutes. TV movie).

The King Is Alive (Denmark 2001). Directed by Kristian Levring, with Miles Anderson. *King Lear*. A Dogme Film. IFC Films. 118 minutes.

Scotland, PA (USA 2001). Directed by Billy Morrissette, with James LeGros, Maura Tierney, and Christopher Walken. *Macbeth*. Lot 47 Films. 104 minutes.

O (USA 2001). Directed by Tim Blake Nelson, with Mekbhi Phifer and Julia Stiles. *Othello*. Lions Gate Films. 91 minutes.

Othello (UK 2001). Directed by Geoffrey Sax, with Keeley Hawes and Christopher Eccleston. CBC/Masterpiece Theater. 100 minutes. TV movie.

King of Texas (USA 2002). Directed by Uli Edel, with Patrick Stewart. *King Lear*. TNT (Turner Network). 95 minutes.

1. Shakespeare quotations are from *The Riverside Shakespeare*, 2nd ed., gen. ed. G. Blakemore Evans (Boston: Houghton Mifflin, 1997).

2. See Anthony Slide, *The Big V: A History of the Vitagraph Company* (Metuchen, NJ: Scarecrow Press, 1976); William Urrichio and Roberta E. Pearson, *Reframing Culture: The Case of the Vitagraph Quality Films* (Princeton, NJ: Princeton University Press, 1993); "Movie Exhibitors Once 'Doubled in Brass,'" *Brooklyn Daily Eagle* (16 February 1933): M2+; and "Bay Shorers Flipped Over Faces in Flicks," *New York Sunday News* (6 February 1972): 21B.

3. Robert Hamilton Ball, *Shakespeare on Silent Film, A Strange Eventful History* (London: George Allen & Unwin Ltd., 1968), 90–91.

4. David A. Cook, *A History of Narrative Film*, 3rd ed. (New York: Norton, 1981), 37.

5. Kenneth S. Rothwell, "The Conspiracy Against Silence: How Movies Began to Talk," unpublished paper presented at the annual meeting of the Modern Language Association, New York City, 2002; see also Edward Abel and Nick Altman, eds., *The Sounds of Early Cinema* (Bloomington: Indiana University Press, 2001).

6. Trade journals consulted include the *New York Clipper, Moving Picture World,* and the *New York Dramatic Mirrror,* either on microfilm or in extensive clipping files at the New York Public Library of Performing Arts, Lincoln Center, or the Museum of Modern Art film library.

7. *Moving Picture World* (17 June 1908), 547.

8 Early Motion Picture Catalogs, Museum of Modern Art, New York City. The Gaumont sound and image projector was another failed device.

9. Frederick B. Warde, *Fifty Years of Make-Believe* (New York: International Press Syndicate, 1920).

10. *Billboard* (27 October 1916).

11. Ray, "WM. Fox's *Romeo and Juliet*," *Billboard* (29 October 1916).

12. "Helen Gardner in *Cleopatra*," *Moving Picture World* (18 January 1913): 32.

13. David W. Menefee, *Sarah Bernhardt in the Theatre of Films and Sound Recordings* (Jefferson, NC, and London: McFarland & Co., 2003), 21.

14. Ball, 253.

15. Press Book for Fox *Cleopatra* (MFLXNC 690) and relevant ephemeral newspaper clippings, New York Public Library of Performing Arts, Lincoln Center.

16. See J. M. Welsh, "Shakespeare with— and without—Words," *Literature/Film Quarterly* 1 (1973): 84–88.

17. See David Bordwell, J. Staiger, and K. Thompson, *The Classical Hollywood Cinema: Film Style and Mode of Production to 1960* (New York: Columbia University Press, 1985).

18. Mary Pickford, *Sunshine and Shadow* (New York: Doubleday, 1955).

19. See Robert Hapgood's informative essay, "Shakespeare and the Included Spectator," in *Reinterpretations of Elizabethan Drama,* ed. Norman Rabkin (New York: Columbia University Press, 1969), 123.

20. Available for viewing by appointment at the Museum of Broadcasting, New York City.

21. For an interesting commentary comparing the Welles and Polanski *Macbeth*s, see Wendy Rogers Harper, "Polanski vs. Welles on *Macbeth*: Character or Fate," *Literature/Film Quarterly* 14 (1986): 203–210.

22. For a slightly out of date but still illuminating essay on the Polanski *Macbeth*, see Jack J. Jorgens, "Roman Polanski's Macbeth," in *Shakespeare on Film* (Bloomington: Indiana University Press, 1977), 161–74.

23. See Alexander Leggatt, "Teen Shakespeare: *10 Things I Hate About You* and *O,*" in *Acts of Criticism: Performance Matters in Shakespeare and His Contemporaries: Essays in Honor of James. P. Lusardi*, ed. Paul Nelsen and June Schlueter (Madison, Teaneck, NJ: Fairleigh Dickinson University Press, 2006), 245–59.

24. Sam Crowl has written an insightful commentary, "The Prince of Manhattan: Almereyda's *Hamlet*," in *Shakespeare at the Cineplex: The Kenneth Branagh Era* (Athens: Ohio University Press, 2003), 187–202.

25. For a full account of this prison movie, see Kirk Melnikoff, "Hank Rogerson, dir. *Shakespeare Behind Bars*," in *Shakespeare Bulletin* 23.3 (2005): 75–80.

26. Background material included in John Wrathall, "Bloody Arcades," *Sight and Sound* 10.7 (2000): 24–26.

27. See Debra Tuckett, "*Love's Labour's Lost.* Directed by Kenneth Branagh, Pathé 2000," *Early Modern Literary Studies* 6.1 (2000): 23. http://purl.oclc.org/emls/06-1/tuckrev.htm.

28. See David Denby, "Bottom's Up: Dreaming with the English Playwrights, from Shakespeare to Rattigan," *The New Yorker* (17 May 1999): 96–99.

29. For a recent analysis of *Scotland PA*, see Elizabeth A. Deitchman, "White Trash Shakespeare: Taste, Morality, and the Dark Side of the American Dream in Billy Morrissette's *Scotland PA*," *Literature/Film Quarterly* 34 (2006): 140–48, and other essays in this same issue.

Production photograph from *Kiss Me, Kate*, 1948.
Sam and Bella Spewack Collection, Rare Book and Manuscript
Library, Columbia University, New York.

Shakespeare and the American Musical
Irene G. Dash

Although Shakespeare was never completely absent from the American stage, he donned a new guise in the twentieth century, dancing, singing, and adding substance and meaning to the American musical theater. Whereas song, dance, and story had often been part of Shakespeare productions, seldom before 1900 had they united to propel the plot forward. Borrowing techniques from a new musical genre, twentieth-century adaptations of Shakespeare's plays especially revealed the importance of the Bard's perceptions of women, power, relationships between the sexes, and societal mores. Five Shakespeare plays and their adaptations solidified the new form: *The Comedy of Errors* (*The Boys From Syracuse*), *The Taming of the Shrew* (*Kiss Me, Kate*), *Romeo and Juliet* (*West Side Story*), *Two Gentlemen of Verona* (a rock musical of the same title), and *Twelfth Night* (*Your Own Thing*).[1]

Tin Pan Alley had provided many of the old form's songs and dances. Its composers wrote music and lyrics on demand, whether a waltz, a march, a ballad, or a love song. According to one critic, Tin Pan Alley was one of the earliest industries that "geared itself to standardization and mass marketing."[2] It evolved a "rigid formula" for the mass market, as publishers "interpolate[d] their songs into vaudeville, burlesque, extravaganzas, 'follies,'" and other variety shows.[3] Imports were also popular on the American stage, especially the operettas of Rudolf Friml and Victor Herbert and Gilbert and Sullivan light operas. Individual performers such as George M. Cohan in the early 1900s presented or acted in brash, breezy, energetic musicals.

Although Tin Pan Alley was the training ground for many of the men who subsequently fashioned the new organic form, Richard Rodgers and Lorenz Hart, the creators of the earliest Shakespeare musical, *The Boys From Syracuse*, in 1938, knew that they wanted a fresh form of expression. For them, Jerome Kern's music hinted at that ideal. "The sound of a Jerome Kern tune was not ragtime; nor did it have any of the Middle European inflections of Victor Herbert. It was all his own—the first truly American theatre music—and it pointed the way I wanted to be led," wrote Rodgers, introducing the term "American" into his description.[4]

The American musical of the twentieth century was thus an original art form. It emerged during the late 1920s, initially in *Show Boat* (1927). With music by Jerome Kern and lyrics by Oscar Hammerstein II, the elements of a story line, music, lyrics, character definition, and dance all fused into something uniquely American. According to Lehman Engel: "[T]he songs and lyrics were integrated into the action; comedy grew out of character and situation; the books had 'reasonable' and contemporary plots and characters; and language was everyday."[5] *Show Boat* also relied on an American literary source, Edna Ferber's novel, for its plot and characterization. Thinking back, Rodgers wrote, "[We] were sure we were not going to make it in the musical theatre . . . with a nondescript play and a couple of satirical songs."[6] Recognizing that their strength lay in their ability to write songs, not stories, the two men began, after *Show Boat*'s enormous success, to look for other likely texts. One of them mentioned Shakespeare. What an idea! They—but particularly Hart—knew the plays. As a twelve-year-old, the story goes, he went to summer camp, his trunk too heavy for his counselor to lift because it was so full of books, particularly the works of Shakespeare. Hart's bunkmates nicknamed him Shakespeare for the rest of the summer.[7]

Richard Rodgers and Larry Hart's *The Boys From Syracuse*, with book by George Abbott, an important writer of the period, was the first to explore the potential of Shakespeare's plays as source material for the emerging organic form. Their musical opened the way. Produced during the period between *Show Boat* in 1927 and *Oklahoma* in 1943, when the form for the American musical is thought to have stabilized, *Boys From Syracuse* exemplifies the new musical form, although its role as a Shakespeare adaptation masks the work's originality. Drawing imaginatively from *The Comedy of Errors*, the musical integrated music, song, dance, and character development. Its characters speak in the American vernacular, although the musical, like the original comedy, is set in the ancient city of Ephesus. Its adapters, nonetheless, insinuated observations about contemporary events—another hallmark of the American musical. In *The Boys From Syracuse*, writer, lyricist, and composer created a parallel between the Ephesian people's delight in a forthcoming execution of a Syracusan and the Anschluss in Austria and the dismemberment of Czechoslovakia. Like that of the people in Europe, the fate of the Syracusans is inexplicable.

By 1948, the Second World War had ended, and the exuberance of those immediate postwar years is reflected in *Kiss Me, Kate,* with lyrics and music by Cole Porter and book by Bella Spewack. Based on Shakespeare's *Taming of the Shrew*, it borrowed the concept of a play-within-a-play from the framing story of Shakespeare's Christopher Sly, a drunken tinker who is thrown out of an alehouse by a woman. In the original play, the story of Kate and Petruchio is performed before Sly and the theater audience. Structurally, the musical expands the play-within-a-play by creating a backstage drama where actors Lilli Vanessi and Fred Graham, formerly husband and wife, not only take the roles of Shakespeare's principals but also resemble them emotionally.

A major influence on this new view of *Taming* grew out of a 1935 production with the husband-and-wife team of Alfred Lunt and Lynn Fontanne, two major American performers of the time.[8] Not only did they revive Shakespeare's drunken tinker and the concept of a play-within-the play, but the diamond-patterned costumes, the sets, and even a procession of players resemble what we later see in *Kiss Me, Kate.*[9] Finally, the close resemblance of Lilli and Fred's names, the lead characters in *Kate,* to Lynn and Alfred has often been noted, despite the denial of the adapters.

Unlike Rodgers and Hart, who had a longtime partnership, Bella Spewack and Cole Porter were known in different areas in the theater—she as a playwright and he as a songwriter and lyricist. Although they had collaborated before *Kiss Me, Kate*, theirs was a comparatively new union in 1948. Initially, Spewack declined to write the book for a musical on *The Taming of the Shrew* because of its seeming sexism; after recognizing the importance of the play-within-the play and the musical's emphasis on a woman's right to independence, Spewack agreed to the task and asked Cole Porter to join her, despite his unsuccessful recent musicals. She appreciated his great skill as a lyricist and composer.

Besides collaborating with Spewack, Porter worked through many of the lyrics alone. Notepads from the Waldorf Astoria Hotel, where Porter lived for many years, show the progression of rhymes and ideas for such songs as "I Hate Men." They move from "I can't abide 'em even now and then" to "rooster-hen" to "I dinna ken—Their worth upon this earth again." Porter's ideas and rhymes eventually tie together into neat lines, supported by tight, fascinating, and challenging concepts and double entendres.[10]

The choreography of *Kiss Me, Kate* also moved the plot forward. Hanya Holm, well-known as a teacher but largely inexperienced on the Broadway stage, created the dances and began a long career in the musical theater. Writing of her choreography for *Kiss Me, Kate*, Walter Terry, the dance reviewer for the Sunday, 9 January 1949, *New York Herald Tribune* observed:

> There is no ballet as such in Kiss Me, Kate, *but there is dancing, all of it firmly integrated into the show to contribute to the achieving of a total theatrical impression. The dancing gives flow to the musical, it provides the*

Cole Porter. List of words for Act 1 of "I Hate Men" from *Kiss Me, Kate*.
Manuscript, ca. 1948.
Courtesy of the Library of Congress.
CAT. NO. 99

Finale First Act,

Knave   reprobate
Snake   rake
scum   bum
dog   hog frog
wretch
imp   pimp   shrimp
whelp   help!
clirt   squirt
lout   (get) out
cail   I laugh
rat   scat
louse   raus (gehen-sie raus)
goon —
scamp   Tramp
Toad)   Kindly drop dead

          rascal

Leonard Bernstein. Musical sequence outline for *West Side Story*.
Manuscript, ca. 1954–55.
Courtesy of the Library of Congress.

CAT. NO. 101

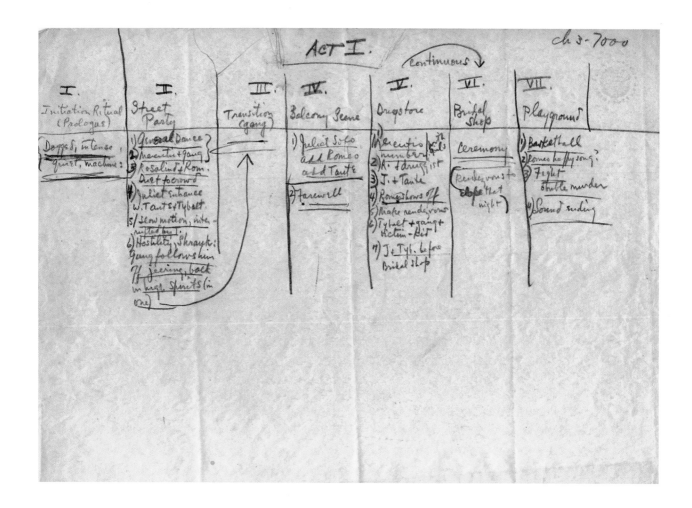

means for transitions in pace, or in mood, or in style, it aids in the definition of character and it accounts for the production's necessary flashes of physical virtuosity.

Thus, every aspect of this new form contributed to the whole.

The next Shakespeare musical reflected the changed tone of its times. By 1957, the optimism of *Kiss Me, Kate* was gone. Shakespeare adapters moved to tragedy with *Romeo and Juliet*. Leonard Bernstein, Jerome Robbins, Arthur Laurents, and Stephen Sondheim translated the hostility between Montague and Capulet of Shakespeare's tragedy into the battles between street gangs in *West Side Story*. The parents of Shakespeare's play disappear, and the clash between Puerto Rican immigrants and natives touches an American nerve. Bias and hatred—as deep as that in Shakespeare's play—enter. Bernstein jotted down at the top of his copy of *Romeo and Juliet*: "an out and out plea for racial tolerance."[11]

Parallels to Shakespeare's play exist throughout. Thus "Somewhere," a song-and-dance sequence, reveals its reliance on the wedding night scene in *Romeo and Juliet*. The newlyweds' hope of an ideal world emerges, their references to the bird of night and not the morning—the nightingale and not the lark, "the herald of the day"—also appears in a holograph draft of *West Side Story*'s lyrics. These include, "Where is darkness gone?/ What is this shining dawn?" And then later on, "What bright Earth are we living on?/ Can it be heaven?"[12]

By the 1950s, dance had become a unifying medium in the musical. Jerome Robbins solidified that tendency and carried it further: "Based on conception of Jerome Robbins," announces the playbill for *West Side Story*, crediting him with the choreography. Robbins writes of the importance of lead characters having major dance roles. Conceding that Romeo and Juliet should be singers, he insisted that Mercutio and Anita as well as some of the prominent gang members be dancers, to avoid the awkwardness of having the principals stand to one side while others danced for them.

Supporting the dancers and dramatizing their work were some of the most amazing set designs of the time. Oliver Smith, the designer, created scenery that captured the bleakness of the tenements where the gangs lived and opened those areas, as if by magic, to the dreams of Romeo and Juliet. In a takeoff on a dream ballet, Smith's city walls fall away to an open field. While the lovers joyously dance, members of the rival gangs enter, observe the openness of the space, and tentatively reach out to one another in an apparent reconciliation. But then the walls of the buildings rise, and the cage of the city squeezes the performers, who face the realities of the murders of Riff and Bernardo (Mercutio and Tybalt). Aware of the limited space and the confrontation that engulfs them, the opposing gangs resume hostilities. Desperately, Tony and Maria (Romeo and Juliet) sing of a place where they can be together. Romeo/Tony offers Juliet/Maria his hand: "Hold my hand and we're halfway there." But the buildings continue to rise, enclosing them. Hostility and hatred take over.

The magic of Smith's designs established yet another new element for the American musical theater. In *Your Own Thing* (1968), based on Shakespeare's *Twelfth Night*, the adapters Hal Hester, Danny Apolinar, and Donald Driver incorporated this new special dimension. The actors' environment included slide projections, film cartoon balloons, and live sound effects— even an onstage band to provide a consistent mise-en-scène. The first of the Shakespeare rock musicals, *Your Own Thing* introduced psychedelic music and new developments in sounds and light, yet retained the basic form of the organic musical, in which all the parts support the plot's overall movement.

Twelfth Night is the story of adult brother and sister twins, separated by a shipwreck. Each believes the other is dead.

Thematically, the play explores what happens when the sister disguises herself as her brother and attracts the love of a young countess, Olivia, who has rejected all suitors, claiming to be in mourning for her recently deceased brother. But Viola herself has fallen for her master, the duke Orsino, for whom she is wooing Olivia. Disguise prevents Viola from revealing herself. Developing hints from Shakespeare's play, the musical also probes contemporary ideas on homosexuality, gender roles, and people's choices in American society of the late 1960s—the problem of people trying to do "their own thing." By focusing on Orson, the Orsino character who lusts for Charlie, the disguised Viola, *Your Own Thing* weaves a lively, humorous tale of misperceptions and misunderstandings.

The comedy's first lines, "If music be the food of love, play on," are spoken in a slide projection of Senator Everett Dirksen, a Republican of the 1960s, while a film shows a raging storm at sea. The combination encloses the audience in dramatic sights and sounds, while on stage, a pair of twins—brother and sister—are arguing. Should they take to the lifeboats or return to their cabin for their orchestration? During this brief moment, the purser insists, "For Christ sakes! Don't just stand there, fella, get your sister to the lifeboat!" This isn't Shakespeare's Viola, but the twentieth century's perception of a dependent woman. The stage darkens and a projected film shows the ship going down.

For Viola's next appearance, the adapters return to Shakespeare's own language. Viola asks the purser who has saved her, "What country, friend, is this?" "This is Illyria, lady," he replies, as the actors are framed by slides of waterfront buildings in semiabstract designs. The mayor of New York, John Lindsay, suddenly appears in a slide projection, coughing (a commentary on cultural and political messages about smoking) and declaring "Illyria is a fun city," but Viola's song complains:

So much glass, so much steel
What's there to care? What's there to feel?
All that glass, all that chrome,
Can I ever call this place home?[13]

Constantly moving slides of steel and glass accompany her as background. Here, the adapters expanded the organic musical with a mixed-media collage. The parts are fractured. A small onstage band replaces the large orchestra; rock 'n' roll and gospel music are heard in the background.[14]

A musical quartet, which has lost one of its members, "Disease," to an army draft needs an immediate replacement. "What good are Death, War, and Famine without Disease" (another political commentary), complains Olivia, the discotheque owner who has booked the Apocalypse quartet into her venue, to Orson, the band manager. Then along comes Charlie, and later, her brother Sebastian. Each has been handed a job card by Buddha, one of the many screen projections, and each has been looking for a job in music—unaware of the other's survival.

The speed and variety of the slide projections reveal the originality and creativity of *Your Own Thing*. Not only Buddha, but Shirley Temple, John Wayne, and others keep the pace moving. The show wowed the critics. Despite its status as an off-Broadway production, usually not considered for awards, *Your Own Thing* won the Drama Critics Circle award for the 1968–69 season. It traveled the country and went abroad, demonstrating the American Shakespeare musical's widespread popularity.

Departing from the example of its predecessors, the musical *Two Gentlemen of Verona* (1971) retained Shakespeare's title but developed new scenes; it dropped some characters, kept others, and laughed at love, yet commented as well on war and abortion—two relevant contemporary issues. John Guare, Mel Shapiro, and Galt MacDermot, the musical's adapters, plunge into Shakespeare's complex plot but add new shades of meaning. Written right after the sexual revolution of the 1960s, the musical changes Proteus's wooing of Julia to an affair; after Proteus leaves for Milan, she finds she is pregnant. "It's very lonely for two ladies in Verona / It must be very nice to be a man / And sail off to Milan," she and Lucetta sing; then Julia continues solo, "It must be nice to be a **man** / And not be preg**nant**" (the emphasized words almost rhyming.) Without relinquishing the original comedy's emphasis on the conflict between love and friendship and a lover's betrayal, the adapters also highlight the plight of a woman made pregnant through the free-love practice of her generation and a duke seeking power by taking his people to war.

Unlike *Your Own Thing*, *Two Gentlemen of Verona* uses neither film nor slides nor voice-over. Instead, it relies on the reportorial roles of its servants and conveys its ideas through rock music. Its explosive opening scene underscores the play's ostensible theme—the rather silly persistence of love. The burst of song from the chorus, the appearance of Cupid "bow and arrowing" everyone, and Lucetta, "pouring thousands of red tissue-paper hearts" down on singers and audience—all set the musical's joyous tone. At the end, snatches of Spanish invade the scene as the lovers are finally reunited. Everyone from the megalopolis is included in the harmonious finale.

In the new and exciting theatrical genre of musical theater, Shakespeare provided complexity to the plots and insights into characters' lives. His original scripts featured soliloquies and taught the value of ambiguity in statements and conversation. He also gave the scriptwriters a remarkable variety of characters on which to draw: the "identical" twins in *The Comedy of Errors* and *Twelfth Night* (in the former, two infant pairs separated at birth; in the latter, one adult pair of brother and sister separated when their ship goes

down) and individualized characters, many of them from Shakespeare's subplots. Shakespeare contributed intriguing husbands and wives, some of them closely connected, others living almost separate lives.

Thematically, too, Shakespeare offered ideas worth exploring. He raised questions about women's roles, power, sexual relations, and the patterns of action in his society. He illuminated the question of a woman's right to self-ownership in such plays as *The Taming of the Shrew* and *Twelfth Night*, leading to a variety of adaptations. In 1948, Bella Spewack and Cole couched their *Kiss Me, Kate* (*Shrew*) in the twentieth-century conflict between marriage and career. Twenty years later, Hester, Apolinar, and Driver approached the topic from an economic standpoint, as well as that of sexual choice, in *Your Own Thing*. In 1971, the protests against the Vietnam War, along with the debate on Roe v. Wade, entered the American Shakespeare musical. *Two Gentlemen of Verona* contained lyrics that advised the pregnant but unmarried heroine, "Don't have the baby" and "You must have the baby," and the show featured politicians who promised to bring the boys home from war, noting sarcastically that "a shroud's a lovely uniform."

Many of Shakespeare's characters have moral flaws. In the best of the adaptations, the script transforms them into recognizable contemporaries. Proteus, the heel in *Two Gentlemen*, remains deceptive in the modern musical. At the musical's opening, Proteus sings "Thou Julia hast metamorphosed me" and speaks of his self-love. Picking up one of Shakespeare's lines from the comedy, the adapters create a song, "I'm very happy / For my best friend / You're looking at a picture of glee / I want my best friend / To be ha-ha-happy / But not happier than me." Quizzical observers and clowns weave in and out of both the comedies and tragedies. They range from comics with sharp tongues, like Petruchio's servant Grumio in *The Taming of the Shrew*, to Feste, the quiet fool of *Twelfth Night*. Minor background characters, such as Sampson and Gregory, who open *Romeo and Juliet* with a series of off-color puns, as well as major characters such as Mercutio, inhabit the plays. "Ask for me tomorrow, and you shall find me a grave man," he quips as he lies dying (*Romeo and Juliet*, 3.1.98).

The adapters transform these characters into contemporary Americans, revealed as such by their mode of expression, their perspective, and their language. Mercutio, for example, becomes Riff, the braggart and sharp leader of the Jets. Bianca's suitor in *Shrew* turns into a gambling hoofer named Bill, pursued by two gangsters straight out of the penitentiary to collect his debt in *Kiss Me, Kate*. The gangsters know the Bard from years in the prison's library. "Just declaim a few lines from Othella, and they'll think you're a helluva fella," they sing in tandem, always addressing themselves to "the girls today in society, [who] go for classical poetry." *Your Own Thing* replaces malcontents, gulls, and schemers of *Twelfth Night's* subplot with visual projections of well-known film actors—John Wayne and Humphrey Bogart—and the Buddha, who hands out calling cards. These are not the comics of Shakespeare's England but rather their reincarnation in new forms by creative American songsmiths, choreographers, and playwrights.

Frequently, the new works followed the form of Shakespeare's original. The long narrative exposition of Shakespeare's *Comedy of Errors* thus emerges in *The Boys From Syracuse*, where Egeon's tale of woe is sung by the guards before he is hustled off to jail. The play-within-the-play that opens *The Taming of the Shrew*, with a drunk evicted from a tavern by the hostess, rescued by a lord, and entertained by the play of Kate and Petruchio, also characterizes the shape of *Kiss Me, Kate*.[15] The larger story concerns a troupe of actors rehearsing for the pre-Broadway tryout of *Shrew*, which itself becomes the play-within-the play.

Similarly, *West Side Story* adopted Shakespeare's opening sequence but changed its form. In Shakespeare's *Romeo and Juliet*, the prologue establishes the plot:

> *Two households, both alike in dignity,*
> *In fair Verona, where we lay our scene,*
> *From ancient grudge break to new mutiny,*
> *Where civil blood makes civil hands unclean.*[16]

Just as this chorus warns of the tragedy that will befall a pair of "star-crossed lovers," *West Side Story* begins with a dance sequence that heralds the ensuing tragedy. Harsh sounds bring us to attention as the dancers leap onto the turf in the musical's opening moments. After he heard Bernstein's music for the opening, Jerome Robbins decided not to use words, but to convey the prologue through dance and movement.[17]

While Shakespeare musicals borrowed plots, characters, and situations from England's best-known poet, they remained essentially "American." For George Balanchine, choreographer of *The Boys From Syracuse*, the dancing of Fred Astaire and Ginger Rogers epitomized his ideal of "American." Balanchine, as ballet master of the Metropolitan Opera, not only introduced ballet into his choreography but also integrated it with tap. In one dance, for example, the two forms were combined as two dancers, one on pointe in ballet and the other in tap shoes seem to be vying for the attention of the male character. Hanya Holm, who designed the dances for *Kiss Me, Kate*, also broke from her training—in her case, German Expressionist dance—and found freedom of movement and expression to epitomize American dance. She believed that anyone can dance, and brought a sense of the democratization of dance to her choreography.

A different kind of reference to "American" appears in a review of Jerome Robbins' early dancing in a Russian ballet. Edwin Denby, the dance critic for the *New York Herald Tribune* in 1943, described Robbins's way of moving as American. While praising Robbins's skill as a dancer, Denby noted that "where everyone else dances with a particular vivacity, he moves with an American deliberateness. The difference," he observed, "is as striking as it used to be in peacetime abroad, when a stray American youth appeared in a bustling French street, and the slow rhythm of his walk gave the effect of a sovereign unconcern."[18] For Denby, the man who was later to choreograph and direct the first Shakespeare tragedy adapted into a musical—*West Side Story* (1957)—walked and moved with an American unconcern. In that musical, the tragic conflict between two warring street gangs leads to the death of the Romeo character. One gang is Puerto Rican, the other claims to be "American." Ironically, it is the young Puerto Rican women who sing "I like to be in America, / OK by me in America," comparing America to life on the island of Puerto Rico, with its "tropical diseases," "hurricanes blowing, and population growing."[19]

Yet another expression of the meaning of "American" appeared in the preface to the adaptation of *Two Gentlemen of Verona* (1971) by John Guare and Mel Shapiro. They stressed the importance of the megalopolis that forces races, colors, and cultures to come in constant contact with each other and ultimately to celebrate each other. The varied accents of the performers reinforce this emphasis on human variety, while the preface helps explain the introduction of some Spanish outbursts in the text, the use of calypso rhythms, and even references to other countries: "We wanted this English play set in Renaissance Italy adapted from a Spanish source to stand as a metaphor for life in New York City in the 1970s."[20] But then the authors clarify their intention—to capture the essence of American life.

They explain the importance of multicultural casting—the physical appearance of the actors, the sounds of their voices, and the assumption that the native sounds in their speech would not be overridden by a uniform English accent. No longer is it merely the language, or the songs, or the beat of the music, but casting too must help produce an American musical.

For the original production, we cast a Puerto Rican for Proteus and Speed, a Cuban for Julia, Valentine and Silvia and the Duke and occasionally Lucetta were played by Blacks, Launce was originally done in Yiddish, then went country western in a cast change, Eglamour was Chinese, Thurio was an Irishman, Lucetta a Russian-Danish girl. The chorus was every color under the sun.[21]

Guare and Shapiro advised future producers of their musical to "look around their city and say who lives here and get them upon this stage," because, they concluded, "In the megalopolis of the 70's, it's so easy not to be noticed, but no longer can anyone be ignored."[22]

Joseph Papp, the producer of *Two Gentlemen of Verona* and founder of Shakespeare in the Park and New York's Public Theater, implicitly agreed with Guare and Shapiro. Papp had begun producing Shakespeare outdoors in the East River Amphitheater in New York in 1956 and then sought a location in Central Park; for him, being American meant bringing free Shakespeare to the people of the city, especially those unfamiliar with live stage productions. Papp therefore jettisoned the idea that his actors mimic—or learn—English pronunciation. They could speak in their own voices and accents, as in *Two Gentlemen of Verona*, where Raul Julia spoke in the lilting tones of his native Puerto Rico. His brilliantly performed Proteus conveyed all the nuances of Shakespeare's instant lover without worrying about his accent.

The great popularity of these plays in America (abroad, too, from the first invasion of *Kiss Me, Kate* overseas) established their place in American culture. Their songs were widely sung. Hailed by the middle class for its exuberance, *Kate* also reflected the optimism of contemporary American life in those early post–World War II years. Audiences in country after country welcomed the American musical—not as a version of a Shakespeare play but as a wonderfully new form of entertainment. Bella Spewack documents *Kiss Me, Kate*'s overseas triumph in her voluminous correspondence with Cole Porter, mentioning contracts in Italy and France; performances in Norway, Denmark, and Sweden; a live TV presentation in Japan, and a production in Israel. By 1961, she delightedly records a moment in Brussels: "EMBRASSEZ MOI, KATHERINE opens at le theatre Royal de la Monnaie in Brussels on June 15. Yes, my love, in French with Belgian opera stars, [and] soloist dancers from the Sadler Wells Ballet. Your orchestra numbers 55!" She observes with pride to Porter, "Ours will be the first American musical to play the opera house in English or French," and "it will mark KATE's thirteenth language!"[23] This most successful modern musical adaptation of a Shakespeare play had acquired a veneer of sophistication and elitism when it traveled abroad, although its roots in Shakespeare's play were often lost.

While the musicals discussed here were the principal and most prominent of the twentieth century, other less successful attempts appeared during the period, works that failed to capture the new movement toward the organic musical. They faltered by remaining in the earlier Tin Pan Alley format, containing individual songs or dances unrelated to the larger movement of the play.[24] Yet as the century came to a close, other composers and writers introduced new ideas into American musicals. One characteristic persisted, however. The musical remained organic; new material took advantage of the established form.

The distinguished critic Philip Edwards recently referred to theater as the interpretation centre of Shakespeare study,[25] observing that "each national culture transmutes what it receives and enhances the totality in which it shares."[26] Totally organic in their fusion of dance, words, music, and design, the American Shakespeare musicals of the twentieth century drew on Shakespeare's plays to give us a new perspective even as they enhanced the totality of his vision. The essential theatrical ingredients—play texts from the late sixteenth and early seventeenth centuries and musicals from the twentieth century—had fused to provide a new view of the earlier works and to increase our understanding of the subtleties of each. American culture transmuted the Renaissance plays into a vibrant new experience in the modern theater.

1. Except as noted, references to Shakespeare's plays are to *The Riverside Shakespeare*, ed. G. Blakemore Evans (Boston: Houghton Mifflin, 1974). The scripts of the adaptations consulted are as follows. (1) *The Boys From Syracuse*, by George Abbott, music by Richard Rodgers, lyrics by Lorenz Hart, choreography by George Balanchine, Alvin Theatre, 23 November 1938, typescript, Theatre Collection, The New York Public Library for the Performing Arts, New York. (2) Cole Porter and Bella Spewack, *Kiss Me, Kate*, typescript, Cole Porter Collection, Library of Congress. This is the 1948 typescript identified as "Cole Porter, Waldorf Tower, 41c." References to the text are to this edition. (The 1948 typescript for *Kiss Me, Kate* in the Spewack collection, the copy in the Cole Porter collection, and the copy at the British Library all contain the attribution "by Cole Porter and Bella Spewack." In contrast, the printed version of 1953 has "Book by Samuel and Bella Spewack, Lyrics by Cole Porter.") I saw three typescripts in the Bernstein Collection in the Music Division of the Library of Congress and used the one with a number 34 on right top corner of the title page and a circled LB in red, also on the title page. (3) *West Side Story*, based on a conception by Jerome Robbins, book by Arthur Laurents, music by Leonard Bernstein, lyrics by Stephen Sondheim and Leonard Bernstein, direction and choreography by Jerome Robbins. I also used the published play *"Romeo and Juliet" and "West Side Story"* (New York: Dell, 1965). (4) The New York Shakespeare Festival, produced by Joseph Papp, presented *Two Gentlemen of Verona*, a musical adapted by John Guare and Mel Shapiro, lyrics by John Guare, and music by Galt MacDermot, Delacorte Theatre, New York, 28 July 1971; "after three weeks TGV was scheduled to travel through the NY boroughs on Shakespeare Festival's Mobile Theatre," St. James Theater, New York, 1 December 1971, New York Shakespeare Festival Archives at the Public Theatre. (5) *Your Own Thing*, musical with book by Donald Driver, music and lyrics by Hal Hester and Danny Apolinar, produced by Zev Bufman and Dorothy Love, opened at Orpheum Theater, New York, 13 January, 1968; Music Division, Special Collections, The New York Public Library for the Performing Arts, New York. Reprinted in *Great Rock Musicals*, ed. Stanley Richards (New York: Stein and Day, 1979), 287–377. All quotations from these musicals are taken from these sources.

2. Philip Furia, *Poets of Tin Pan Alley: A History of America's Great Lyricists* (New York: Oxford University Press, 1992, 13.

3. Furia, 41.

4. Richard Rodgers, *Musical Stages: An Autobiography* (New York: Random House, 1975), 20.

5. Lehman Engel, *The American Musical Theater*, rev. ed. (New York: Macmillan, 1975), 10.

6. Rodgers, 53.

7. Frederick Nolan, *Lorenz Hart: A Poet On Broadway* (New York: Oxford University Press, 1994), 9–10.

8. Typescript, William Shakespeare, *The Taming of the Shrew*, 1935. Produced by the Theatre Guild at the Guild Theatre, New York, 30 September 1935. Billy Rose Collection of the New York Public Library for the Performing Arts.

9. *Kiss Me, Kate*, book by Bella Spewack, music and lyrics by Cole Porter, typescript 30 October 1948.

10. Cole Porter Collection, Box 11/folder 1, Holograph Lyric Sheets. Music Division, Library of Congress.

11. Annotated copy, *The Tradgedy of Romeo and Juliet*, ed. George Lyman Kittredge (Boston: Ginn, 1940), Prologue, 1–4. Leonard Bernstein Collection, Writings, 1954–55, Box 73, Folder 9.

12. Bernstein's manuscript notes for the song in the Leonard Bernstein Collection, Music Division, Library of Congress.

13. *Your Own Thing* in Richards, 302.

14. Scott Warfield, "From *Hair* to *Rent*: Is 'Rock' a Four-Letter Word on Broadway?" in *Cambridge Companion to Musicals*, ed. William A. Everett and Paul R. Laird (Cambridge: Cambridge University Press, 2002), 231–45.

15. For an in-depth discussion of this play see my chapter, "Challenging Patterns," in *Wooing, Wedding, and Power: Women in Shakespeare's Plays* (New York: Columbia University Press, 1981), 33–64.

16. *Romeo and Juliet*, ed. Kittredge, Prologue, 1–4. Leonard Bernstein Collection. Music Division, Library of Congress.

17. Jerome Robbins Collection, Box 563, Folder 7, Manuscript for the Dramatists' Guild Symposium on *West Side Story* of the collaborators in 1985. Jerome Robbins Dance Division, New York Public Library for the Performing Arts.

18. This Denby reference appeared in *Jerome Robbins: His Life, His Theater, His Dance* by Deborah Jowitt (New York: Simon and Schuster, 2004), 66.

19. Act 1, scene 5 in the printed edition.

20. Guare and Shapiro, adapters, *Two Gentlemen of Verona* typescript.

21. Guare and Shapiro.

22. Guare and Shapiro.

23. Cole Porter Letters, Box E. Letter from Bella Spewack, 30 May 1961. The Bella and Sam Spewack Collection, Columbia University Rare Book Library.

24. An example was *Swingin' the Dream*, based on *A Midsummer Night's Dream*. Music and lyrics by Jimmy Van Heusen and Eddie DeLange, book by Gilbert Seldes. Produced 29 November 1939, Center Theatre of Rockefeller Center. It was set in 1890 Louisiana. The predominantly black cast included Louis Armstrong as Bottom. Settings were based on Walt Disney drawings. Whereas the producers hoped to fill the huge Center Theatre (capacity 3,500), the work itself lacked taste (for example, a flit-gun was used to hypnotize the queen). It was not a work moving toward the new American organic Shakespeare musical, but it was instead a late attempt to build on individual songs.

25. Philip Edwards, "*Shakespeare Survey:* Beginnings and Continuities." *Shakespeare Survey,* 51 (1998): 141–46, esp. 144.

26. Edwards, 146.

Photograph of Langston Hughes.
CAT. NO. 91

Jazzing Up Shakespeare

Douglas M. Lanier

In 1942, at the height of the swing craze, Langston Hughes published a collection of poetry entitled *Shakespeare in Harlem*, a volume filled with poems modeled on African-American music. Here is the title poem:

> *Hey ninny neigh!*
> *And a hey nonny noe!*
> *Where, oh, where*
> *Did my sweet mama go?*
>
> *Hey ninny neigh*
> *With a tra-la-la-la!*
> *They say your sweet mama*
> *Went home to her ma.*[1]

Rather daringly for its day, Hughes offers a melding of Shakespearean song and Harlem blues, lamenting the fickle nature of love. The poem is also an assertion of parity between the cultural achievement of two different Renaissances, that of early modern England and jazz-age Harlem, then at its zenith. In the collection's title, Hughes, chronicler of the Harlem Renaissance, makes the even more daring claim that an African-American poet working in the quintessential idiom of his culture might claim the mantle of the exemplar of the earlier Renaissance— Shakespeare. This claim is not without tension—"hey ninny neigh" has the ring of parody as much as homage—but this poem and the volume's title nonetheless suggest that for Hughes conjoining Shakespeare and black music was potentially empowering.

This poem needs to be set against another of Hughes's poems, "Note on Commercial Theatre," which appeared in his next collection, *Jim Crow's Last Stand* (1943). In it, the narrator complains that his blues have been stolen: "You sing 'em on Broadway / And you sing 'em in Hollywood Bowl, / And you mixed 'em up with symphonies / And you fixed 'em / So they don't sound like me." To demonstrate such expropriation, he singles out three theatrical examples—"*Macbeth* and *Carmen Jones* / And all kinds of *Swing Mikados*," referring to Orson Welles's 1936 black-cast production of *Macbeth*, Oscar Hammerstein's 1943 adaptation of Bizet's *Carmen*, and Mike Todd's 1939 *Hot Mikado*, a jazz adaptation of Gilbert and Sullivan's operetta. Here, Shakespeare (along with classical music) serves an altogether different function. He becomes a vehicle for domesticating African-American culture for mainstream consumption, treating that culture as mere musical styling for "jazzing up" highbrow classics rather than as an expression of black experience. At the poem's end, Hughes defiantly vows to "write about me— / Black and beautiful— / And sing about me, / And put on plays about me!" Unlike *Shakespeare in Harlem*, Hughes insists here that to maintain faith with authentic African-American culture he must *resist* its being yoked with Shakespeare.

Langston Hughes's contradictory attitude responds to a characteristically American ambivalence about jazzing up Shakespeare and to the long history of African-American music's status in the nation's culture. Until recently, Shakespeare and jazz were widely seen as representative of two different cultural registers, highbrow and lowbrow. Shakespeare epitomized high culture: European in origin, imbued with classical literature, and demanding close study, his works were regarded as aesthetically and thematically sophisticated, laden with enduring moral values universal in their application. By contrast, jazz was identified with American popular entertainment. Geared to bodily pleasures and the speed of urban life rather than to the contemplative intellect, it was regarded as simple, direct, even raw in its modes of expression; improvisatory and thus of the moment; somewhat scandalous and counter-cultural in its reputation; and specific to a racial subculture. Bringing Shakespeare and jazz together meant sacrificing what was essential to both or forcing together idioms that were best kept apart. Little wonder, then, that jazzed-up Shakespeare would become symbolically significant in twentieth-century debates about the relationship between high and popular culture. Some worried that the meteoric rise of jazz, like other forms of popular culture, would displace inherited cultural tradition, of which Shakespeare was an oft-cited exemplar. For others, jazz provided a means for making the antiquated bard newly relevant to mass audiences and revivifying a safely out-of-copyright commodity that had grown stale.

This drive to popularize Shakespeare, a leitmotif throughout the twentieth century, operates alongside two complementary developments during the same period: the institutionalization of Shakespeare as an academic subject and the displacement of the theater by radio, film, and TV as the dominant performance media, particularly in America. Without the stage as a mass venue and increasingly regarded as the purview of scholars, Shakespeare would require jazzing up if he were to remain vital in public life. For those black artists who produced jazz-oriented art, there was the added benefit that Shakespeare's authority offered cultural respectability by association to their own productions. Yet using pop culture to re-brand Shakespeare was not without its costs. It potentially undermined his special stature, the very quality that made him attractive. Moreover, no small part of Shakespeare's usefulness for popular culture was as a foil to pop's antielitist, modern, and or subversive nature. Harmonizing Shakespeare with popular culture threatened to blunt both pop's street credibility and Shakespeare's usefulness as pop's defining Other.

In the case of jazz, these issues were complicated by the complex intertwining of Shakespeare and African-American music in the nineteenth century, particularly in the minstrel show, America's first contribution to world theater. Born in the 1830s out of the enormously popular "Jim Crow" character developed by Thomas Dartmouth "Daddy" Rice,

the minstrel show grew from modest musical reviews in the 1840s to full-fledged blackface variety shows after the Civil War. Although African-American-style music remained the centerpiece of these extravaganzas, minstrel shows included acrobatic and dance acts, comedy routines, and so-called "Ethiopian" burlesques, which were parodies of popular melodramas, operas, and classical plays, performed in blackface and with plantation dialect.

It was through the minstrel show that African-American music first entered wider cultural consciousness. Indeed, despite the virulent racism of minstrelsy, many practitioners saw themselves as promoting, not denigrating, black culture, and a few identified themselves as abolitionist sympathizers. Early on, the minstrel show was regarded as offering access to actual African-American musical practice and thus to an indigenous, authentically American culture. In 1845, in the midst of the initial minstrel show craze, an essay in the *Knickerbocker Magazine* argued, not entirely seriously, that "our negro slaves" were artists of natural genius unsullied by education or cosmopolitanism: "*That* is the class in which we must expect to find our original poets, and there we *do* find them. From that class come the Jim Crows, the Zip Coons, and Dandy Jims, who have electrified the world. From them proceed our ONLY TRUE NATIONAL POETS." Later in the essay, the author sets the extraordinary popularity of the American minstrel against the cultural reach of the British Empire: "Compared with the time occupied by Great Britain in bringing [its cultural dominance] to pass, 'Jim Crow' has put a girdle round the earth in forty minutes."[2] The tone of the *Knickerbocker* article underlines the divided attitude toward African-American music in the minstrel show. It was lauded as a distinctively American form of popular entertainment, the upstart *doppelgänger* of "proper" British culture, but not to be raised to the level of legitimate art except ironically.

The content of the minstrel show featured various racist, ethnic, and gender stereotypes; nostalgia for an utopian vision of antebellum plantation life; and different forms of class-oriented parody. This last element grew with expansion of the roles of the end men, Mr. Tambo and Mr. Bones, who served as both buffoons and unruly tricksters, and with development of the olio, the second section of the minstrel show. The olio featured short pieces lampooning forms through which the genteel exerted their cultural and political authority, including the stump speech, lecture, soiree, opera, and legitimate theater. Like British Shakespearean burlesques, these minstrel parodies tweaked the elite by transposing their discourses into a "low" register, at once mocking upper-class decorum while stressing the anarchically "low" nature of the working classes. These burlesques reinforced the cultural divide between high and low, even as they used one register to mock another. While in Britain the cultural divide was dominated by social class, in supposedly democratic America that divide turned on race, with "Ethiopian" idioms serving as the preferred low register by which "proper" culture was mocked. Thus, the terrible paradox of the minstrel show: it showcased African-American music at a moment when blacks might be culturally and politically enfranchised, but that music was presented within a context that reinforced the idea that African-American culture was immutably "low," never more than popular entertainment.

Given how central Shakespeare was to nineteenth-century conceptions of art and culture, it is unsurprising that Shakespeare would be a perennial target for the minstrel show. Although minstrel songs feature various passing references to Shakespeare, straight and parodic, it was in the olio that the relationship between Shakespeare and African-American culture was first codified.[3] Minstrel burlesques of Shakespeare combined knockabout farce and racist humor with elements of the British Shakespearean burlesque. The Shakespearean content of these parodies was often minimal, sometimes no more than a few key characters, scenes, or speeches. It typically served as a mere armature on which to hang topical satire—*Julius the Snoozer* (1875), for example, lampoons Boss Tweed's political corruption—or to recycle commonplaces of racist stereotyping. In *Hamlet the Dainty* (1866), where jokes about liquor abound, the appearance of old Hamlet's ghost sends Horatio, Marcellus, and Hamlet into bug-eyed fright.

Again and again, these skits demonstrate the incapacity of blacks to perform Shakespeare without turning his works into farce. Indeed, a number of these works have a metatheatrical element, featuring African-Americans who, motivated by easy money or outsized ambition, desire to become Shakespearean actors, with the invariable result that they mangle the text, misunderstand the plot, and reduce the play to a comic brawl (the typical ending of "Ethiopian" burlesques). For example, in Henry Llewellyn Williams's *The Black Forrest* (1882), when the eminent American Shakespearean Edwin Forrest doesn't arrive for a performance at a provincial theater, aspiring black actor Jerry Mander decides to impersonate him, leading eventually to his exposure as a charlatan. The skit provides ample opportunity for parodies of Shakespearean lines, Forrest's acting style, and the social pretensions of the theater's manager, but as is always the case with minstrel burlesques of Shakespeare, it also makes clear that Mander's attempts to perform Shakespeare lead inevitably to self-deflating farce.

Behind these burlesques lurks the influence of *Othello*, another tale of a black man who at first lays claim to full citizenship in white culture, only to eventually reveal his native barbarism. *Othello* provided minstrelsy not only the motif of blackface and a favorite target for burlesque, but also a crucial ideological narrative of cultural delegitimation, a narrative all the more authoritative because it was Shakespearean. In order to trade upon the fame of his Jim Crow character, "Daddy" Rice adapted Maurice Dowling's 1834 British burlesque *Othello Travestie* in 1844 as a comic opera, including many of the distinctive components soon to be shaped into the minstrel show: blackface, plantation dialect, popular American songs with allusions to slavery, topical references, sight gags, and slapstick. In the many minstrel burlesques of *Othello* that followed before minstrelsy faded in the late 1880s, fears about miscegenation in *Othello* were intermixed with anxieties about African-American cultural enfranchisement, and so minstrel burlesques of *Othello* typically remake Shakespeare's tragedy into a travesty of mobility, portraying Othello or the black actors who try to present him as buffoons with inappropriate aspirations. Clearly influenced by minstrelsy, the illustrations for Alexander DoMar's *Othello: An Interesting Drama, Rather!* (1850) picture Othello in the garb of Zip Coon, the foolish urban dandy who was a stock blackface character. As if in testimony to the seductive popularity of minstrel music, this Othello woos his Desdemona by strumming a banjo, and the poem's coda uses Shakespeare's plot to deliver a mock moral about that music's power:

> *Remember that, though they are all pleasant fellows,*
> *Yet, like Mister Othello, all Blacks are jealous.*
> *Believe me, the banjo that produces such tones,*
> *Is made, from Mistress O's skin and Mister O's bones.*[4]

"Ethiopian" burlesques of Shakespeare work to undermine African-American aspirations to cultural legitimacy on two fronts: first, through their treatment of Othello as a signal example of black overreaching, comically absurd rather than tragically noble; and second, through their lampooning of black efforts to stage Shakespeare and thus to lay claim to cultural prestige. In the minstrel show, Shakespeare becomes a symbolically powerful means for denying cultural legitimacy to African-Americans.

Shakespeare's relationship to the minstrel show was to haunt efforts to meld Shakespeare to African-American music throughout the twentieth century. "That Shakesperian Rag," a novelty song from 1912, sets various famous tag lines and references to characters to a ragtime melody, promising tongue-in-cheek that the result will be "most intelligent, very elegant" and that Romeo, Juliet, Shylock, and "the Moor" will dance in the modern way. As if with a vestigial memory of minstrelsy, the lyrics conclude with a parodic reference to *Othello*, substituting for Desdemona's handkerchief the jazzy tune to which Othello dances: "Feeling gay, he [Othello] would say, / As he started in to sway, / 'Bring the rag, right away.'" When T. S. Eliot (mis)quotes this song in "The Waste Land," it becomes a cardinal example of the catchy popular "nothing" that displaces an authentic Shakespearean quotation— "Those are pearls that were his eyes"—in the narrator's mind, a portrait in miniature of the process of cultural ruin that Eliot laments.

It was the ascendancy of swing music in the 1930s and 1940s that especially invigorated efforts to jazz up Shakespeare. By virtue of its wide cross-racial and cross-class popularity during this period, swing came to be regarded as an African-American musical style with universal appeal, democratizing and popularizing whatever it touched. That potential is trumpeted in a 1936 Warner Brothers short, *Shake, Mr. Shakespeare.* In an extended dream sequence, various Shakespeare characters celebrate their "goin' Hollywood" by dancing and singing to swing music. Jazz and film, the short suggests, are forms interchangeably emblematic of American modernity, capable of transforming even the stuffy, antiquated bard into something hip; at the urging of his characters, Shakespeare himself obligingly joins the group of dancers at the film's end. As is often the case with such pieces, *Shake, Mr. Shakespeare* entertains the possibility of jazzing up Shakespeare for profit while it simultaneously parodies it.

A very different understanding of hybridizing Shakespeare and African-American music can be found in *Paradise in Harlem*, a 1939 "race" film directed by Joseph Seiden. Seiden's movie addresses the gap between the utopian promise for African-American culture symbolized by Harlem and the degrading reality of black life in mid-century America. As it opens, we meet Lem Anderson, a black actor working as a blackface comedian at a New York nightclub. Backstage, Lem confides in his nephew that he dreams of leaving behind "cork and comedy" to play Othello. When he witnesses a gangland killing, Lem is forced by thugs to move South where he tries to pursue his theatrical aspirations while working menial jobs, eventually descending into despair and alcoholism. Determined to succeed, Lem returns to Harlem only to have his dream of performing Shakespeare again threatened by gangsters, who attempt to discredit him by framing him for the shooting of a kingpin's girlfriend.

As the gangsters' plot unravels at film's end, Lem is finally allowed to play his Othello under police custody. Despite the nobility of Lem's rendition of the play's final scene, the black audience heckles him; one man shouts, "yeah, put out the light so we can all go home." But as Desdemona pleads for her life, the performance slowly transforms from Shakespearean oratory to a slow blues, first sung by women audience members, built upon the refrain, "no, no, she shan't die." Soon the chorus transforms into a moving choral spiritual that includes the voices of former hecklers. After Desdemona's death, the tune shifts yet again, this time becoming an up-tempo, hot swing number to which the audience dances in delight. The scene becomes the unproblematic triumph of Lem over insurmountable obstacles, not least of which is Shakespeare's incompatibility with his black audience's sensibilities. To underline that triumph, Lem's gangster nemesis, Rough Jackson, is exposed and then killed, and Lem is exonerated. The performance of *Othello* becomes Lem's act of self-redemption, purging his blackface past and uniting African-American culture with Shakespeare without resorting to minstrel travesty. The final moments of his performance of *Othello* break decisively with the tragic nature of the role Lem plays and with the path of degradation he suffers; his adaptation does not include the revelation of Othello's mistaken jealousy, his confrontation with Iago, or his final speeches and suicide. That redemptive trajectory is also signaled by the musical sequence to which the scene is set: blues, then spiritual, and then swing. Lem's Shakespearean performance, the film imagines, foreshadows wider cultural legitimacy, for Lem learns afterward that he has been offered a chance to play Othello on Broadway "with a jazz band and a choir." The resonance of this extraordinary film is deepened when we realize that this is the first mass-market film performance of Othello by a black actor.

Even so, to overemphasize the significance of *Paradise in Harlem* is to underestimate the legacy of Shakespeare and minstrelsy. That legacy hangs over an ambitious example of jazzed-up Shakespeare that also dates from 1939, the Broadway musical *Swingin' the Dream*. This grand production drew on earlier efforts to adapt Shakespeare to modern musical form, most notably *The Boys from Syracuse*, a Rodgers and Hart musical version of *The Comedy of Errors* which had run successfully on Broadway the year before. Using *A Midsummer Night's Dream* as its template, *Swingin' the Dream* placed jazz and African-American culture at center stage. It used a swing adaptation of Mendelssohn's music and various big band numbers as the score's basis; it featured a cast of such black luminaries as "Moms" Mabley, Maxine Sullivan, Butterfly McQueen, the Dandridge sisters, and, most famously, Louis Armstrong as Bottom. The play's action was transposed from Athens, seat of Western high culture, to 1890s New Orleans, the mythic birthplace of jazz, suggesting that jazz was the foundation of a new American cultural empire. By all accounts, the production was lavish: Gilbert Seldes and Erik Charell wrote the book, the Bud Freeman Band and Benny Goodman's sextet played the music, and Agnes de Mille choreographed dancers such as Bill Bailey and the Rhymettes.

Yet despite this astonishing gathering of talent, the show closed after only thirteen performances. One reason for the failure can be traced to Seldes and Charell's too-faithful adherence to Shakespeare's plot and language, a decision that only highlighted the anachronisms generated by converting the play to modern musical and spoken idioms. Equally off-putting was the choice of Mendelssohn as the basis for Jimmy Van Heusen's jazz score, for it too evoked the very gentility that the show sought to dispel. But the shadow of minstrelsy also figured in the unsympathetic reception. The inability of African-American actors to speak Shakespeare "properly" surfaced in several notices, as did the expectation that the adaptation would be, in the words of the *New York Times* reviewer, "a Negro carnival." The transposition of the action to the Old South unintentionally evoked the plantation setting of the minstrel walkaround. Singled out for praise were the instrumental music, the "dark-skinned steppers who take to rhythm as though it were created for them,"[5] and the passing moments of travesty provided by Butterfly McQueen's squeaky-voiced Puck. Because *Swingin' the Dream* used African-American music, actors, and milieus to update, rather than lampoon, Shakespeare, the show was regarded as overly serious, inappropriately grandiose, even incoherent. If *Paradise in Harlem* held out the promise that melding Shakespeare and black music might codify African-American cultural prestige, the sad fate of *Swingin' the Dream* seemed to confirm their fundamental incompatibility.

It is against this backdrop that Duke Ellington created a milestone in the relationship between jazz and Shakespeare, his 1957 jazz suite *Such Sweet Thunder*. By the mid-1950s, the precipitous postwar fall of swing and rise of bop, changes in personnel in his band, and a creeping conservatism in his repertoire had made Ellington seem a relic of jazz's past. His career's second chapter, most jazz historians agree, began with his band's electrifying performance of "Diminuendo and Crescendo in Blue" at the 1956 Newport Jazz Festival, a performance which prompted the press to dub Ellington an elder statesman of jazz.[6] *Such Sweet Thunder* was composed a year later, after a series of concerts for the Stratford, Ontario, Shakespeare Festival, performances which affirmed Ellington's stature as a hip classic. Stratford's invitation of jazz musicians of an older generation to the festival reinforced the perception that pre-bop jazz constituted an art form akin in cultural stature to that of Shakespeare. Ellington's suite acknowledges this act of legitimation, but it also deepens the affinities between Shakespeare's art and Ellington's own, suggesting in several ways that the analogy is not superficial but thoroughgoing.

In his program notes for the first performance of *Such Sweet Thunder*, Ellington worries that, as classics, he and Shakespeare labor under the misperception that their arts are for the cultural elite, making some reluctant "to expose themselves and join the audience." In the 1930s and 1940s, swing was seen as the very voice of popularization, reaching (problematically) across racial divides and rendering whatever it touched modern, American, and immediately appealing. But in 1957 the "classicizing" of Ellington's music by linking it to Shakespeare risked making jazz a coterie form, the property of connoisseurs. In his program notes Ellington seeks to navigate these concerns. On the one hand, he stresses that "whether it be Shakespeare or jazz, the only thing that counts is the emotional effect on the listener"—no special knowledge is required. The power of the performance's "immediate impact on the human ear" aligns both Ellington and Shakespeare with popular culture and potentially democratizes their respective audiences. On the other hand, Ellington claims that his art and Shakespeare's are sufficiently sophisticated to reward repeated encounters, an assertion which differentiates their arts from mere pop ephemera. Here, Ellington articulates the musical ambitions of his later career,–to create a music with the prestige and virtuosity of other "classics" and the inclusive immediacy of popular culture.

Ellington's *Such Sweet Thunder* consists of eleven numbers, each of which is linked to Shakespearean characters:

"Such Sweet Thunder" [Othello]

"Sonnet for Caesar" [Julius Caesar]

"Sonnet to Hank Cinq" [Henry V]

"Lady Mac" [Lady Macbeth]

"Sonnet in Search of a Moor" [Othello]

"The Telecasters" [The Three Witches and Iago]

"Up and Down, Up and Down, I Will Lead Them (Up and Down)" [Puck]

"Sonnet for Sister Kate" [Katherine]

"The Star-Crossed Lovers" [Romeo and Juliet]

"Madness in Great Ones" [Hamlet]

"Half the Fun" [Cleopatra]

A final number, "Circle of Fourths," added later, offers a musical tribute to Shakespeare himself. The suite addresses the challenge of wedding Shakespeare to African-American music in several ways. First, the suite is entirely instrumental, sidestepping the issue of setting Shakespearean language in an African-American idiom. Even so, a few sections have a conversational quality, as in the opening number "Such Sweet Thunder," which musically depicts the seductive stories Othello tells Desdemona. Ellington tends to choose characters known for their oratorical power or verbal facility, a quality mirrored in his witty arrangements and playful titles. Second, Ellington thinks of Shakespeare

as a portrayer of individualized personalities. He conceives of his suite as a series of musical portraits of Shakespearean characters, ending coda-like with a portrait of Shakespeare himself—it is essentially a suite of solos. The well-worn conception of Shakespeare as a creator of distinctive characters accords with Ellington's own compositional methods, for he famously used the distinctive sounds of individual band members as starting points for his compositions. Strikingly, Ellington plays down the tragic trajectories of Shakespeare's plots, reserving indication of their fates for a single ominous final note or unresolved chord. Emphasis falls rather on the vitality of their distinctive voices, even when, as in his "sonnets" for Othello and Kate, those voices engage in a blues-laden lament.

Most importantly, Ellington stresses Shakespeare's affirmation of black characters and his works' formal affinities with African-American music. Ellington's suite begins and ends with black characters—Othello in "Such Sweet Thunder" and Cleopatra in "Half the Fun" (as the liner notes wryly observe, Antony seems to be on hiatus). A third portrait, "Sonnet in Search of A Moor," also concerns Othello, this time depicting his tenderness and pathos rather than his oratorical skill. All three portraits actively celebrate black erotic power—as the pun on "a moor / amour" suggests—defying stereotypes of black sexuality by stressing these characters' sly charm and sophistication. Since Shakespeare is popularly known as a poet of love, this emphasis on black sensuality also provides a rationale for placing Othello and Cleopatra at the center of his artistic achievements. And Shakespeare's depictions of blacks, Ellington's portraits suggest, are affirming—Ellington barely acknowledges Othello and Cleopatra's tragic ends, and Aaron from *Titus Andronicus* and the Prince of Morocco from *The Merchant of Venice* are nowhere to be found. Ellington also foregrounds Shakespeare's women in his suite, particularly those women who are verbally assertive

Duke Ellington. Manuscript music from *Such Sweet Thunder*.
Duke Ellington Collection, Archives Center, National Museum of
American History, Behring Center, Smithsonian Institution
CAT. NO. 94

or subversive—Lady Macbeth, Katherine Minola, the three witches, Cleopatra. The parallel between Shakespeare's spunky women and his black characters becomes clearest when Ellington musically quotes from "Such Sweet Thunder" in the opening and closing phrases of his "Sonnet to Sister Kate." When he turns to "The Star-Crossed Lovers," Ellington gives the majority of the beautiful melody line not to Romeo but to Juliet, portrayed by Johnny Hodges's alto sax.

Ellington's assertion of the affinity between Shakespeare's art and the black experience also extends to artistic form. Throughout are little musical touches that elegantly transpose Shakespearean styles and forms into an African-American musical idiom. The suite includes four "Sonnets," each of which sets a fourteen-line melody (a Shakespearean "sonnet") into a modified twelve-bar blues framework, that most quintessential of African-American musical forms. Puck's taunting of the lovers in "Up and Down" is portrayed by mocking call-and-response sequences between dissonant instrumental pairs and Clark Terry's solo trumpet. In its original release, the piece ends with Terry musically quoting "Lord, what fools these mortals be." "Circle of Fourths," the final number which traverses all the musical keys in less than two minutes, slyly suggests an analogy between Shakespeare and Ellington himself. If Shakespeare was renowned for his universal poetic facility, his ability to mime any verbal idiom, so too Ellington demonstrates his ability to think in any musical key and freely, deftly move between them.[7] Ellington's sophistication and craft in the arrangements thoroughly reject the notion that transposing Shakespeare into an African-American idiom leads only to travesty.

The suite's title, *Such Sweet Thunder*, makes the point forcefully and wittily. The phrase is taken from Hippolyta's description of Hercules' baying dogs in *A Midsummer Night's Dream* (4.1.111–15):

. . . never did I hear
Such gallant chiding: for, besides the groves,
The skies, the fountains, every region near
Seem'd all one mutual cry: I never heard
So musical a discord, such sweet thunder.

This phrase acknowledges the historically denigrated status of African-American music, the idea that jazz was mere "discord"—Ellington's early jazz was originally dismissed as "jungle music." But the phrase also asserts the possibility that such "thunder" could be labeled "sweet," the adjective most often applied to Shakespeare's style. It is telling, then, that the title "Such Sweet Thunder" is used both for the entire suite and for the opening number in which Othello, a black man like Ellington, tells "the sweet and swinging, very convincing story" of his life with which he wooed Desdemona, a story so compelling that, Ellington notes with pride, the Venetian Duke declares "if Othello had said this to his daughter, she would have gone for it too."[8]

The phrase's original context, with its reference to music filling "every region," resonates with Ellington's ambitions for jazz in his late career. *Such Sweet Thunder* illustrates how Ellington sought to assimilate other cultural traditions while keeping faith with his music's African-American nature. Ellington's approach to jazzing up Shakespeare (as well as many other traditions) was to emphasize points of cultural contact—his adaptations were mutually affirmational rather than confrontational or revisionary. *Such Sweet Thunder* inaugurated Ellington's drive to establish jazz as an international modernist style rooted in African-American culture into which other traditions might be fruitfully translated. That would become a hallmark of Ellington's later writing—*The Nutcracker Suite* (his adaptation of Tchaikovsky, 1960), *The Peer Gynt Suite* (his adaptation of Grieg, 1960), *The Far East Suite* (1966), *The Latin American Suite* (1968),

85

The Afro-Eurasian Eclipse (1971), and his *Sacred Concerts* (1965, 1968, and 1973).

Several large-scale attempts to jazz up Shakespeare followed *Such Sweet Thunder*—the film *All Night Long* (1961, a transposition of *Othello* into the bop scene), Ellington's own incidental music for a Stratford production of *Timon of Athens* (1963), and George Russell's *Othello Ballet Suite* (1967), as well as a smattering of projects in the decades following. Even so, Ellington's *Such Sweet Thunder* marks the ending, albeit a glorious one, of the cultural drive to bring Shakespeare and jazz together, except as a part of the occasional high-concept production of Shakespeare or an allusive title for the occasional jazz tune. By the early 1960s, jazz had moved decisively away from dance music and into the avant-garde, so that its once-dominant position in popular culture was replaced by rock and roll, a fact which fueled a new phenomenon, the Shakespeare rock musical. What is more, jazz's growing affiliation with Afrocentrism, the civil rights movement, and counterculturalism made Shakespeare, still an icon of mainstream culture, seem inhospitable territory. Ellington's affirmational style was increasingly at odds with the confrontational social politics of the 1960s; indeed, at the time Ellington was accused of being above the civil rights movement, a comment which caused him pain. But equally so, Ellington's towering stature as a modern "classic" made it difficult for other composers to follow his example. Indeed, when the 1990s jazz revival led by Wynton Marsalis and others made large-scale jazz Shakespeare potentially commercially viable again, creators Cheryl West and Sheldon Epps turned to Ellington, with *Play On!* (1997), a musical adaptation of *Twelfth Night* based upon the Duke's music. Although the reviews and box office were lukewarm, *Play On!* offers evidence of the ironic success of the Duke's elevation in American culture to the level of the Bard. Where jazzed-up Shakespeare once had the frisson of cultural dissonance and iconoclasm,

it has now (to my mind, unfortunately) become passé, the stuff of revival, not innovation. But that it should be so might also be seen as evidence of a not inconsiderable cultural achievement—the dual acknowledgment by mainstream American culture that jazz indeed is one of its "classics," an African-American cultural form that deserves the appellation "art," and that Shakespeare can be, if one chooses to claim him, the cultural property of all Americans.

1. *The Collected Works of Langston Hughes*, ed. Arnold Rampersad, vol. 2 (Columbia: University of Missouri Press, 2001), 66.

2. "Salt-Fish Correspondent" [J. Kennard], "Who are Our National Poets?," *Knickerbocker Magazine* (1845); reprinted in *Inside the Minstrel Mask: Readings in Nineteenth-Century Blackface Minstrelsy*, ed. Annemarie Bean, James V. Hatch, and Brooks McNamara (Hanover, NH: Wesleyan University Press, 1996), 52 and 55.

3. For more on blackface burlesques of Shakespeare, see William J. Mahar, "Ethiopian Skits and Sketches: Contents and Contexts of Blackface Minstrelsy, 1840–1890," *Prospects* 16 (1991):) 241–79, esp. 248–62.

4. Alexander Do Mar, *Othello: an interesting drama, rather!* (London : T.L. Marks, ca. 1850), 5.

5. Brooks Atkinson, review of *Swingin' the Dream*, *The New York Times*, 30 November 1939, 24.

6. For biographical details, see John Edward Hasse, *Beyond Category: The Life and Genius of Duke Ellington* (New York: Da Capo, 1993), as well as Ken Vail's comprehensive *Duke's Diary: The Life of Duke Ellington, 1950–1974* (Lanham, MD: Scarecrow Press, 2002), 103–13.

7. For a detailed musical analysis, see Stephen M. Buhler's "Form and Character in Duke Ellington's and Billy Strayhorn's *Such Sweet Thunder*," in *Borrowers and Lenders* 1.1 (2005), online at http://atropos. english.uga.edu/cocoon/borrowers/request?id=118083.

8. This quotation and other details about the suite are taken from Irving Townshend's liner notes for *Such Sweet Thunder*, Columbia Legacy CK 65568 (1957).

(Foreground) John Livingstone Rolle as Bottom and Lisa Tharps as
Titania with (background) Shawn Winslow Lyles and Gamal Palmer as
fairies in The Shakespeare Theatre Free For All production of *A
Midsummer Night's Dream.* Photo by Scott Suchman.
CAT. NO. 120

Shakespeare Festivals
Yu Jin Ko

America's first two Shakespeare festivals, the Oregon Shakespeare Festival (OSF) and the San Diego National Shakespeare Festival at the Old Globe, were born in 1935. The Oregon festival began in the small town of Ashland as the First Annual Shakespearean Festival, reflecting in its optimistic title what its founder, Angus Bowmer, confessed to be his "wildly ambitious" and "grandiose schemes."[1] Its actual scope was decidedly more modest: three shows over the course of three days for audiences that numbered in the hundreds. The festival that eventually took root at the Old Globe was originally just a temporary attraction at the 1935 California Pacific International Exposition in San Diego, where a medley of fifty-minute versions of several Shakespeare plays appeared in a replica of the original London Globe.

While these early forays were sufficiently successful to give some life to the vision of a Shakespeare festival, the idea spread slowly. Although a handful of new festivals emerged in the following two decades, and Shakespeare plays continued to be produced in professional theaters in America, Shakespeare was most frequently performed in academic settings. By the mid-1970s, however, several dozen festivals existed in America, with the pace of new festival births accelerating dramatically by the end of the decade. By 1995, when an international guide to Shakespeare festivals was published, the United States boasted more than one hundred festivals, dwarfing, for example, Great Britain's fifteen. In the decade since that last count, the American number has nearly doubled, with over two hundred Shakespearean festivals and total attendance figures in the millions. From Fairbanks, Alaska, and Honolulu, Hawaii, to Spring Green, Wisconsin, and Staunton, Virginia, festivals of all sizes—from start-ups on a shoestring to megaplex institutions on multimillion-dollar budgets—cover the American cultural landscape. We are presently in the midst of an explosion that goes beyond Angus Bowmer's wildest imagination. This astonishing growth is easier to document than explain, but tracing the history of the Shakespeare festival in America will point to some of the forces behind the phenomenon.

As cultural historians have taught us, there existed two Shakespeares in nineteenth-century America—the highbrow and the lowbrow. There was the Shakespeare who belonged to the oral world of the various towns that sprouted along the Oregon Trail and the routes that the Gold Rush took. This was the Shakespeare of Jim Bridger, the illiterate Army Scout credited with being the first white man to visit the Great Salt Lake in 1863; he is said to have offered a yoke of cattle to purchase a volume of Shakespeare and then to have paid a German boy $40 a month to read it to him. This was the Shakespeare especially, though not exclusively, of the West, where an actor could earn the most money (up to $3,000 a week in San Francisco) performing in venues ranging from grand theaters to the most rough-and-tumble of makeshift stages in mining camps or over saloons. The audiences were boisterous, driven by a populist demand for their money's worth.

Then there was the highbrow Shakespeare of the so-called legitimate theater, especially in the East, where patrons were increasingly separated by class. For those who embraced the more egalitarian Shakespeare, this was the snobbish, aristocratic Shakespeare of England, as the Astor Place Riot attested (when a visit to New York City by the English actor William Macready set off a riot by largely working-class New Yorkers to protest his presence). Not surprisingly, this was the Shakespeare who came to define *culture*, and literary culture in particular. This was also the Shakespeare who came out on top by the beginning of the twentieth century and was, as man of letters and college president A. A. Lipscomb predicted in 1882, "destined to become the Shakespeare of the college and university."[2]

By the time Angus Bowmer was dreamily contemplating a festival that would become the "Salzburg of the West," the highbrow, archaic Shakespeare of the learned had become firmly entrenched in the broader culture of America. Shakespeare was also a huge box-office risk, especially as the Depression beset the country and newer forms of popular entertainment, especially the movies, competed for scarce dollars. Bowmer took a flexibly divided approach to this Shakespeare that defined not only the Oregon festival but also of many others after it and would also contribute to their phenomenal success. On the one hand, Bowmer maintained a reverential posture toward Shakespeare as a classic to be approached only through devoted study and training. Bowmer was determined, for example, to make education a crucial part of the festival experience, and as he was on the faculty of Southern Oregon Normal School (precursor to Southern Oregon University), he used its resources to advance this goal. As a theater practitioner, Bowmer was directly influenced by Englishman Iden Payne, who was part of the so-called "Elizabethan revival" that sought to replace the labyrinthine trappings of the English Victorian stage with Elizabethan simplicity and vigor. Payne's rehearsal practices, however, were guided by a draconian sense of theatrical rectitude and included read-through after read-through, which he accompanied with hectoring lectures and demonstrations. If his actors complained, they were not alone: in classrooms of the time, students and teachers often deplored a similarly toilsome march through the plays. Nonetheless, influenced by Payne, Bowmer staged the plays in a style that would today be called straight.

Bowmer, however, was also deeply averse to what he thought of as the clinical aura of academia and was determined to keep his theater from becoming a museum. Indeed, in tension with high straightness were the material conditions and cultural circumstances behind the perform-ances. The first Oregon festival took place as part of a Fourth of July celebration that the Ashland Chamber of Commerce sponsored to attract attention and tourist dollars. As Bowmer tells the story, his actors—mostly amateurs collected from the community—had to compete with the fireworks on the Fourth of July in order to be heard by the audience, as the performance took place in a domeless building formerly used for the Chautauqua, a gathering of performers and lecturers that sought to bring culture to the rural masses. At the first festival, that is, high art was presented in a distinctly populist environment.

A similar dynamic occurred in San Diego, where the medley of plays at the open-air replica Globe for the California Exposition was also directed by Iden Payne. As for the Exposition, it was, like the many expos that preceded and followed it, a thoroughly American fair that employed entrepreneurship and entertainment to showcase technological innovations, commercial successes, and sheer carnival fun for a popular audience. It included the Palace of Electricity as well as a Ripley's Believe-It-or-Not exhibit, and a "Zoro Garden" where fifty nudists read books, although the women were required by the Chief of Police to wear "brassieres and G-strings." From the very outset, a uniquely American tension between elite and popular culture lay at the heart of the festival experience. To a great extent, the Shakespeare festival's ability to negotiate this tension has transformed Shakespeare from box-office poison to the most popular playwright in America.

In 1955, nonetheless, Shakespeare scholar Alfred Harbage lamented that audiences at Shakespeare plays often acted as though they were attending church, "gratified that they have come, and gratified that they now may go," remaining all the while "reverently unreceptive." That was partly because the overwhelming majority of Shakespearean performances took place on college campuses (as *Shakespeare Quarterly* reported somewhat ruefully in 1955). Although

Souvenir program for the Oregon Shakespearean Festival.
Ashland, Oregon, 1963.
Courtesy of the Oregon Shakespeare Company.
CAT. NO. 111

intense scholarly work on Shakespeare opened up his plays in unforeseen and invaluable ways and although the college productions, especially those affiliated with drama programs, were richly varied, the academic dominance of Shakespeare reinforced the pervasive image of his works as a source of education and cultural refinement rather than popular entertainment. The journalist Gerald Nachman echoed the experiences and sentiments of many when he recalled that Shakespeare in American schools had become "theatrical spinach: He's good for you. If you digest enough of his plays, you'll grow up big and strong intellectually like teacher."[3] The festival would not easily counter this reflexive attitude to Shakespeare and develop into more than an isolated cultural force.

But slowly the task was performed. Much of it took place in towns that developed along the Oregon Trail in locations that would prove perfectly suited to spread the spirit of the Oregon and San Diego Festivals. In Boulder, Colorado, in 1958, the Colorado Shakespeare Festival officially came into existence, after fourteen years as an informal venture. Not surprisingly, the Festival was intimately affiliated with the University of Colorado at Boulder and drew upon its rich resources for everything from space and funding to personnel. The Festival was determined from the outset, however, to reach far beyond the university, indicated by its decision to follow the OSF and the Old Globe by performing in an outdoor amphitheater to take advantage of its festive, open-air populism. Like the OSF Elizabethan Stage nestled at the base of the Siskiyou mountains in Ashland and the Old Globe in the heart of San Diego's Balboa Park, Colorado Festival's primary venue (the Mary Rippon Theatre) was also on a campus surrounded by the stunning, snow-capped beauty of the Rockies. It was a place worth visiting. Similarly, in Cedar City, Utah, the Utah Shakespearean Festival took root in 1961, led by Fred Adams, who made a cultural pilgrimage to Ashland to learn from the OSF. The Utah Festival was also associated with a university (Southern Utah University), but it began on an outdoor platform stage and eventually settled into an Elizabethan-style outdoor theater. Located near attractions such as Zion and Bryce Canyon National Parks, it also sought to become a destination to visit.

New festivals also emerged in the East. In the aptly chosen town of Stratford, Connecticut (although this had not been the first choice), a group of enterprising people from the arts world founded the American Shakespeare Theatre (AST) in 1955 after raising the enormous cost of a 1,550-seat theater, dubbed the Festival Theatre. (This festival should not be confused with Canada's premier Shakespeare Festival, the Stratford Festival of Canada, which was founded in 1952 and led for its first three years by Tyrone Guthrie, who would later found the Guthrie Theatre in Minneapolis. Because of its location outside the United States, the Canadian Stratford Festival falls beyond the scope of this survey.) The AST enjoyed immediate success under artistic director John Houseman, with instant classics such as *Much Ado about Nothing* with Katherine Hepburn and *The Merchant of Venice* with Hepburn and Morris Carnovsky. The theater would cease operation in 1982 (for the usual reasons that besiege theaters—creative differences and financial woes), but during its twenty-seven-year run, it established itself as an important center for innovation on the East Coast.

The biggest jolt of energy from the East Coast would come from a slight, perennially combative man from New York who considered theaters like Stratford's an opportunity wasted on the overprivileged. Joseph Papirofsky or, as he later became, Joe Papp was raised by his immigrant Jewish parents in rundown tenements of various ethnically mixed neighborhoods of Brooklyn. He was the kind of Jew, by his own account, who was "despised" by assimilated, prosperous, "uptown" Jews.[4] As he liked to recall, no one in his family was a lawyer or a doctor, and he never went to college. He had certainly never been to the New York City Ballet, the cofounder of which (Lincoln Kirstein) had been an early supporter of the American Shakespeare Theatre. But Papp, driven by his early experiences, sought to revolutionize festival Shakespeare by reaching the kind of people he grew up with—the "great dispossessed audience"—with shows that had casts who looked like those people. He was determined to bring Shakespeare closer to the urban populace and re-Americanize Shakespeare as a democratic contemporary. As he was to say later, "I believe that great art is for everyone—not just the rich or the middle class. When I go into East Harlem or Bedford-Stuyvesant and see the kids who come to our shows, I see nothing so clearly as myself." After a series of fitful starts, Papp established the New York Shakespeare Festival (NYSF) in 1954. His first shows—staged in amphitheater settings in different parks and transported on flatbed trucks to the outer boroughs of New York—had many of the features that would become trademarks of the NYSF: multiethnic casts and the kind of gutsy staging that enabled actors to engage audiences that had never seen a Shakespeare performance. (The Festival would soon launch the careers of actors ranging from Colleen Dewhurst and Meryl Streep to James Earl Jones and Raul Julia.) The shows were also free, as the summer shows still are.

Eventually, the NYSF settled in Central Park in an amphitheater, Delacorte Theatre, that Papp fought bruising battles to build, but it also established a year-round home around the corner from the Astor Place of the nineteenth-century theater riot. As the Festival evolved, it continually struggled to maintain its egalitarian character and mass appeal. It borrowed, for example, the practice of celebrity casting from the AST to bring recognized Hollywood stars to the stage (sometimes back to the stage), such as Al Pacino and Michelle Pfeiffer. But the Hollywood glamour was often coupled with an edgy, urban sensibility that lent a stylish excitement to Shakespeare. The NYSF would also become a leader in a theatrical practice that was already growing when the Festival was established. The 1955 issue of *Shakespeare Quarterly* that noted the extraordinary number of Shakespeare performances on college campuses also hinted at something else on the landscape: "a comic strip *Comedy of Errors*, another staging of the same play as a study in abnormal psychology, a science fiction *Tempest*, a hillbilly *Hamlet*."[5] Eclectic experimentation—which would come to be known and sometimes derided as "concept" Shakespeare—had arrived. Whatever one may think of this practice, it involved, at its heart, translating Shakespeare on stage into more accessible idioms. Such experimentation was often driven by a kind of mantra, especially for educators who wanted to make Shakespeare more palatable to resistant students: cultural relevance. From the outset, the AST, for example, was given to reshaping Shakespeare, as it did by designing its *Much Ado* (with Katherine Hepburn) with gestures toward Texas. Later, with Michael Kahn as artistic director, it would embark on productions of political plays (*Henry V, Julius Caesar*) that drew on the Vietnam War and a version of *Romeo and Juliet* that reflected on the hippie generation. The Colorado Shakespeare Festival was noticed for it's diverse approaches to production. But of all the Shakespeare Festivals of the 1950s, and 1960s, the New York Shakespeare Festival was perhaps the boldest in its experimentation. Its *Hamlet* of 1968, the year in which the NYSF also produced the musical *Hair*, revealed that spirit in its cutting of the text and its choice to make *Hamlet* a kind of Puerto Rican street prince. Many balked at the radical nature of some of the experiments, but the continually evolving, sometimes restless, sometimes buoyant and cheery spirit of exploration would draw new fans to the venues with the news that Shakespeare spoke a language they could understand.

Program for the New York Shakespeare Festival.
New York, 1976.
Courtesy of the Joseph Papp Public Theater.
CAT. NO. 114

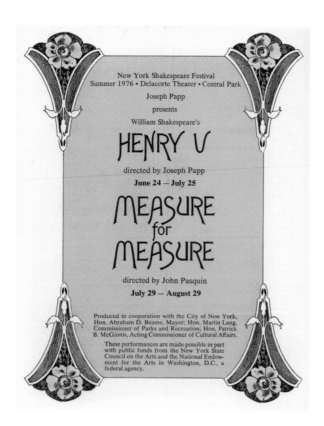

Still, even as a democratic spirit generally reigned, the festivals reminded their audiences of Shakespeare's iconic status as a sacred repository of the Western world's highest cultural and aesthetic values. It became customary to develop ambitious education programs that often collaborated with universities. These (generally very popular) programs provided a genuine service to audiences and enabled the festivals to trade on the benefits; as William Patton, the first full-time, paid general manager of the Oregon Shakespeare Festival put it, Shakespeare is "certified as good for you, so audiences can congratulate themselves on their intellectuality." What all this ultimately meant was that audiences during this period of early growth were surprised into discovering, again and again, that Shakespeare was spinach that actually tasted good. The explosive growth of festival Shakespeare over the next decades can be attributed in large measure to more people discovering a taste for Shakespeare against a cultural backdrop that continued to equate him with the pinnacle of high culture.

One cannot, however, overlook some of the economic and social forces that contributed to the success and spread of festivals during the 1950s and 1960s. Populist as the festivals were in spirit, their audiences were largely middle class. This amorphous group, whose numbers grew rapidly in the boom years following World War II, enjoyed new forms of mobility. There was, first of all, economic mobility that allowed an increasing segment of the population to buy, for example, new appliances. Second, a consequence of economic prosperity was the physical mobility afforded by the automobile and the ever-expanding interstate highway system. In the two decades under consideration, the number of automobiles in the United States nearly tripled, reaching 119 million by 1972. Third, after the Federal Highway Act of 1956, the last of the major trails that were opened in the nineteenth century essentially became highways and thus enabled, not frontier adventurism, but tourism. Fourth, there was the kind of cultural mobility that came with the broadening of access to higher education and the various social institutions that dispensed cultural capital. Festivals benefited from and finessed this mobility in remarkably prescient and efficient ways.

Angus Bowmer's early decision to incorporate the Oregon festival as a not-for-profit organization also had a tremendous impact on the subsequent history of Shakespeare festivals. The impact is still felt today on the bottom line; pricey as some festivals are (tickets range up to $65), they remain within a middle-class budget, especially compared to costs for attending commercial theaters and many sporting events. As festivals developed, they reaped the benefits of increasing middle-class wealth (in both ticket sales and philanthropic donations), but without the more urgent profit motive of firmly commercial theaters, they kept ticket prices within reach of a large percentage of the population. This wealth also went hand in hand with the long-standing American tradition of small-town community involvement in civic development. It is no coincidence that, with notable exceptions, festivals developed in secondary cities or rural towns: Ashland, San Diego, Boulder, Cedar City, Anniston, Odessa, Spring Green, and so on. From the earliest days of Bowmer himself, the selling points of festivals have been economic revitalization and community building. Ironically, what made it possible for many of the less populated areas to thrive and to become destination festivals was the physical mobility that allowed tourists to come. Ashland still has a population of only about 20,000, roughly five percent of the number of tickets sold annually by the OSF; similarly, Spring Green, Wisconsin, home of the American Players Theatre, has a population of about 1,600, while attendance reaches 100,000 annually. Residents and visitors enjoyed the cultural mobility enabled by a thriving Shakespeare festival.

As America entered the 1970s and 1980s, success bred more success for the Shakespeare festival, and patterns were repeated, though sometimes the ruins of one venture gave rise to a new one. Many of the older festivals went through ambitious expansions that established them as performance and research centers with multiple stages. After rebuilding its outdoor Elizabethan Stage in 1959, the OSF, for example, went on to add the indoor Angus Bowmer Theatre in 1970 and The Black Swan in 1977. And the pace of growth would only accelerate. In 2001, the OSF would celebrate the sale of its ten-millionth ticket; in the following year, the Black Swan would be replaced by the impressively modern, in-the-round New Theatre. The Old Globe and the Utah Shakespearean Festival experienced similar expansions into multiple-show destinations. Some companies that started later, like the New Jersey Shakespeare Festival (1963), traded their hard-won reputations for new, bigger venues and longer seasons in the 1970s. Some simply grew, like the Carriage House Players, which staged a Shakespeare play in Central Park—in Louisville, Kentucky, that is—for the first time in 1960 as part of an arts fair. The following year, they produced Kentucky's first—and first free—Shakespeare festival with a season of three plays, giving birth to a new tradition. Shakespeare in Central Park, as the festival came to be called, continued to suffer growing pains as its audience expanded and funding needs intensified, until it was rechristened the Kentucky Shakespeare Festival in 1984 and, with new funding from private sources and the city of Louisville, expanded its amphitheater capacity to 1,000 seats in 1988. Today, it boasts a record of forty-six straight years of "Free Will in Central Park," in the same location in inner-city Old Louisville with its ethnically mixed population.

Still other companies emerged when veterans from one festival went elsewhere, as in the case of the Oklahoma Shakespearean Festival. Molly Risso, its founder, had been an actress at the OSF and watched some of her colleagues help Cedar City establish the Utah Shakespearean Festival. Inspired by this, while she was teaching theater at Southeastern Oklahoma State University, she founded the Oklahoma Shakespearean Festival in 1980 in the hamlet of Durant, which like Ashland and Cedar City is close to a natural tourist attraction (Lake Texoma) that draws hundreds of thousands of visitors each year.

The movement of talent benefited some existing festivals as well, such as the Shakespeare Theatre at the Folger. This company was founded in 1969 as the Folger Theatre Group (FTG) and mounted its first season in 1970 in the reduced-scale, model Elizabethan indoor theater at the Folger Shakespeare Library. Early success (12,000 spectators for the first season) generated more success and larger ambitions; by 1976, the season had expanded to thirty-two weeks. As was the case with many other companies in traditional replica spaces, the stagings were often far from traditional (its first Shakespeare production—*Twelfth Night*—was modern dress and featured an aluminum geodesic dome and soft-rock incidental music). However, burdened by its very success and rapid growth, as well as its limited seating capacity, the theater's financial situation deteriorated; by 1985, the FTG verged on bankruptcy and jeopardized the fiscal health of the Folger Shakespeare Library. Through the efforts of Washington power brokers like Senator Patrick Moynihan of New York, the FTG was reorganized as The Shakespeare Theatre at the Folger and was made financially independent. Equally significant, a new artistic director was named: Michael Kahn, who had been instrumental in bringing innovation to the American Shakespeare Festival at Stratford but had resigned in 1977 over philosophical differences. Kahn worked quickly to revive the theater, staging fresh and imaginative shows while also pulling out some old tricks like celebrity casting (e.g., Sabrina Le Beauf, Sondra Huxtable of "The Cosby Show," as Rosalind).

By 1992, the theater had balanced its $4.3 million budget and moved into a spanking-new, state-of-the-art theater (The Lansburgh) and renamed itself simply The Shakespeare Theatre. The company's departure from the Folger created, in turn, an opportunity for the Folger itself to develop a new theater initiative: the Folger Theatre, which has grown since its founding in 1992 to perform a three-play season in the Elizabethan theater. As for The Shakespeare Theatre, today it awaits the opening of its new home, an eleven-story, truly state-of-the-art, $77 million complex to be called the Harman Center for the Arts.

Many of the festivals simply started from scratch. In 1971, a young man fresh out of college, Martin L. Platt, went to Anniston, Alabama (population, 30,000) to direct its community theater. The following year, he started a Shakespeare festival with $500 borrowed from his mother and an initial company of fifteen actors for four plays in the multipurpose auditorium-gymnasium of the former Anniston High School. On opening night, which served up *The Comedy of Errors* inside the sweltering auditorium (temperatures climbed to over 100 degrees), only two people attended—a critic and his wife. Despite that inauspicious beginning, by 1985—thirteen years after its founding—the festival would move to Montgomery, where its newly constructed, eight-level, $21.5 million theater complex awaited. The budget for that first year would be $4.2 million, the season would run year-round, and the performances would number over four hundred. Today, the festival annually attracts 300,000 visitors from all fifty states.

With the number of festivals expanding so rapidly during the two decades of the 1970s and 1980s, the variety of festivals also grew considerably richer. In 1978, in the town of Lenox, Massachusetts, in the heart of the Berkshires (also home to the Tanglewood Music Festival), Tina Packer, a veteran of the Royal Shakespeare Company, and Kristin

Linklater, a legendary but idiosyncratic Scottish-born voice teacher, cofounded Shakespeare & Company. Packer stated early on that that "she wanted a year-round classically-trained repertory company based on the English model but with an energy and emotional truth that she saw as distinctly American."[6] But she would try to tap into this American emotional truth by freeing the actor's voice, to borrow the title of one of Linklater's books. Packer's method borrowed from many sources—including Linklater's, and the American method—but it was unique in its intense focus on connecting individual words and syllables to the whole voice (the physical sound and all the emotional and intellectual power and history that could be packed into a sound). In the words of Shakespeare & Company's early mission statement,

> Shakespeare & Company is committed to creating a permanent American Shakespeare company which will perform with the same intense understanding of language and verse, the same physical grace in dance, the same exploration in violence, and the same lust for exploring universal truths as did the Elizabethans. At the heart of this commitment is the principal aesthetic upon which the company is founded—the aesthetic of language—its power, its import, its visceral impact on humankind's emotions and intellect.

Today, the company is in the middle of a capital campaign to raise the funds necessary to build a replica of the Rose playhouse on its grounds. It continues its effort to revive the English past by making it deeply contemporary and American.

Packer was not alone in the 1980s in taking an idiosyncratic, originalist approach to Shakespeare. From the early 1970s, Ralph Cohen, a Shakespeare professor at James Madison University in Virginia's Shenandoah Valley, would take his students to London to see Royal Shakespeare Company (RSC) productions. Over the years, he grew less and less satisfied with the RSC productions as they grew larger in scale with more elaborate sets and trappings. He and his students discovered that simpler, lower-budget, fringe productions engaged them and their imaginations far more. This experience, and a seminar in which Cohen and his students staged *Henry V* in a manner that took the simpler aesthetic to an extreme, led to the founding in 1988, with his student Jim Warren, of a company dedicated to original Elizabethan practices: the Shenandoah Shakespeare Express. The company alternated between touring the country and performing in its hometown of Harrisonburg, but their productions always contained several features: universal lighting (a wash of stage lighting that approximates the unchanging light of an open-air space) and no set except for a few movable boxes, minimal props, and plentiful audience contact. For Cohen and Warren, this was popular theater in its highest form. It demanded total imaginative participation from the audience to create the playworld in the moment of performance, but because the boundary between actor and audience was so permeable (without the lighting that separates the stage illusion from the audience), it enabled the actor to develop the mutual relationship with the audience that is possible only in an informal, truly populist environment (as in a vaudeville house or a ballpark). In 2001, after a dozen years of success, Cohen changed the organizational structure, creating the American Shakespeare Center and rechristening its resident playing company Shenandoah Shakespeare; the company also began performing in its new theater, the Blackfriars Playhouse, a replica of the indoor theater in which Shakespeare's company performed its winter seasons. In this handsome and elegant space, in the curious comfort of plaster, timber, and two-tiered galleries, echoes of the past mix with the most festive sounds when the actors are on stage.

Since the 1990s began, trigger points seem to have accelerated the self-replicating process of festival expansion. Many companies disappeared, but many more sprang up anew, which in turn spawned new companies. Some explored directions suggested by previous undertakings, like the African-American Shakespeare Company in San Francisco, which began in 1995 with the motto of "Envisioning the Classics with Color" and the goal of making them more "accessible" to minority communities. In 1993, the Los Angeles Women's Shakespeare Company began its mission of creating all-female, multiracial productions that involved collaboration between adult women and younger girls. Some simply followed traditions they inherited. In 1991, the Heart of America Shakespeare Festival was created in Kansas City, Missouri, by two women, one who was sent back home to Kansas City from New York by Joseph Papp with the explicit exhortation to start a Shakespeare festival, and another who approached the former artistic director of the Shakespeare Festival of Dallas for advice about a free Shakespeare festival. This festival is held under the stars in Southmoreland Park and is free. Still other festivals exist about which little can yet be written because they are fledgling projects in the most remote corners of the country. Taken all together, however, one can say that the festival has evolved collectively over the past seventy years to provide more access for more people to Shakespeare's greatness. The immense, continually changing diversity of festivals today is a living, organic reflection of Shakespeare's infinite variety. Indeed, the vitality of Shakespeare as a playwright who continues to speak to us will depend in no small measure on sustaining the vigor of the festival.

FOR FURTHER READING

On the cultural history of Shakespeare in America:

Carrell, Jennifer Lee. "How the Bard Won the West." *Smithsonian* 19.5 (1998): 99–107.

Koon, Helene Wickham. *How Shakespeare Won the West.* Jefferson, NC: Mcfarland, 1989.

Levine, Lawrence W. *Highbrow/Lowbrow: The Emergence of Cultural Hierarchy in America.* Cambridge, MA: Harvard University Press, 1988.

Sturgess, Kim C. *Shakespeare and the American Nation.* Cambridge: Cambridge University Press, 2004.

On Shakespeare festivals, collectively and individually:

Bowmer, Angus. *As I Remember, Adam: An Autobiography of a Festival.* Ashland: Oregon Shakespearean Festival Association, 1975.

Engle, Ron, Felicia Hardison Londré, and Daniel J. Watermeier. *Shakespeare Companies and Festivals.* Westport: Greenwood Press, 1995.

Epstein, Helen. *Joe Papp: An American Life.* Boston: Little, Brown & Co., 1994.

_____*The Companies She Keeps: Tina Packer Builds a Theatre.* Cambridge, MA: Plunkett Lake Press, 1985.

Houseman, John, and Jack Landau. *The American Shakespeare Festival: The Birth of a Theatre.* New York: Simon & Schuster, 1959.

Loney, Glenn Meredith. *The Shakespeare Complex* New York: Drama Book Specialists, 1975.

1. For the story of Oregon Shakespeare Festival in Angus Bowmer's own words, see his *As I Remember, Adam: An Autobiography of a Festival* (Ashland: Oregon Shakespearean Festival Association, 1975).

2. Quoted in Lawrence W. Levine, *Highbrow/ Lowbrow: The Emergence of Cutural Hierarchy in America* (Cambridge, MA: Harvard University Press, 1988).

3. For Harbage and Nachman, see Levine.

4. For Joe Papp's story, see Helen Epstein, *Joe Papp: An American Life* (Boston: Little, Brown & Co., 1994).

5. "Current Theater Notes," *Shakespeare Quarterly* 6 (1955): 67–88, esp. 69.

6. For the story of Shakespeare & Company, see Helen Epstein, *The Companies She Keeps: Tina Packer Builds a Theatre* (Cambridge, MA: Plunkett Lake Press, 1985).

Additional sources for this essay include festival web sites, press materials and interviews with festival personnel conducted by the author.

Portrait miniatures of Mr. and Mrs. H. C. Folger.
Folger Archives.
CAT. NO. 138

Duty and Enjoyment: The Folgers as Shakespeare Collectors in the Gilded Age
Georgianna Ziegler

In April 1911, the elderly Shakespeare editor Horace Howard Furness wrote to Henry Clay Folger, "Tell me, that I may have it in black and white, how many First Folios you have. I long to be pea-green with envy."[1] Hoping to entice the Folgers to visit him again in his country house at Wallingford, Pennsylvania, Furness adds that they should come down when his nephew Owen Wister visits, as Wister will probably bring along Henry James. Here, in a few sentences, a window opens to us on American cultural life just before the First World War. One collector writes to another about the extent of his library, playfully expressing the spirit of competition, which is part of what makes collecting a game. The literary world to which Furness belonged and which he held enticingly open to the Folgers included two American novelists, one of whom—James—was a master at understanding and writing about the acquisition of wealth and the nuances of collecting.

Steeped in Shakespeare himself and influenced by the dispersal of great wealth he saw in collectors such as his friend Isabella Stewart Gardner, Henry James anatomized the subject of collecting in a number of places, including his early novel, *The Portrait of a Lady*. Here, Henrietta Stackpole tells the wealthy American ex-patriot, Ralph Touchett, what he has done to Isabel Archer, "You were Prospero enough to make her what she has become. You have acted on Isabel Archer since she came here, Mr. Touchett."[2] Ralph has educated the naive Isabel and then provided her with a fortune, but she has the ill grace to throw it away by marrying the dilettante collector Gilbert Osmond. Only late in the novel does Isabel realize how different she is from her husband. James writes: "Her notion of the aristocratic life was simply the union of great knowledge with great liberty; the knowledge would give one a sense of duty and the liberty a sense of enjoyment. But for Osmond it was altogether a thing of forms." Osmond wished to add her to his collection as another

object of great value, along with her inheritance. But Isabel understands that wealth brings more than the power to acquire. It frees one up to enjoy life, but it also brings obligations, or in her words, "knowledge [that] would give one a sense of duty."[3] James's novel was published in 1880, the "Gilded Age" of American society, and here, as in much of his writing, he explores the effects of wealth—old and new—on its possessors.

This combination of enjoyment and duty, which might be traced to America's Anglo-Protestant roots, lies at the heart of some of the major collections formed in this country during the late nineteenth century by the likes of art collectors Isabella Stewart Gardner and Henry Clay Frick and book collectors J. P. Morgan, Henry Huntington, and Folger. All of these families made their money in the hard-driving days of American industry, on the backs of steel, coal, railway, and oil workers. All but one of the collectors inherited wealth; only Mr. Folger came from humble beginnings and gradually built his own much smaller fortune. And all but one of the collectors diversified; only the Folgers seem to have collected as a team, both focused on and passionate about one subject—Shakespeare.

Henry Clay Folger was born on 18 June 1857, the eldest of eight children, descended on his father's side from Peter Folger, sire of an old Nantucket family, whose members included Benjamin Franklin's mother. In the fall of 1875, Henry entered Amherst College. His letters, college scrapbook, and essays show his reading in the current novels of Dickens, Hawthorne, and Bulwer-Lytton, his interest in musical events, and his sense of the dramatic, including one occasion when he and his friends donned costumes for a supper party. For Christmas of his freshman year, his brother gave him a one-volume edition of Shakespeare's *Complete Works*, which still survives, full of quotations about the Bard by Folger's contemporaries—Thomas Carlyle, Elizabeth Barrett Browning, Abraham Lincoln, and especially Ralph Waldo Emerson—that Folger copied in over the years. By the time he was a senior, he had written essays on Portia and Shylock, won a prize for an oration on Tennyson, whom he compared to Shakespeare, and bought a ticket for 25 cents to hear the aging Emerson give a talk. It was Emerson who made all of Folger's brushes with Shakespeare coalesce into a passion that would remain the focus of the rest of his life.

After graduating from Amherst in 1879, Folger worked for an oil company while pursuing a law degree at Columbia University. He also met Emily Clara Jordan, a recent graduate of Vassar College, and they were married on 6 October 1885. Folger could not have found a better companion. Also interested in books, music, and the theater, Emily Jordan, like many intelligent women of the period, adopted her husband's intellectual passion as her own and prepared herself to work with him. She wrote to Furness, asking him to set her a reading list so that she could work towards a master's degree in Shakespeare. Furness replied with some suggestions, adding, "Take Booth's Reprint of the First Folio, and read a play every day consecutively. At the end of the thirty seven days you will be in a Shakespearian atmosphere that will astonish you with its novelty and its pleasure, and its profit. Don't read a single note during the month."[4] After a detailed and demanding course of self-study, Emily Folger produced a thesis on "The True Text of Shakespeare" and received her M.A. from Vassar in 1896. Having lost his own wife and scholarly companion, Furness was delighted by the enthusiastic young couple dedicated to Shakespeare. In 1897, he wrote to them, "the sight of husband and wife, both eager in the same pursuit, always touches me deeply."[5]

In the meantime, Henry Folger had kept up a private course of reading while he attended law school. We know, through Emily Folger, that after hearing Emerson speak, Henry went back to read Emerson's talk on the 300th anniversary of Shakespeare's birth.[6] It includes the following passage, which may have struck the young man about to make his way in the world:

Wherever there are men, and in the degree in which they are civil, have power of mind, sensibility to beauty, music, the secrets of passion, and the liquid expression of thought, [Shakespeare] has risen to his place as the first poet of the world.[7]

Folger's notebooks, preserved in the Library's archives, show that he was reading Thomas Carlyle and the American author James Russell Lowell on both Emerson and Carlyle. On 13 December 1879, six months after graduating from college, Folger bought a copy of Carlyle's *On Heroes*. Though he was not given to extensive annotations in his books, his markings in Carlyle's essay "The Hero as Poet," are especially interesting. He twice underlines Carlyle's estimation of Shakespeare as "the grandest thing we have yet done." What really seems to have captured Folger's imagination, however, is Carlyle's Victorian appraisal of Shakespeare as the greatest representative of English culture. Folger marks the passages that include such sentiments as "For our honour among foreign nations, as an ornament to our English Household, what item is there that we would not surrender rather than him? . . . this Shakspeare does not go, he lasts forever with us." Writing in the days of empire, Carlyle sees Shakespeare as the linchpin that will hold together the English-speaking world, and Folger takes note. "This King Shakspeare, does not he shine, in crowned sovereignty, over us all, as the noblest, gentlest, yet strongest of rallying-signs . . . 'Yes, this Shakspeare is ours; we produced him, we speak and think by him; we are of one blood and kind with him.'"[8] Folger has emphasized "King Shakspeare" and "ours" by underlining, but while admiring Carlyle's high opinion of Shakespeare's

Composite image: Letter to Mrs. H. C. Folger. Manuscript, 1894;
Contemporary photograph of Horace Howard Furness.
CAT. NO. 137-138

influence, Folger was no imperialist. His beliefs lay elsewhere, in Emersonian democracy.

Reading Lowell on the two men, Folger discovered that Carlyle was deemed the less human, while Emerson "tended much more exclusively to self-culture and the independent development of the individual man." Folger wrote Lowell's estimation of Emerson on the title page to his copy of the *Essays*: "If it was ever questionable whether democracy could develop a gentleman, the problem has been affirmatively solved at last."[9] It was Emerson's understanding of the ideal and the real, the transcendental and the material in American life, that spoke to Folger. He quotes from Lowell again: "What then is his secret? Is it not that he out-Yankees us all? . . . that he is equally at home with the potato-disease and original sin . . . that his mysticism gives us a centerpoise to our superpracticality?"[10] Bringing together these different forces to create a modern gentleman appealed profoundly to Folger as he left law school and began his career in the oil business.

On the title page of Emerson's *Essays*, Folger also wrote, "Build therefore your own world," taken from the "Essay on Nature." Building his own world is what Folger set out to do. As he compiled his commonplace books, he seemed to be on a moral and spiritual search, trying to find the principles that would guide him to be not a rapacious or a great man, but a good man. He was twenty-five years old, reading Jean Jacques Rousseau's *Confessions*, David Friedrich Strauss's *Life of Jesus* translated by George Eliot, John Ruskin's *Fors Clavigera*, Robert Browning's *The Ring and the Book*, as well as books about Transcendentalism, Emerson, Goethe, Schiller, and Charles Lamb. From Rousseau he noted, "I would exhibit to my fellows a man in all the truth of nature, and that man—myself," and from F. M. Robertson's lecture on Shakespeare he copied out: "Shakespeare is an universal poet, because he utters all that is in men." Ironically, the clearest statement of his purpose may be in a mundane piece of verse that he jotted down from the October 1868 issue of *Harper's* magazine. The author was a Michigan writer, Mary Frances Tyler.

Not to the man of dollars,
Not to the man of deeds,
Not to the man of cunning,
Not to the man of creeds;
Not to the one whose passion
Is for the world's renown . . .

But to the one whose spirit
Yearns for the great and good; . . .
Unto the one who labors,
Fearless of foe or frown:
Unto the kindly hearted,
Cometh a blessing down.[11]

Already, then, at the very beginning of his career, Henry Folger seems to have been looking for a center and purpose to his life that would be more than making money. In the next few years, that center focused more and more on Shakespeare.

As time goes on, Folger's commonplace books show that he began reading about Shakespeare and Elizabethan literature: works by Samuel Taylor Coleridge, William Hazlitt, Victor Hugo, Edward Dowden, and even Delia Bacon. He quotes from Victor Hugo: "Shakespeare has emotion, instinct, the true voice, the right tone. . . . His poetry is himself, & at the same time it is you." And he adds from Hugo, "England has two books, one which she has made, the other which has made her.—Shakespeare and the Bible."[12] It is such reflections as these by Hugo, combined with Emersonian idealism, that I believe created Folger's understanding of what Emily Folger later described as "the relation of Shakespeare to the Bible and to English literature in general and to American idealism in particular. It fascinated him, just as it had fascinated Washington and Lincoln."[13] And these were the sentiments that led the Folgers to conceive of a library.

About the time of their marriage, Henry Folger had acquired a copy of the Halliwell-Phillipps facsimile edition of the First Folio for $1.25. The book inspired him and became, as Emily Folger said, "the cornerstone of the Shakespeare Library."[14] By 1896 when Emily received her master's degree, their collection was underway, beginning on the day in 1889 when Henry made his first appearance in an auction house and purchased a Fourth Folio for $107.50 on credit.

The Folgers never had children and thus were able to devote themselves wholeheartedly to their project. After his working hours, Henry Folger would relax by going through catalogs from bookdealers, deciding what to order, and handling the correspondence with dealers, agents, and auction houses. The Philadelphia dealer A.S.W. Rosenbach remembered that Emily Folger contributed to the effort by researching bibliographical details and frequently offering her advice on purchases.[15] Beginning in 1891, the Folgers made eleven trips to England to add to the collection, traveling frequently on an old-fashioned merchant ship, the SS *Minnehaha*. On one such trip, obviously inspired by the sea air, Folger wrote an essay that began: "Shakespeare's *The Tempest* reads well anywhere but especially so at the seashore, and best of all in mid-ocean. It is fragrant with salt spray picked up from wave crests by driving winds. The enchanted island of Prospero seems to have risen out of the surf."[16]

In 1897, Folger had the opportunity to purchase his first major collection. This was the Shakespeare library originally gathered by the great nineteenth-century collector, James Orchard Halliwell-Phillipps. He sold the collection to the Earl of Warwick in the 1850s but continued adding to it,

at least until 1870, and published several catalogues updating its contents. For Folger, trying to build up his own Shakespeare library, it must have been the dream collection. In addition to eight copies of the first four Folios of Shakespeare's plays, it included the 1599 quarto of *Romeo and Juliet*, the 1600 first quarto of *The Merchant of Venice*, and hundreds of other volumes of literature published in Shakespeare's time. An extremely important early seventeenth-century manuscript in the collection offers perhaps the earliest handwritten transcription of one of Shakespeare's plays *1 Henry IV*. In addition, the collection had many works about Shakespeare and his times, including biography, history, and criticism. Always shying from publicity, Mr. Folger carried out his transaction for the Warwick Castle Library in such secrecy that it was not noted by the *Times Literary Supplement* until many years later in 1923, though the *New York Times* listed *The Merchant of Venice* quarto among book sales in 1897 without giving the name of the purchaser.[17]

Also shrouded in some secrecy had been his purchase two years earlier of two lots of Shakespeareana from Halliwell-Phillipps's collection that were offered for sale by Sotheby's.[18] These included sixty folio-sized volumes into which Halliwell-Phillipps had pasted thousands of engravings, maps, letters, portraits, and other materials relating to Shakespeare and his times. The rest of that collection was sold to another American collector, at that time unnamed, who turned out to be Marsden J. Perry. Perry was a banker and financier, resident of Providence, Rhode Island, who was descended from Richard Perry, a grantee of the Massachusetts Bay Company, and John Brown, a founder of Rhode Island.[19] A lover of Shakespeare, like Mr. Folger, Perry had acquired a fine collection, including Halliwell-Phillipps items. In 1907 when the stock market plunged, Mr. Folger had his chance and was able to purchase part of Perry's collection. Still downsizing in 1919, Perry sold more of his collection to Rosenbach, who turned around and offered Folger "the greatest prize of the Perry collection," the earliest known compilation of Shakespeare quartos by a private individual.[20] They had been purchased and bound together around 1619 by Edward Gwynne, who had his name stamped on the binding. Now, three hundred years later, they found a new home with an equally passionate collector of Shakespeare.[21]

Some of the Folgers' best purchases were serendipitous and depended on being in the right place at the right time. One morning in 1904, Folger saw a notice in the New York *Sun* announcing the discovery of a 1594 edition of *Titus Andronicus*. The existence of such a book had been reported in the late seventeenth century, but no one had ever seen a copy. Now one had appeared in the possession of a Swedish family. Folger recalled that he wired his London agent to send someone immediately to Sweden, then he walked the streets of New York, trying to decide how much he should offer for the book. Having decided on £2,000, he then waited for a week or so, in the meantime receiving word from two other dealers that they would be able to offer him this book. Finally he learned that his own man had purchased the volume, because he was the only one who had turned up with ready cash.[22]

According to Rosenbach, Mr. Folger was eager to acquire more Shakespeare quarto editions, having captured the prized *Titus*. Again, he was lucky. Reading in a footnote of an article by Sidney Lee that Dr. John Gott, bishop of Truro, had a collection of quartos, Folger asked his London dealer to go to Wales and view the books. The dealer demurred, in British fashion, that this was not how things were done, but Folger, using the persistence of an American businessman, insisted. Eventually the dealer met the bishop's son-in-law, a barrister, who allowed a viewing of the books, admitting that his father-in-law was not well and was low on cash. Mr. Folger made an offer; the barrister brought the

books to London and received a check in return. The next day, the bishop died. If Folger had not been ready to pay with money up front, the books most probably would have been lost to the Chancery court and auction.[23]

Rosenbach worked with both Folger and Huntington in their collecting, but he states that their competition "was . . . a most amiable one." Although both men were interested in volumes from the great Britwell Library sale in London, neither bid against the other, and when Rosenbach acquired the Marsden Perry collection, he gave Mr. Folger first choice, asking only that he leave some good items for Mr. Huntington, which was done. Although Huntington purchased a "collection of Shakespeare plays formed by [the actor] John Philip Kemble" which had belonged to the Duke of Devonshire, he sold Folger some of the duplicate quartos.[24] Both men used their business acumen in their dealings with booksellers and auction houses, but Huntington took up collecting mostly after retirement, whereas for Folger it was a lifelong passion.[25] It was through Rosenbach that Folger had access to another American collector's choice Shakespeare quartos. William A. White of Brooklyn had a fine library which he generously lent to scholars over the years. Rosenbach had suggested to him that Folger would be interested in his quartos, and eventually Folger acquired a number of early English books from White's library, including the first edition of *The Rape of Lucrece* (1594).[26]

As he became more involved in business and in the process of collecting, Folger had less time for reading. In 1899 he wrote to the secretary of his Amherst class: "A business position with the Standard Oil Co. has called for my best efforts to meet added responsibilities; while for diversion, the gathering of a modest library—for the most part as yet unread—has helped to keep me interested in matters literary."[27] Unlike Furness or the Ohio collector Joseph Crosby the Folgers did not look on their collection

William Shakespeare. *The most lamentable*
Romaine tragedie of Titus Andronicus.
London, 1594.

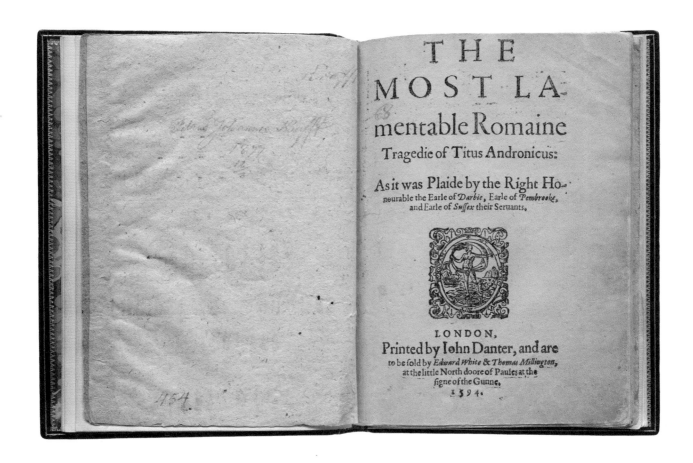

as a research tool for themselves, although Furness tried to push Folger in this direction by asking him to check references in his folios.[28] The middle-class backgrounds of Furness and Crosby were more like those of the Folgers— none of them had the wealth of a Huntington or a Morgan.[29] But Furness, Crosby, and the Philadelphian J. Parker Norris all enjoyed collecting Shakespeare books and Shakespeareana, which they arranged in libraries in their American homes that became comfortable shrines to the great British Bard.[30] Furness wanted the Folgers to do the same. In 1911, he wrote to them,

> *Would that this taste of putting your books to their befitting use would induce you to stop piling up any more hard food for Midas. Build yourself a fine library, wherein you and Emily may ensconce yourselves into a corner, like a couple of brave and industrious mice, and nibble at the contents of your treasures and let the rest of the world share your pleasures.[31]*

But the Folgers chose to live most of their married life in rented houses, and although they kept some of their Shakespearean treasures at home and filled the walls of 24 Breevort Place in Brooklyn with playbills and pictures of David Garrick, Kitty Clive, and other actors, for years they kept most of their collection in numerous crates, scattered among storage facilities.

By the early years of the twentieth century, however, the Folgers were quietly planning to do something important with their collection. Every five years, Folger reported to the secretary of his Amherst class. By 1909, he could write,

> *I have found the means for adding to my collection of Shakesperiana until it is probably the largest and finest in America and perhaps in the world. That is really saying a great deal, for collecting Shakesperiana has been*

the life-work of many students during the past 100 years, and the results of their labors have found permanent homes in the great public libraries of Europe and America. To rival these collections is a real achievement.[32]

In the meantime, Folger had to deny scholars' requests to consult items in his collection. A typical request came through Morgan's librarian, Belle da Costa Greene, asking if David Little, chairman of Harvard's English Department, could consult Folger's collection of Garrick material for a biography of the actor.[33] Folger replied, "I hope, at some time in the near future, to have a proper place for storing my collection, so that it will be accessible to all who wish to make use of it. At present it is all packed up in some 1,700 cases and put away in several warehouses."[34] Ms. Greene wrote back, "As you doubtless surmised, my purpose in writing was largely to have just such a statement from you, which I could quote. If you have no objection, I will retain and use this letter for the large quantity of similar requests which come to me!"[35]

As the Folgers considered locations for their library, New York City and even Stratford-upon-Avon were possibilities, but Washington they chose. In explanation, Mrs. Folger wrote: "That city is the common capital of the whole United States; it belongs to all the people. It is advantageously situated, it is beautiful, and it constantly is growing in cultural significance." Once during the First World War when the Folgers were on the way to their vacation spot, the Homestead in Hot Springs, Virginia, they found themselves "delayed by dislocated railroad schedules," and spent the time walking around Washington in the rain, looking for possible sites to build their library.[36] They finally chose the block of East Capitol Street adjacent to the Library of Congress. It took nine years to purchase the properties then standing on that block and to obtain permission to use the land for a private institution, since it had been earmarked for an addition to the Library of Congress. Finally in 1928 Congress passed a resolution allowing the Folgers full use of the plot for their own library.

Henry Folger worked closely on the building plan with Philadelphia beaux-art architect Paul Philippe Cret, consulting also with Alexander B. Trowbridge. Taking a clue from a long-ago passage from Emerson that he had copied— "Every book is a quotation; and every house is a quotation" —Folger designed his library building to be read, sprinkling it with citations from Dante, Hugo, Garrick, Goethe, and of course Emerson and Shakespeare. Soon after the cornerstone was laid in, Mr. Folger entered the hospital for a minor operation and unexpectedly died on 11 June 1930. About a week later the *New York Times* made public the contents of his will, and only then did the Trustees of Amherst College become aware that they were to administer the bulk of Folger's fortune as a trust for the new Folger Shakespeare Memorial Library. Because Folger's will had been drawn up in 1927 before the great stock market crash, his assets were somewhat depleted. Nevertheless, with careful planning by the Trustees and with the generosity of Emily Folger, who contributed some of her own funds, work on the library went forward. Emily Folger was totally committed to seeing the project through. She wrote, "We had been together so long and had been so much at one in our thought that I knew what he desired and was prepared to take up the task in his name."[37] Their relationship might be described like that between Portia and Bassanio in *The Merchant of Venice*, outlined long before by Folger in his college essay: "The poet has delicately admitted the reader into the secret of their mutual affection. We see depicted their adaptation for each other, and every noble trait in Bassanio or Portia reflected in the other."[38]

The library was dedicated on Shakespeare's birthday, 23 April 1932, with President Herbert Hoover heading the list of distinguished guests from around the world. For her own untiring efforts towards the completion of their joint dream, Emily Folger was awarded an honorary Doctor of Letters degree from Amherst College in 1932. She continued to remain active in organizing the administration and contents of the library until her death in 1936. In talking about the relationship between collectors and the objects they collect, Susan Pearce has written that "in a very real sense, we and our collections are one." This feeling is especially strong with the Folgers, who collected Shakespeare because they saw reflected in his works the moral and spiritual qualities in which they themselves believed.[39] But the oneness of collector and collection is *literally* true with them as well, for the ashes of both Folgers are buried together in the grand reading room within their living Shakespeare monument, and their portraits, painted by Frank Salisbury, hang beneath the memorial bust of Shakespeare himself.

After his death, Emily Folger wrote of her husband's "sense of responsibility to God and man. He did not feel that he had been sent into the world merely to live and prosper to himself alone."[40] The focus of his early reading and thinking, as we have seen, was on the development of moral character; through the guidance of Emerson, Carlyle, and others, he found in Shakespeare the cultural, ethical, and social values he sought, and which he thought fit well with American idealism. Placing his library one block from the Capitol made the statement that he felt, as Emily said, that "the poet [Shakespeare] is one of our best sources, one of the wells from which we Americans draw our national thought, our faith and our hope."[41]

1. Horace Howard Furness to Henry Clay Folger, Wallingford, Pennsylvania, 18 April 1911. On Furness, see James M. Gibson, *The Philadelphia Shakespeare Story: Horace Howard Furness and the New Variorum Shakespeare* (New York: AMS Press, 1990), passim.

2. Henry James, *The Portrait of a Lady*, ed. Leon Edel (Boston: Houghton Mifflin, 1963), 108. For this reference and a general discussion of Shakespeare in the works of Henry James, see Adeline R. Tintner, *The Book World of Henry James* (Ann Arbor: UMI Research Press, 1987), 45, and chapter 1 in general.

3. Henry James, *Portrait*, 354.

4. Horace Howard Furness to Emily Folger, Wallingford, Pennsylvania, 25 July 1894.

5. Furness to Emily Folger, Wallingford, Pennsylvania, 2 January 1897. In the same letter, Furness sends the Folgers Mary Cowden Clarke's address. He must have imagined them in the company of the Cowden Clarkes and of himself and his own wife as marital "teams" of Shakespeare scholars. Helen Kate Rogers Furness had published a *Concordance to Shakespeare's Poems* in 1874.

6. Emily Folger, "The Dream Come True," corrected typescript of paper presented at the Meridian Club, 1933, 5–6.

7. Ralph Waldo Emerson, "Shakespeare," *Miscellanies*, vol. 11 of *Complete Works*, ed. Edward Waldo Emerson (Cambridge: Riverside Press, 1904). Emerson originally delivered this address at the Saturday Club in 1864.

8. Thomas Carlyle, *On Heroes, Hero-Worship and The Heroic in History* (London: Chapman and Hall, n.d.), 104–5.

9. From Lowell's essay on "Thoreau" as copied on the flyleaf and title page of vol. 1 of Folger's copy of R[alph] W[aldo] Emerson, *Essays*, 2 vols. (Boston: Houghton, Osgood and Company, 1880).

10. From James Russell Lowell, *My Study Windows*, as quoted on front flyleaf of Folger's copy of Emerson's *Essays*, vol. 1.

11. These quotations are cited in the Diary dated April 1882, which Folger used for some time, as several of the sources he is quoting were published in the 1880s; pp. 23, 141, 139.

12. Diary for 1884, 2:11, 17.

13. Emily Folger, "Dream," 13–14.

14. Emily Folger, "Dream," 13.

15. A. S. W. Rosenbach, "Henry C. Folger as a Collector," *Henry C. Folger* (New Haven: privately printed, 1931), 105.

16. Henry Clay Folger, "From Ariel to Caliban," typescript, 1 Folger Collection, Box 30.

17. References to Folger's purchase of the Warwick Castle collection are from Rosenbach, "Collector," 78–79; "Notes on Sales: the Warwick Castle Shakespeares," *Times Literary Supplement* (25 October 1923): 712; "Book and Art Sales," *New York Times* (12 June 1897); and Papers of A.B. Railton, ABR/5/1, John Rylands University Library, University of Manchester, Collection Description. The Warwick Castle collection itself is described in the catalogue compiled by Thomas Simmons, *Warwick Castle Library Shakespearian Collection* (1889–90), Folger MS M.b.31.

18. "In a Sotheby's auction of July 1895, Folger purchased some Halliwell-Phillipps Shakespeareana (lots 666 and 667) for £1,200, through the agency of H. Sotheran [London bookseller]. The main bulk of the collections, listed as lots 668–73, were however withdrawn from sale. Folger offered £11,000 through his agent Sotheran, but was told that they were not for sale. In 1897 they were finally sold to Marsden J. Perry" (Papers of A.B. Railton, Collection Description).

19. Marsden J. Perry obituary, *The Providence Journal* (16 April 1935): 1, 9.

20. Edwin Wolf 2nd with John F. Fleming, *Rosenbach: A Biography* (Cleveland, New York: World Publishing, 1960), 117. See 114ff. for a discussion of Rosenbach's purchase and sale of the Perry Collection.

21. Folger paid $100,000 for this one book, causing it to be estimated as "the highest priced book in the world" (Wolf and Fleming, 121).

22. Folger's own account of this acquisition is quoted at length in Rosenbach, "Collector," 80–81.

23. Rosenbach, "Collector," 81, 82–84. Rosenbach quotes from Folger's own account of acquiring the quartos from Dr. Gott. Folger's original notes and a typescript are in Folger Collection, Box 30.

24. Rosenbach, "Collector," 85.

25. Louis B. Wright, "Huntington and Folger: Book Collectors with a Purpose," *Atlantic Monthly* 209 (April 1962): 72.

26. Rosenbach, "Collector," 86.

27. Quoted in George F. Wicher, "Henry Clay Folger and the Shakespeare Library," rpt. from the *Amherst Graduates' Quarterly* (November 1930): 11.

28. Furness to H. C. Folger, Wallingford, Pennsylvania, 21 November 1911. "As one of my boys, I feel responsible for your intellectual life, which I greatly fear will 'rot itself at ease on Lethe's wharf;' so, I am going to give you some work that will put to some use all of your fourteen thousand First Folios. . . . I shall try you first with these from 'Cymbeline.'"

29. On the building of Morgan's library see Jean Strouse, *Morgan: American Financier* (New York: Random House, 1999), 487ff.

30. See *One Touch of Shakespeare: Letters of Joseph Crosby to Joseph Parker Norris, 1875–1878*, ed. John W. Velz and Frances N. Teague (Washington: Folger Shakespeare Library, 1986); and John W. Velz, "Joseph Crosby and the Shakespeare Scholarship of the Nineteenth Century," *Shakespeare Quarterly* 27 (1976): 316–28.

31. Furness to H. C. Folger, 28 November 1911.

32. *History of the Class of 1879 in Amherst College: From 1904 to 1909,* comp. [J. Franklin Jameson] Secretary of the Class (Brunswick, ME: Record Press [1909]).

33. Belle da Costa Greene to H. C. Folger, New York, 9 November 1927.

34. Folger to Greene, [n.p.], 14 November 1927.

35. Greene to Folger, New York, 21 November 1927.

36. Emily Folger, "Dream," 17.

37. Emily Folger, "Dream," 21. In the original version she added, "I think no prouder privilege ever was granted to any woman," but she revised this to read, "It was a twice blessed privilege." Emphasizing her position as a woman would have made sense when delivering the talk to the women's Meridian Club.

38. H. C. Folger, "Portia," autograph, Folger Collection, Box 29.

39. Susan Pearce, *Museums, Objects and Collections* (Washington, DC: Smithsonian Institution Press, 1993), 55. Appropriately, Pearce points out that this concept of oneness came from William James in 1890.

40. Emily Folger, "Dream," 47.

41. Emily Folger, "Dream," 14.

14. DETAIL

Catalogue of the Exhibition

Henry Clay Folger and Emily Jordan Folger situated their library in the United States capital because they believed Shakespeare was essential to American culture. This exhibition, Shakespeare in American Life, *proves their prescience. The items displayed here reveal a myriad ways in which, from the era of colonization to the present day, Americans have made Shakespeare their own. Whether in political rhetoric and satire, stage performance, musical comedy, film, poetry, parody, or shtick, Shakespeare has deeply enriched the American scene. Displayed in the exhibition are samples from the Folger Shakespeare Library's multifaceted collection: books, of course, but also playbills, play programs, engravings, portraits, and scrapbooks, as well as material artifacts from everyday life (quilts, puzzles, comic books, and advertisements)—all signaling how widely Shakespeare is enmeshed in our national consciousness.*

Shakespeare's final solo play, The Tempest, *drew inspiration from the wreck of the* Sea Venture *on Bermuda and the survival of everyone aboard. That dramatic episode was described most extensively and vividly by one of the passengers, William Strachey, after his arrival at Jamestown in 1610. By then, a few English immigrants may have brought a Shakespeare play or poem to the New World, but not for another century would Shakespeare become a literary staple in English America, and not until the 1760s were his plays regularly staged. Thereafter, he was the colonies' favorite dramatist.*

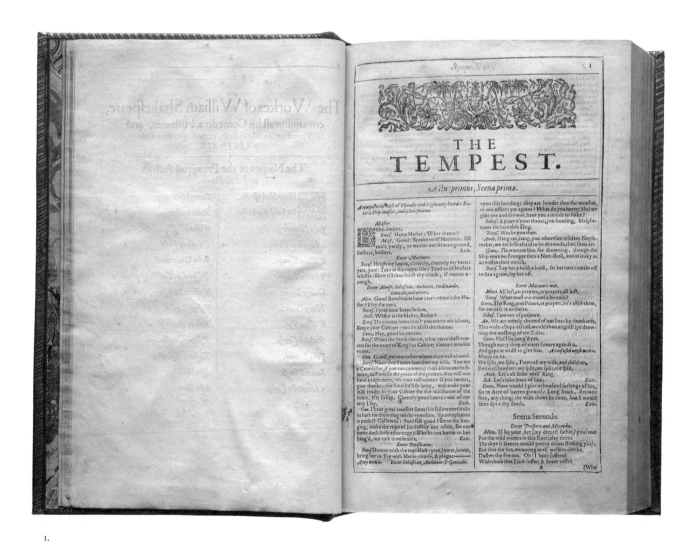

1.

1

William Shakespeare (1564–1616)

Mr. William Shakespeares comedies, histories, & tragedies,
published according to the true originall copies

London: Isaac Iaggard, and Ed. Blount, 1623

Folger STC 22273 Fo. 1 no. 41

Sig. A1r

The Tempest's earliest known printed version is the opening
play in Shakespeare's collected works, the First Folio of
1623. *Actus primus, scena prima* poignantly portrays a
storm-tossed ship "Mercy on us!—We split, we split!" with
frequent echoes of William Strachey's letter (see cat. no. 3),
as do several passages in scene 2.

——————

2

Pewter Candlestick

English, ca. 1609

Graciously lent by the Bermuda Maritime Museum

William Strachey recalled that at the height of the tempest
that blew the *Sea Venture* to Bermuda, the crew, "with
candels in their hands," searched for leaks inside the ship's
hull. This candlestick is among the very few surviving
artifacts from the wrecked ship.

——————

3

William Strachey (1572–1621)

"A true reportory of the wracke, and redemption of
Sir *Thomas Gates* Knight; upon . . . the Ilands of the
Bermudas," in Samuel Purchas (1577–1626), *Purchas his
pilgrims,* vol. 4

London: William Stansby for Henrie Fetherstone, 1625

Folger STC 20509 c.1 vol. 4

P. 1734

2.

William Strachey addressed his lengthy letter of July 1610
to an "Excellent Lady" (probably Dame Sarah Smith, wife
of Sir Thomas Smith of the Virginia Company) to inform
her—and the many friends with whom she would surely
share the exciting tale— of recent events on Bermuda and
in Virginia. Strachey described not only the storm, the
shipwreck, and the island's wonders, but also murders, conspiracies, rebellions, and harsh retributions. Such candor
delayed publication of the letter until 1625, following the
demise of the Virginia Company.

3.

Captain John Smith, president of the Virginia Colony in 1608–9 and its principal historian from 1608 until his death in 1631, included revealing maps and illustrations in his book. The map of early Virginia locates the important Indian communities as well as the major geographic features. Some literary critics have argued that in creating *The Tempest*'s "savage and deformed slave" Caliban, as he is described in the list of characters, Shakespeare drew on such ambivalent pictures and derogatory descriptions of American natives.

4

Map of Virginia

Engraved by William Hole

In Captain John Smith, *The generall historie of Virginia, New-England, and the Summer Isles*

London: J. D[awson] and J. H[aviland] for Michael Sparks, 1631

Folger STC 22790 c.2

Following sig. Y4

5

Hugh Gaine, printer

"This day is published . . . the following plays, . . . The Tempest . . . King Lear"

Advertisement in *New-York Mercury*

27 July 1761

Facsimile courtesy of the American Antiquarian Society, Worcester, Massachusetts

The first known printing of Shakespeare's plays in America is announced by Hugh Gaine in the weekly *New-York Mercury*. Gaine, who printed this newspaper as well as books, ran this advertisement for plays he had produced, including *The Tempest* and *King Lear*, on 20 and 27 July 1761. See p. 15.

6

Deryck Foster

Sea Venture and Consorts at Sea, 1609

Painting, 1994

Reproduction courtesy of the Bank of Bermuda Foundation and the Bermuda Maritime Museum

The English fleet shown in this painting was under the command of Sir George Somers and was carrying settlers and supplies to Virginia when it was struck by a hurricane

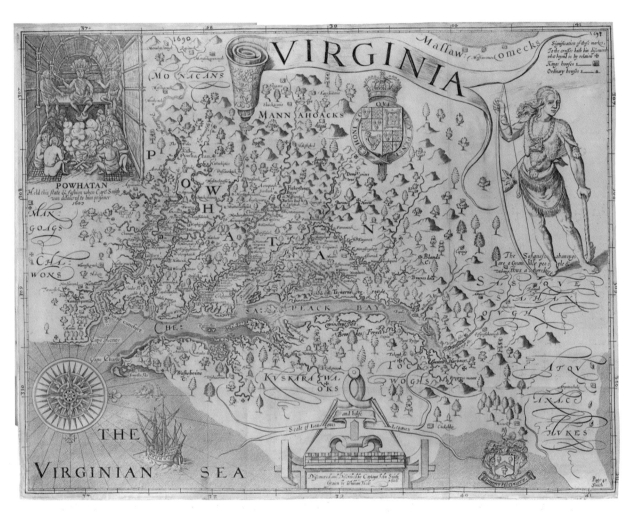

4.

in July 1609. Seven of the nine vessels would eventually reach Jamestown; one sank, while the *Sea Venture* grounded on the Bermuda reefs. See p. 10.

In this painting, the *Sea Venture* is separated from the rest of the fleet and caught in the tempest that drove it onto the coast of Bermuda.

7

W. H. Harrington

Wreck of Sea Venture

Painting, 1981

Reproduction courtesy of the Bermuda National Trust and the Bermuda Maritime Museum

During the colonial period and well into the early republic, impoverished British actors traveled to America hoping to strike it rich. Playbills advertised the arrival of such English celebrities as George Frederick Cooke, Edmund Kean, and William Charles Macready. Eventually, Americans challenged the English hegemony. Edwin Forrest, the most formidable American actor of the early nineteenth century, saw Macready as his rival and often performed the British actor's favorite roles, sometimes on the same night but at a different theater with a less elite audience. The dueling Macbeths, as it were, reached a crescendo on 10 May 1849, when a mob of Forrest enthusiasts rioted outside the Astor-Place Theatre in New York where Macready was performing. By one account, twenty-two people died in the melee.

☛ BROADWAY THEATRE

E. A Marshall...Sole Lessee

Also of the Walnut Street Theatre, Philadelphia.

Thomas Barry...Stage Manager

Unprecedented Success ! 36th Night

MR. FORREST

THE AMERICAN TRAGEDIAN,

Positively for the last time, prior to his departure for the South, in his great Shakspearian character of

MACBETH!

Being the 36th Night of his Engagement.

Notice---The Manager respectfully announces that the **Intense Anxiety** to witness the performance of this **Great Artist,** exceeding all **former precedent,** the **Box Book** has been opened **Three Days in Advance,** and the patrons of the Drama are requested to secure their Tickets at an early hour in the day, as **Many Hundred Persons** have frequently been unable to obtain admission shortly after the opening of the doors at night.

11. DETAIL

8

The Theatre, Baltimore, Maryland

Playbill, *Catherine and Petruchio* (*Taming of the Shrew*)

5 September 1786

Folger Bill Box U7 m2 B21bt 1786–87

Although pre-1800 playbills are extremely rare, other evidence reveals that Shakespeare was frequently presented on American stages during the late eighteenth century. This playbill announces performances of the Old American Company in Baltimore. Built by English actor Thomas Llewelyn Lechmore Wall, Baltimore's Theatre was a substantial brick building that marked the importance of theatrical entertainment in the city's cultural life.

———————

9

The John Street Theatre, New York

Playbill, *Much Ado About Nothing*

19 March 1787

Folger Bill Box U4 J66 1787

Much Ado About Nothing is advertised on this playbill as a play which had never before been performed in America. *Catherine and Petruchio* (*Taming of the Shrew*), *Hamlet*, *Romeo and Juliet*, and *Richard III* were regularly offered in eighteenth-century American theaters, but as this playbill attests, acting companies sometimes expanded the standard repertoire.

———————

10

Alexandria, Virginia

Playbill, *Macbeth*

12 July 1799

Folger Bill Box U7 v2 A51t 1799 no. 1

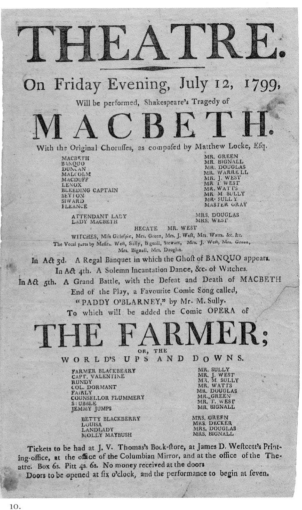

10.

Although the playbill doesn't mention the exact location of the performance, it announces *Macbeth*, performed "with the original choruses as composed by Matthew Lock," in a theater in Alexandria, Virginia. The bookseller, J. V. Thomas, and the printer, James D. Westcott, both named on the bill, worked in Alexandria during the late eighteenth century. The *Columbian Mirror*, where tickets could be bought, was also located in Alexandria. It is conceivable that George Washington, an avid playgoer who lived nearby at Mount Vernon, attended this performance.

11

Broadway Theatre, New York

Playbill, *Macbeth*

23 March 1852

Folger Bill Box U4 B78 1851–52, no. 7

Identifying Edwin Forrest as the "American Tragedian,"
this playbill announces his "unprecedented success" and his
36th night, when he will perform "positively for the last
time, prior to his departure for the South, in his great
Shakespearian character of Macbeth!"

———

12

"Riot at the Astor-Place Opera House"

Engraving, New York, 1849

Folger Art File N567.7 no. 2

A playbill in the foreground of the engraving announces
William Charles Macready's performance as Macbeth that
evening (10 May 1849) at the Astor-Place Theatre. Outside
the theater, Edwin Forrest's supporters riot. See p. 25.

———

13

H. Tracey

"Mr. Macready as Macbeth"

Engraved by Sherratt from the original painting by
Tracey in the possession of the publishers

London, New York: John Tallis & Company, undated

Folger Art File M174.4 no. 20, c.1

William Charles Macready's Macbeth wears the costume
of a Scottish laird, complete with shield, tartan, and tam-
o'-shanter.

11.

14.

14

A. Robin

"Edwin Forrest as Macbeth"

Engraving, undated

Folger Art File F728 no. 18

Edwin Forrest appears to have copied his rival's costume for Macbeth, including a similar round shield, dagger, and feathered tam-o'-shanter.

15

Peter E. Abel

Theatrical Scrapbook, *Forrestiana*

"Collected by (up to this date) Peter E. Abel"

Philadelphia, 10 August 1875

Folger Scrapbook B.24.2

P. [71]

The compiler of this scrapbook followed the Forrest-Macready rivalry closely, collecting numerous clippings about the actors and the exploits of their numerous supporters. Included are clippings about the Astor Place Riot.

16

Promptbook, *Macbeth*

New York: Berford and Co., 1847

Property of Joseph J. Salmon, Boston

Marked by Wm. McFarland, 15 May 1852

Folger Prompt Mac. 56

P. 37

William McFarland, a supporting actor in many of Edwin Forrest's productions, marked this promptbook of *Macbeth* with stage business for Banquo, the role he probably performed against Forrest's Macbeth. Stage business for Banquo's ghost (3.4.22–60) appears on the left, while Shakespeare's text is on the right.

17

"James H. Hackett as Falstaff, *Henry Fourth,* Act IV,
scene II"

Gravure, Gebbie & Co., undated

Folger Art File H121 no. 8

James Henry Hackett (1800–71), the first great American
comedian, was celebrated for his impersonation of
Shakespeare's Falstaff, both in the United States and in
England, where he frequently toured.

18

Washington Theater, Washington, DC

Playbill, *Hamlet*

16 February 1861

Folger Bill Box U7 d2 W27wt 1860–61

Charlotte Cushman (1816–76) was the first internationally
recognized American actress. This playbill proudly
announces her appearance "in compliance with the request
of many distinguished senators, representatives and citizens" in three of her best-known roles at the Washington
Theater. In particular, she is to perform the role of Hamlet
on 16 February.

19

Thomas Sully (1783–1872)

Portrait of Charlotte Cushman

Oil on canvas, 1843

Folger FP b47

Gift of Mrs. Victor N. Cushman

18.

After attaining public acclaim in Philadelphia, New York, and Boston, Charlotte Cushman (1816–76) traveled to England where she was embraced by London audiences as a great Shakespearean actress. In addition to Shakespeare's most prominent female roles, she often portrayed Romeo and Hamlet. She commissioned this portrait from Thomas Sully in Philadelphia in 1843. See p. 22.

20
Booth's Theatre, New York
Playbill, Edwin Booth as Hamlet
February 1870
Folger Bill Box U4 B62 1869–70 no. 3

Edwin Booth, the most talented American actor of the nineteenth century, opened his own theater in New York lin 1869. This playbill uses his portrait—a mark of his celebrity—to advertise a production of *Hamlet*, in which he played the title role.

21
Winter Garden, New York
Playbill, *Julius Caesar*
25 November 1864
Folger Bill Box U4 W78 1864–65 (2a)

Three brothers, Junius Brutus Booth, Jr., Edwin Booth, and John Wilkes Booth, joined in a production of *Julius Caesar* to raise money for a statue of Shakespeare in New York's Central Park. In hindsight, John Wilkes Booth's rendition of Marc Antony, the Roman who decries Julius Caesar's assassination, seems sadly ironic. On 14 April 1865, John Wilkes Booth shot and killed President Abraham Lincoln. See p. 26.

The Folger Library's vast holdings in theatrical memorabilia illustrate how Americans have memorialized their experience of Shakespeare onstage—by collecting press clippings, photographs, play programs, and other ephemera. The wealthy theatrical entrepreneur Augustin Daly kept numerous scrapbooks, including one for each of the Shakespeare plays he produced; in addition to a program and reviews of performances, he included engravings of scenes and characters and critical writings about each play. A modest scrapbook compiled by a thirteen-year-old girl stands in vivid contrast to Daly's collections. She seems to have been a fan of Daly and of the actress Ada Rehan, for most of her material is concerned with Daly's company and his productions of the 1890s. Two twentieth-century programs provide a pictorial record of their owners' evenings at the theater and are souvenirs that can be considered works of art in their own right.

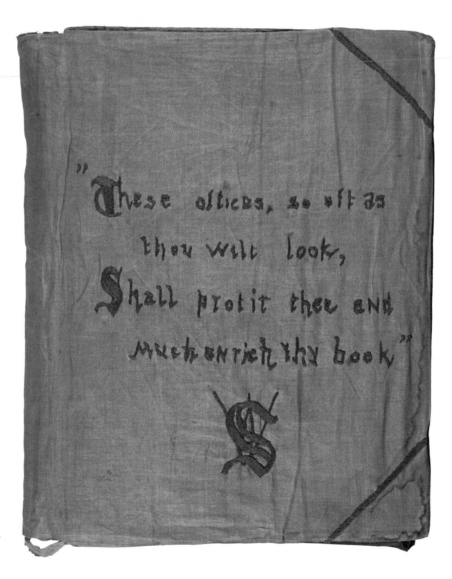

23.

22

William Shakespeare (1564–1616)

Love's Labor's Lost . . . arranged . . . in 4 Acts for the
present stage by Augustin Daly. Produced at Daly's
Theatre, March 28, 1891, and here printed from
the prompter's copy

New York: Privately printed, 1891

Folger Art Vol. b25

Folios 10v–11r

Theatrical impresario Augustin Daly compiled scrapbooks
for each of his major Shakespeare productions. This
one for *Love's Labor's Lost* contains a letter to Daly from
the actress Louisa Drew. Writing from Philadelphia on 17
February 1874, she says that *Love's Labor's Lost* was never
acted in America until it was produced at the Walnut Street
Theatre. Next to her letter is a clipping from a Philadelphia
newspaper that reproduces an 1827 advertisement for
Junius Brutus Booth's production of *Richard III.* In that
production, the nine-year-old Louisa Lane (later Louisa
Drew) played the Duke of York.

23

Emma Patten Beard

Theatrical Scrapbook

New York, ca. 1890s

Folger Scrapbook B.133.1

Gift of Patten Beard

Cover and p. 1

Not only did the thirteen-year-old Emma Patten Beard
reuse newspaper articles, playbills, and magazine illustrations in her theatrical scrapbook, she carefully covered
it with leftover fabric, embroidering a quote from one of
Shakespeare's sonnets on the front. This patchwork
details a young girl's fascination with the stage and the

Shakespearean revivals of the 1890s—in particular, the
final years of Augustin Daly's company and the intriguing
actress Ada Rehan.

On the first page of her scrapbook, Beard uses satin
ribbon, scraps from the *New York Tribune,* and paint to
depict two hearts "linked by a never-broken chain." In
one heart she places her initials; in the other those of
Rehan. Beard and other children like her documented
Shakespeare's continued ability to enliven the imagination
and touch the heart, while making their own artworks in
the process.

ALFRED LUNT *and* LYNN FONTANNE

24.

24

The Theatre Guild, New York

Program, *The Taming of the Shrew*

1925

Folger Program Collection

Alfred Lunt and Lynn Fontanne met in 1924, married, and spent most of their careers as an acting team. Lunt and Fontanne designed much of this production of *The Taming of the Shrew*, counting on their star appeal to draw audiences to Shakespeare's most rollicking comedy. They may also have served as the inspiration for the characters Fred Graham and Lilli Vanessi in Cole Porter's musical comedy *Kiss Me, Kate*, based on *Shrew*.

25

The Broadway Theatre, New York

Program, *Troilus and Cressida*

1932

Folger Program Collection

This program cover from 1932 for The Players production of *Troilus and Cressida* represents Cressida as a seductress who lures the battle-ready Troilus away from the fighting to her bed. The classical figures are recast here in the art deco style popular in 1932, the year that the Folger Shakespeare Library opened in Washington, DC.

Nineteenth-century American travesties and minstrel shows are important markers of Shakespeare's role in popular culture; parody works best when the audience recognizes discrepancies between the original and the lampoon. The Shakespeare plays most often parodied were standards of nineteenth-century touring companies—Macbeth, Othello, Hamlet, The Merchant of Venice, and Julius Caesar.

Edwin P. Christy, founder of Christy's Minstrels, who flourished from 1842 until the late 1880s, established the format of the minstrel show. A group of performers (usually white men in black makeup) was introduced by a white interlocutor. The show that followed was in sections, three of which were the "olio," a series of variety stunts. These sequences alternated with "fantasia," which allowed for individual comic routines and burlesques. Aimed principally at white urban audiences, minstrel shows were blatantly racist, reinforcing white stereotypes about black people as ignorant, indolent, and shiftless. Yet as uneducated as they might seem, Mr. Tambo and Mr. Bones were smart tricksters who lampooned white pretensions. The travesties and minstrel shows collected here reveal nineteenth-century America's ambivalence about elite culture and a growing tendency to identify Shakespeare with polite society.

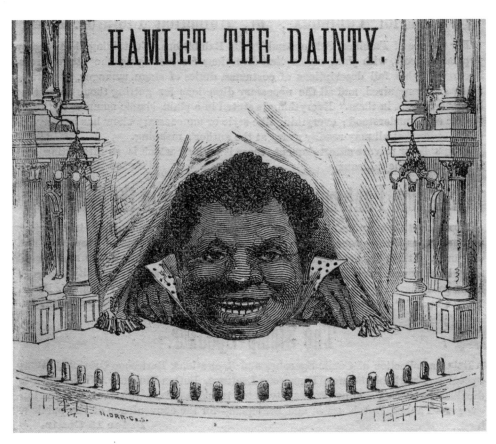

29. DETAIL

26.

29.

26

Desdemonum: An Ethiopian Burlesque
New York: Happy Hours, 1874
Folger PR2829 A72 D4
Title page

This brief musical travesty of *Othello* features a tambourine-playing Moor and a banjo-strumming Roderigo, plus several dances and jigs.

27

"Othello": A Burlesque
As performed by Griffin and Christy's Minstrels
Clyde, Ohio: A. D. Ames, ca. 1870
Folger PR2829 A72 O7
P. 3

The Christy's Minstrels' musical talents are spotlighted in this *Othello* burlesque. Several speeches are set to popular tunes, including Iago's "air" that begins the play:

When first I Desdemona saw, I thought her very fine,
And by the way she treated me, I thought she'd soon
be mine.

———————

28
Dar's De Money
New York: Samuel French, ca. 1880
Folger PR2829 A72 D2
Pp. 22–23

In *Dar's De Money*, dialogue between two blackface characters, Jake and Pete, uses bits and pieces of recognizable
Shakespeare quotations. Broke and down on his luck, Jake
decides to earn money by acting: "I play de lovers—and
de fervency of my emotions covers all my defishingcies."
See p. 38.

———————

29
Hamlet the Dainty, an Ethiopian Burlesque
Performed by George Griffin and Christy's Minstrels
New York: Happy Hours, 1870
Folger PR2807 A72 G8
Title page

The appearance of the ghost of Hamlet's father terrifies the
blackface characters—Horatio, Marcellus, and Hamlet—in
this burlesque of Shakespeare's play.

———————

30
W. K. Northall
Macbeth Travestie
New York: William Taylor, 1852
Folger PR2823 A72 N7 1852
Pp. 34–35

Macbeth Travestie relies upon the audience's familiarity
with the play's original language. Macbeth's most famous
speech, "Tomorrow and tomorrow and tomorrow"
(5.5.21–31) is transformed into a reflection on whiskey
punches and overdue bills:

To-morrow—and to-morrow—and to-morrow—
Aye, that's well thought of—I've a note to pay,
And the last recorded dollar to me lent,
Was yesterday in whiskey-punches spent!

———————

31
George Edward Rice
An Old Play in a New Garb
Boston: Ticknor, Reed, and Fields, 1853
Folger PR2807 A72 R5 1853A
Pp. 10–11

Here, Hamlet's opening soliloquy, "O that this too, too solid
flesh would melt" (1.2.133–64) becomes a song:

Oh, would this flesh would melt
And resolve itself to dew,
That I as once I felt
Could feel, and not so blue!

———————

32
The (Old Clothes) Merchant of Venice: or, The Young Judge
and Old Jewry. A burlesque sketch for the drawing room
New York: DeWitt, ca. 1870
Folger PR2825 A72 O6
Pp. 4–5

Burlesques like this spoof of *The Merchant of Venice* were
popular home entertainments and diversions for literary
societies.

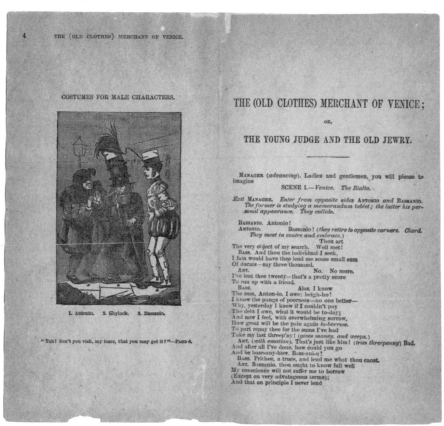

32.

33
R. W. Criswell
The New Shakspeare and Other Travesties
New York: American News Company, 1882
Folger PR2878 C85
P. 9

By the late nineteenth century, American school children were often required to memorize passages from Shakespeare's plays. Antony's funeral oration from *Julius Caesar* was a popular choice. This parody of that famous speech no doubt delighted those who had been forced to learn it by rote.

Friends, Romans, countrymen! Lend me your ears;
I will return them next Saturday. I come
To bury Caesar, because the times are hard
And his folks can't afford to hire an undertaker.
The evil that men do lives after them,
In the shape of progeny, who reap the
Benefit of their life insurance.
So let it be with the deceased.

Shakespeare has long been a touchstone in American political rhetoric. Many early leaders read him avidly, recommended him to friends, and quoted him in their speeches. Later politicians found themselves praised or mocked in Shakespearean metaphors and caricatured as Hamlets, Macbeths, or King Lears. The examples chosen for the exhibition represent two centuries of Shakespeare's connection to American political culture.

TO BEE OR NOT TO BEE ; THAT, MY FRIENDS, IS THE QUESTION!

36.

34
"A Proslavery Incantation Scene, or Shakespeare Improved"
Lithograph, ca. 1856
Folger Art File S528ml no. 86

This antislavery cartoon of circa 1856 depicts a cluster of proslavery sympathizers mixing a witches' brew to thwart the Free-Soil advocates. Beginning with Stephen Douglas on the left, each man parodies lines from *Macbeth* that apply to such contemporary events as South Carolina Representative Preston Brooks's assault with a cane on Massachusetts Senator Charles Sumner.

———————

35
"Franklin Delano Roosevelt Ponders a Purge of His Cabinet"
Washington, DC, *Evening Star*, 23 November 1938
Folger Scrapbook E.5.1

As part of his implementation of the New Deal, Franklin Delano Roosevelt tried unsuccessfully to prevent the re-election of several recalcitrant senators and then pondered (with Hamlet-like uncertainty, the cartoonist suggests) a purge of his cabinet. He also attempted to "pack" the Supreme Court.

———————

36
Clifford Kennedy Berryman (1869–1949)
"FDR [as Hamlet] Considers a Third Term"
Pen and ink, ca. 1940
Folger Art Box B534 no. 5

Roosevelt knew he would face strong resistance to an unprecedented third term. A ground swell of support and criticism eventually forced his hand, but not until political cartoonists lampooned his indecision.

37
William Shakespeare (1564–1616)
Lines from *Julius Caesar* in the autograph of John Adams
(1735–1826)
Undated
Folger MS Y.d.246

When and why John Adams copied these lines from Act 2, scene 1, of *Julius Caesar* is not known, but the lines illustrate the second president's reliance on the author he called "great Shakespeare." Adams' diaries and correspondence are replete with such allusions and quotations.

———————

38
John Quincy Adams (1767–1848)
Autograph letter, signed, to John B. Davis
5 January 1830
Folger MS Y.c.10 (2)

The sixth president was, like his father, an avid reader of Shakespeare and almost certainly at an earlier age. His mother, Abigail Adams, kept the complete works on her nursery table; by age ten, John Quincy Adams (as he later recalled) was thoroughly familiar with Shakespeare's plays. In this letter of 1830 to John B. Davis of Boston, Adams quotes from *Two Gentlemen of Verona* (5.4.79–80).

———————

39
From *Frank Leslie's Budget of Fun*
"John Bull in his favorite character of Iago"
New York, April 1863
Facsimile courtesy of the American Antiquarian Society, Worcester, Massachusetts
Civil War Cartoon Collection, Box 1: Folder 2: Humors of War: 1863, no. 44

Ambition.

Brutus in J. Caesar of Shakespeare.

    'Tis a common Proof
that Lowliness is young Ambitions Ladder
Whereto the Climber upwards turns his face;
But when he once attains the Upmost round,
He then unto the Ladder turns his back,
Looks in the Clouds, Scorning the base degrees
By which he did ascend. So Caesar may.

    I have no autograph signature to spare, but the above
is in the handwriting of John Adams.

37.

As John Bull (England), playing *Othello*'s Iago, watches the fight between Cassio and Roderigo (the American North and South), he muses: "Now, whether HE kill Cassio, or Cassio kill HIM, or each do kill the other, every way makes my gain."

———————

40

"Abraham Lincoln . . . Shakespeare Applied to Our National Bereavement"
Broadside
Boston, 9Massachusetts: B. D. Russell, 1865
Folger Sh.Misc. 390

Three quotations from *Macbeth* pay tribute to the slain president, while the third passage also calls for an investigation into "this most bloudy piece of woe." Legend has it that Lincoln had reread *Macbeth*, his favorite Shakespeare text, shortly before the assassination.

———————

41

Barbara Garson
MacBird
Berkeley, California: Grassy Knoll, 1966
Folger Sh.Misc. 1822

Lyndon Johnson takes a verbal beating in this parody of presidential politics, 1960–67. His principal tormentors are the three Kennedy brothers, the Egg of Head (Adlai Stevenson), and the Earl of Warren. *MacBird* enjoyed a measure of popularity before the assassination of Robert F. Kennedy rendered it inappropriate.

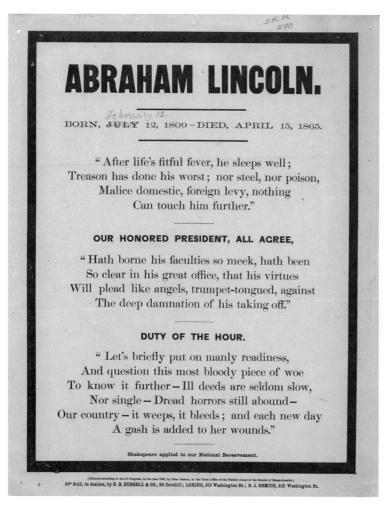

40.

42

Robert John Myers

The Tragedie of King Richard, the Second; the Life and Times of Richard II (1367–1400), King of England (1377–1399) Compared to Those of Richard of America in His Second Administration

Washington, DC: Acropolis Books, 1973

Folger Sh.Misc. 1866

The cast of this parody "On the moral similarities between the reign of Richard II in England . . . and that of Richard II in America (1968–)" includes Queen Pat; Princess Tricia; Lords Haldeman, Ehrlichman, and Kissinger; Duke Agnew; Sir John Dean; and the Bishop of Graham.

As settlers pushed the boundaries of the United States westward, they took editions of Shakespeare with them; even the illiterate mountain man, Jim Bridger, carried Shakespeare's plays into the Rockies and paid people to read them to him. Eminent actors such as Edwin Forrest, Charlotte Cushman, and Edwin Booth attained fame and fortune by taking Shakespeare's plays on tour throughout the country. Booth went as far as the mines of California. When a full-scale theatrical production was impractical, audiences satisfied their appetite for Shakespeare by attending a reading of his work by a professional actor or by hearing a public lecture. By the end of the nineteenth century, prominent American actors also toured England. Then, as now, Shakespeare kept on the move.

54.

HAMLET'S SOLILOQUY.

44.

43

Frances Anne Kemble (1809–1893)
Three tickets to Fanny Kemble's readings from
Shakespeare, signed by her, with an engraving of Thomas
Sully's portrait of her, 1832
Folger MS Y.d.443 (1–3)

Fanny Kemble, the daughter of English actor-manager
Charles Kemble, captured the hearts of American audiences
when she toured the eastern United States in 1832. After
her disastrous marriage to the southern slaveholder Pierce
Butler ended in divorce, she made her living by reading

from Shakespeare's plays in Boston and other American
cities. Displayed here are several "guest tickets" she wrote
on the back of her calling card, offering free admission to
her friends and admirers.

44
Mark Twain (1835–1910)
Adventures of Huckleberry Finn
New York: C. L. Webster and Company, 1885
P. 178
Graciously lent by the American Antiquarian Society and
reproduced with the permission of the Society

In this famous passage from *Huckleberry Finn,* Twain
parodies the actors who toured America. Huck listens to
the "Duke" recite fractured lines from *Hamlet.*

45
William Hussey Macy
Letter to his cousin, Susan Burdick, "on board ship
Alpha, at sea, Oct. 8, 1848 . . . 27 months out," on the
South Seas, with a handwritten playbill, Act 5 of *Othello*
Graciously lent by the collection of the Nantucket Historical
Association and reproduced with the Association's permission

This letter from William Macy, on board the whaling ship
Alpha, to his cousin back in Nantucket, describes the
sailors' theatrical activities, including a performance of the
last scenes of *Othello.* The handwritten playbill shows
how the sailors, far from home and "twenty-seven months
out," used amateur theatricals to while away the time.

ALPHEAN MARINE

THEATRE.

Saturday EVENING, October 15"

Wind, Weather, and Whales permitting, will be presented

The last scene from the tragedy of

OTHELLO, THE MOOR OF VENICE!

Othello. Mr Stewart		Gratiano,	Mr Wood
Desdemona, wife of Othello	Mr Macy	Ludorico,	Mr Squier
Iago. an officer under Othello,	Mr Blackstock	Cassio	Mr Baker
Emilia, wife of Iago,	Mr Bailey	Francisco	Mr Peters

Song "Wery Ridiculous" by Mr Macy

Recitation "The Mariner's Dream" by Mr Stewart

After which the farce of

THE BOSOM FRIENDS,

OR

Unrequited Affection!

Nicholas Nickleby	Mr Squier	Matilda Price,	Mr Bailey
John Browdie	Mr Stewart	Fanny Squeers	Mr Macy

Dramatised for the occasion.

Original Song for the occasion by Mr Stewart

First appearance of Messrs Peters, & Blackstock!

New stars, in the firmament !!

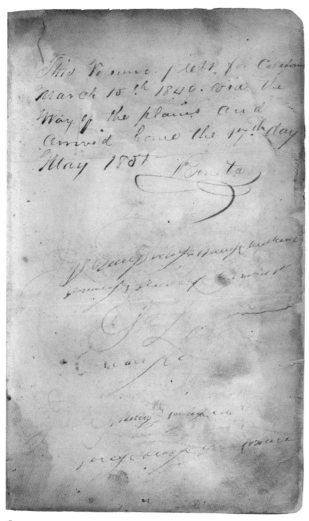

48.

This scrapbook tracks the touring career of Thomas Wallace Keene (1840–98), an actor best known for his robust style, particularly as Richard III, Hamlet, Othello, and Romeo. Keene spent 1875–80 with the California Theater Stock Company in San Francisco, often supporting Edwin Booth, and from 1880 to his death in 1898, Keene toured the United States and Canada. The wide extent of his travels is apparent from this collection of clippings.

47

Jefferson Winter (b. 1878)

Scrapbook

Stratford-upon-Avon, 26 August 1890

Folger Scrapbook B.54.1

Jefferson Winter, son of famed drama critic William Winter, toured with Augustin Daly's company to Stratford-upon-Avon in 1890. He kept a postcard showing the Avon River and Trinity Church as a souvenir of his visit, adding a handwritten note indicating the location of the stage and the spot where "we dressed in the bushes."

48

William Shakespeare (1564–1616)

The Dramatic Works

Hartford: Andrus & Judd, 1834

Folger PR2754 2a1 c.2 Sh.Col.

Endleaf

46

Theatrical scrapbook of clippings about the actor

Thomas Keene

1880s

Folger Scrapbook 260162

P. 27

By the 1830s Shakespeare's texts could be found in many American households, and when settlers moved west, they took along Shakespeare and the family Bible. A handwritten inscription in this edition of Shakespeare's *Dramatic Works* states that "This Volume left for California March 15, 1849 via the Way of the plains and arrived here the 17th day May 1851. Boneta."

CHARLESTON THEATRE.

This Evening, Friday, December 20,

WILL BE PRESENTED

(By Particular Desire,) Shakspeare's Celebrated *TRAGEDY* of

HAMLET;

PRINCE OF DENMARK.

TO WHICH WILL BE ADDED,

The Musical Entertainment, of

The PRIZE;

Ten Thousand Pounds!!

OR,

2, 5, 3, 8.

DOORS to be opened at half paft five, and the curtain to rife at half paft fix o'Clock, precifely.

BOX and PIT, 4s. 8d.—GALLERY, 2s. 4d.

TICKETS and places for the BOXES to be had at Mr. G. G. Bailey's, Meeting-Street; where Subscribers for the Season, are requested to send for their Tickets, *before Dusk.*

☞ *The Proprietors are requested to send for their Tickets, to Mr. W. P. Young's,* before Dusk.

People of Colour cannot be admitted to any part of the Houfe.

Smoaking in the Theatre, Prohibited.

PRINTED BY W. P. YOUNG, No. 41, BROAD-STREET.

50.

49

California Theatre, San Francisco

Playbill, *Coriolanus*

4 April 1873

Folger Bill Box U7c1 S19 ct

The California Theatre of San Francisco attracted many famous actors from the East, including Edwin Booth.

———

50

Charleston, South Carolina

Playbill, *Hamlet*

20 December 1805

Folger Bill Box U7s1 C38 ct

This early playbill declares that "People of Colour cannot be admitted to any part of the House," suggesting that some of Charleston's African Americans would have attended the theater if they had been permitted to do so.

———

51

Providence Opera House, Providence, Rhode Island

Playbill, *Hamlet*

20 November 1872

Folger Bill Box U7r P94 po 1872–82, no. 3

This playbill advertises the appearance of Edwin Booth for five nights only and, in particular, on 22 November as Hamlet.

———

52

St. Charles Theatre, New Orleans

Playbill, *The Merchant of Venice*

25 March 1864

Folger Bill Box U71 N47 sc

A double-header program, featuring John Wilkes Booth as Shylock in *The Merchant of Venice* and Petruchio in *The Taming of the Shrew*, is announced here. The notice at the bottom, which encourages people to get their tickets in advance, implies that the St. Charles Theatre expected Booth to be a big draw.

53

Baltimore Armory, Baltimore, Maryland

Playbill, *The Merchant of Venice*

8 August 1862

Folger Playbill 261129

The Baltimore Armory was the site for a performance of
the trial scene (Act 4) of *The Merchant of Venice* by the "7th
Regiment Amusement Association" for Union Army troops
during the Civil War.

54

Mary Jo Tydlacka

Chesapeake Shakespeare Company in *Much Ado about
Nothing* at the Patapsco Female Institute Historic Park,
Ellicott City, Maryland, 2004

Watercolor and gouache, 2005

Folger Art 262099

The American flag over the stage in Mary Jo Tydlacka's
watercolor of a performance of *Much Ado about Nothing* at
the Patapsco Female Institute Historic Park in Maryland
reminds us that Shakespeare in the park—or any outdoor
venue—has become as American as apple pie.

53.

Americans from all walks of life have adopted and adapted Shakespeare. New Americans who immigrated to the United States during the nineteenth century translated Shakespeare's plays into a host of European languages. In New York, for example, Shakespeare became a staple of the Yiddish theater. The effort to make Shakespeare one's own by rewriting his language continues today; The Bomb-itty of Errors *translates the dramatist's* Comedy of Errors *into the explosive rhythms of hip-hop. Many Americans feel a personal affection for the Bard as well, writing poems about him and his work, collecting illustrations, essays, play programs, and ticket stubs to ponder in leisure hours and attending readings and lectures.*

Grace Before Shakespeare

Lord, I am thirsty; fill for me a cup
Whence I may sup.
And supping, feed; and feeding break the bars
That shut me from the stars;
And breaking bonds, reach with a growing span
The utmost level of my fellow-man;
And reaching, stoop, and feel the piteous need
Where broken hearts do bleed;
And stooping, pour libation ere I quaff
To those that laugh.

Thou Heaven, despite of my unworthiness,
How Thou dost bless!
Filling to overflow the gracious Cup
Wherefrom I sup!
Will Shakespeare's wizard wine upon my board.
I thank Thee, Lord!

Dec 27, 1913

56.

55
Charles Lamb (1775–1834) and
Mary Lamb (1764–1847)
Shekspier's oysgevehlte verk
Tales from Shakespeare in Yiddish
Translated by D. M. Hermalin
New York: Sh. Drukerman, 1912
Folger 247331
P. 37

By the early twentieth century, Jewish immigrants to
New York had established their own theaters in which they
presented Shakespeare's plays in Yiddish. Among the staples
was *The Merchant of Venice.* This Yiddish translation of
Charles and Mary Lamb's *Tales from Shakespeare* was probably read by adults, as well as by children.

———————

56
William Shakespeare (1564–1616)
The Complete Dramatic and Poetic Works
Edited by William Allan Neilson
Boston: Houghton, Mifflin Co., 1906
Helen Coale Crew (1866–1941), former owner
Folger 260939
Front endleaf

Americans' personal copies of Shakespeare's works sometimes served as commonplace books. Their owners annotated the text with comments and reactions and sometimes
pasted in illustrations or articles of interest. Helen Coale
Crew annotated her copy of Shakespeare with a poem
thanking the Lord for Shakespeare's "wizard wine" that fills
her cup with inspiration.

57
Jordan Allen-Dutton, Jason Catalano, Gregory J. Qaiyum,
and Erik Weiner
The Bomb-itty of Errors
Typescript performing text, 2000
With the permission of Lou Viola, producer
Prologue

Inspired by their high school English teacher, four students
in 2000 adapted Shakespeare's *Comedy of Errors* into the
incantational rhythms of hip-hop. Since then, *The Bomb-
itty of Errors* has been performed frequently in New York
and other cities.

———————

58
J. Woods Poinier, Jr.
Theatrical scrapbook
1872
Folger Scrapbook B.113.36
P. 1

"A thing of shreds and patches"—J. Woods Poinier, Jr., gives
this fitting epithet to his scrapbook devoted to lectures,
notices, plays, and other clippings about Shakespeare and
his works. Scrapbooks, primarily comprising ephemeral
materials from newspapers, magazines, and leaflets, were
often intended to preserve the most useful writings on the
most worthwhile subjects. Poinier confides that he, like
many others, collected these disparate Shakespearean pieces
out of "reverence for the mightiest intellectual genius
that ever lived" whose works "are destined to instruct and
amuse the children of men as long as the language in
which they are written lasts."

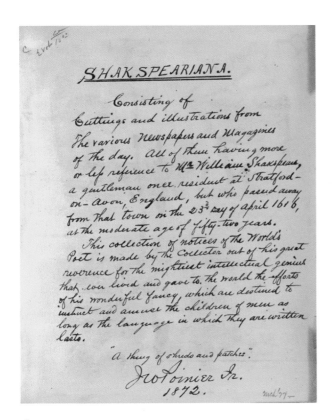

Edward H. Southern at the "absolutely fireproof" Knickerbocker Theatre. Later, he clipped illustrations of the play by the famous American artist E. A. Abbey from *Harper's* series of Shakespeare's comedies and tragedies and reused them to illustrate his own theatrical ramblings.

60

William Shakespeare (1564–1616)

The Complete Works from the text of George Steevens

Cincinnati, Ohio: Rickey and Carroll, 1864

Folger PR2752 1864h Sh.Col.

Front endleaves

Like the family Bible, an edition of Shakespeare's complete works was a prized possession, often handed down from generation to generation or presented as a gift for a special occasion. This copy of Shakespeare's plays was presented to Clara Barton, founder of the American Red Cross, at the end of the Civil War in gratitude for her efforts in war relief.

61

William Shakespeare (1564–1616)

The Complete Works [edited by] W. G. Clark and W. Aldis Wright

Chicago: Morrill, Higgins & Co., 1892

Folger PR2752 1892c Sh.Col.

Inside front cover

The bookplate on this edition of Shakespeare's complete plays indicates its service during the Spanish-American War in the War Service Library: "This book is provided by the people of the United States through the American Library Association for the use of the soldiers and sailors."

58.

59

Horace Fish

Theatrical scrapbook

New York, 1904

Folger Scrapbook B.133.36

An avid theater goer at the turn of the century, Horace Fish compiled this scrapbook of programs, playbills, illustrations, and ticket stubs from plays he attended, not just those by Shakespeare. Meticulously charting his theatrical tastes, this scrapbook maps Fish taking in play after play in New York—a geography of his love affair with the stage. On 31 October, for example, he saw a production of *Much Ado about Nothing* featuring Julia Marlowe and

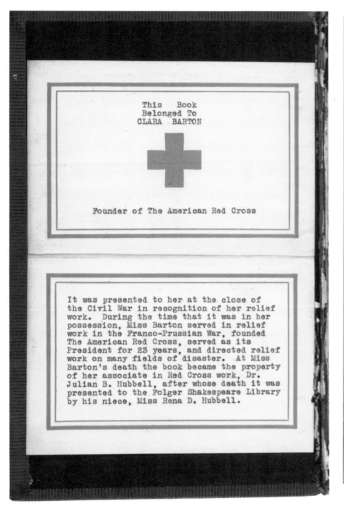

This Book
Belonged To
CLARA BARTON

Founder of The American Red Cross

It was presented to her at the close of
the Civil War in recognition of her relief
work. During the time that it was in her
possession, Miss Barton served in relief
work in the Franco-Prussian War, founded
The American Red Cross, served as its
President for 23 years, and directed relief
work on many fields of disaster. At Miss
Barton's death the book became the property
of her associate in Red Cross work, Dr.
Julian B. Hubbell, after whose death it was
presented to the Folger Shakespeare Library
by his niece, Miss Rena D. Hubbell.

60.

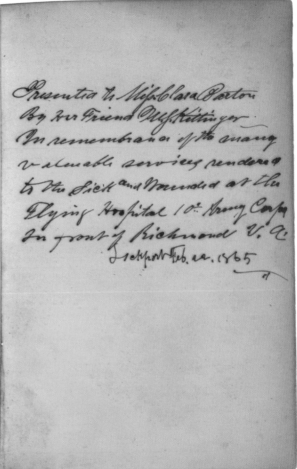

Presented to Miss Clara Barton
By her Friend W.S. Kittinger
In remembrance of the many
valuable services rendered
to the Sick and Wounded at the
Flying Hospital 10th Army Corps
In front of Richmond V. A.
Lockport Feb. 22. 1865

"A thing of shreds and patches": Memorializing Shakespeare in American Scrapbooks

Leigh Anne Palmer

This collection of the notices of the World's Poet is made by the collector out of his great reverence for the mightiest intellectual genius that ever lived and gave to the world the efforts of his wonderful fancy, which are destined to instruct and amuse the children of men as long as the language in which they are written lasts.

In 1872, J. Woods Poinier, Jr., inscribed this dedication on the opening page of his scrapbook (cat. no. 58). He was deliberate in his collecting, plainly describing his book as "Shakspeariana. Consisting of cuttings and illustrations from the various newspapers and magazines of the day. All of them having more or less reference to Mr William Shakspeare, a gentleman once resident at Stratford-on-Avon, England, but who passed away from that town on the 23d day of April 1616, at the moderate age of fifty-two years." Poinier's admiration of the Bard inspired him to devote his leisure time to clipping news articles, squirreling away mementos, and then pasting these fragments into a Shakespeare scrapbook. He called his creation "a thing of shreds and patches," a physical memorial to a man who lived across the Atlantic Ocean three hundred years before. Poinier's pastime was not unusual. During the nineteenth and early twentieth centuries, scrapbooking became wildly popular among American men, women, and children. In this period when newspaper and magazine consumption exploded, books were cheap, and everyday Americans had more access to the printed page than ever before, people of every ilk found new ways to save and store meaningful print ephemera. While magazine articles and ticket stubs were certainly cheap and disposable,[1] they remained enticingly valuable to nineteenth-century Americans. Readers treasured these scraps as pieces of information to be reread, as keepsakes of memorable occasions, and as great works of art—the best of what modern culture had to offer. Saved from the oblivion of the dustbin by careful readers, the scraps were thoughtfully organized and pieced together, telling a fascinating story of collectors and the items they collected.

Theater goer Horace Fish (cat. no. 59), for example, didn't dream of discarding his theater programs and ticket stubs. Instead, he saved them, along with portraits of actors and illustrations of the plays. He pasted the stub and program of each play he attended onto a white page of a blank book. Fish illustrated his scrapbook, gluing pictures that he had found in magazines and inexpensive, disposable editions onto bright crepe paper, then tipping those in as adjacent pages. When the book is closed, the colorful crepe pages resemble vibrant bookmarks, separating one performance from another, marking the moments in one man's life in the world of the New York theater. In cutting and pasting these bits into books, readers like Fish made the ephemeral permanent, canonizing their tastes in book form and producing original creations from old materials.

Briefly scanning a list of nineteenth- and twentieth-century scrapbooks, it's easy to draw conclusions about the tastes of the time. If scrapbooks can be understood as an "index to the popular heart,"[2] the sheer number dedicated to Shakespeare that are preserved in the Folger Library's collection remains a very real reminder of his popularity in America in this period. They number in the hundreds and are dedicated to specific actors (cat. no. 15, and 46), particular plays (cat. no. 22), the theater habits of individuals (cat. no. 23, and 59), and Shakespeare clubs in large cities and small towns (cat. no. 79). They record the many ways in which Shakespeare was a meaningful force in American life: a bellwether of taste; a social bond connecting people and communities; an inspiration, touching individuals and motivating them to create their own works of art.

Thirteen-year-old Emma Patten Beard was certainly touched by the Bard. Motivated by an interest in the Shakespeare productions of the Daly Company, Beard created one of the more stirring scrapbooks in the Folger's significant collection. Fascinated by Ada Rehan's roles—Rosalind in *As You Like It*, Katherine in *The Taming of the Shrew*, Viola in *Twelfth Night*—Beard collected portraits and news of the star. It is obvious that she felt a personal connection to the actress, so much so that she used satin ribbon, scraps from the *New York Tribune*, and paint to construct two hearts "linked by a never-broken chain." In one heart, she placed her initials; in the other, those of Rehan.

In 1942, when she donated the scrapbook to the Folger Library, Beard explained that it was her habit "to take from old magazines the pictures that illustrated plays—some being less popular than others, it was a difficult matter to illustrate them fully."[3] Piecing together her scrapbook was a pleasurable labor, one that perhaps readied her for her future career writing children's books and craft manuals. Lessons of economy learned by scrapbooking (valuing what can be salvaged and reused; transforming everyday materials into art) would be particularly helpful. During the height of the Great Depression, for example, Beard recommended in a *New York Times* article using what a woman could find for free, such as a book of wallpaper samples, to create decorative items for the home.[4] She explains, "With a sample book, some glue and a pair of scissors one may design colorful posters, fire screens, ornamental lampshades. . . . They may even be used for the covers of books."

Like Emily and Henry Clay Folger, these modest, often anonymous, scrapbook authors teach a valuable lesson: "We preserve what we value." And although purchasing costly editions would have been impossible for most of these Americans, they nevertheless paid homage to the Bard by amassing their own humble collections from snippets and sharing them with family, friends, and future generations. Their collections do not consist of rare folios and quartos but are filled with cuttings printed in the hundreds, if not thousands. However, these scrapbooks are anything but common. Each tells a unique story of Shakespeare's place in American life, and the ways in which everyday Americans were, and continue to be, inspired to make Shakespeare their own.

1. The affordability of paper and the subsequent rise of the periodical press are products of the introduction of paper-making machinery during the early nineteenth century. "By about 1813," Philip Gaskell writes, "a typical machine would turn out as much paper as eight hand vats, and productivity per employee in a machine mill was already about two-and-a-half times that in a hand mill." See *A New Introduction to Bibliography* (New Castle, DE: Oak Knoll Press, 1995), 220.

2. Ellen Gruber Garvey, "Scissoring and Scrapbooks: Nineteenth-Century Reading, Remaking, and Recirculating" in *New Media, 1740–1915*, ed. Lisa Gitelman and Geoffrey B. Pingree (Cambridge, MA: MIT Press, 2003), 207–28, esp. 214.

3. Emma Patten Beard, Letter of Gift, 29 July 1942.

4. Emma Patten Beard, "Wall-paper 'Cut-Outs': Designs are Used as Basis for Decorative Crafts," *New York Times*, 31 January 1937.

Soon after the Revolutionary War, Americans began to print their own editions of Shakespeare's plays instead of relying on those imported from England. By the mid-nineteenth century, America had a "Shakespeare industry" of its own. Ralph Waldo Emerson, Richard Grant White, and Walt Whitman, among others, lectured on the Bard and wrote commentaries on his work for popular magazines. After lecturing on Shakespeare and British culture throughout the Northeast, the self-educated New England spinster Delia Bacon sparked the Shakespeare authorship controversy (still going strong) in her campaign to prove that the lowly actor from Stratford-upon-Avon could not have written the plays known as Shakespeare's. In Philadelphia, the more circumspect Horace Howard Furness accumulated a Shakespeare library that enabled him to compile variorum editions of Shakespeare's plays, each volume summarizing the history of critical commentary in England, America, and continental Europe. Today, American scholars, joined by colleagues from around the world, practice their craft at the Folger Shakespeare Library.

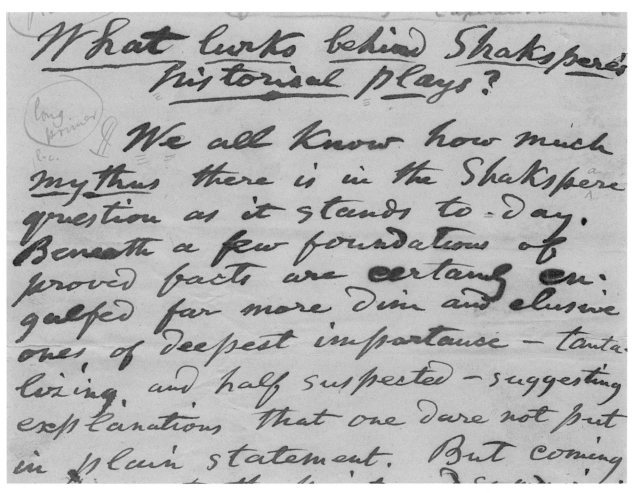

62. DETAIL

62
Walt Whitman (1819–92)
"What Lurks Behind Shakespeare's Historical Plays?"
Autograph manuscript signed, ca. 1884
Folger MS S.b.89
Fol. 1

In this short essay (published in *The Critic*, 27 September 1884), Walt Whitman argues that Shakespeare's history plays portray the predatory arrogance of England's medieval aristocracy; the dramatist's powerful critique of the feudal caste system, he concludes, might even be interpreted as the "inauguration of modern democracy."

———————

63
Delia Salter Bacon (1811–59)
Autograph letter signed, to Ralph Waldo Emerson
4 April 1853
Folger Ms Y.c.2599 (83a)

By 1853, Delia Bacon had become convinced that only a small coterie of gifted aristocrats—Edmund Spenser, Francis Bacon, and Sir Walter Ralegh, among others—could have composed the texts we know as Shakespeare's. She argued that these gentlemen then conspired to have the plays performed and published under the name of the man from Stratford. In the spring of 1853 Bacon wrote to Ralph Waldo Emerson about her theories. The kindly sage of Concord encouraged her to travel to England to continue her investigations and even gave her a letter of introduction to his friend, Thomas Carlyle. Despite Carlyle's efforts to assist her in England, Bacon became an impoverished recluse. After she was hospitalized in an insane asylum, her nephew brought her home to the United States, where she died in 1859.

64
William Shakespeare (1564–1616)
Shakespeare's plays . . . Illustrated with . . . wood-cuts . . . by H. W. Hewet, after designs by Kenny Meadows.
Edited by Gulian C. Verplanck
New York: Harper & Bros., 1847
Folger PR2752 1847c c. 1 vol. 1
Title page

Gulian Crommelin Verplanck's illustrated edition of 1847 is a milestone in American editing of Shakespeare. Verplanck included more original material than his American predecessors had, and he was the first American editor to present a chronology of Shakespeare's plays.

———————

65
William Shakespeare (1564–1616)
The Tempest (A new variorum edition by Horace Howard Furness)
Philadelphia: J. Lippincott, undated (ca. 1892)
Folger PR2833 A375 Sh.Col.
Pp. 16–17: Act 1, scene 1

By the end of the nineteenth century, Horace Howard Furness was the nation's most important Shakespeare scholar. His extensive collection of rare books and early editions (now housed at the University of Pennsylvania) enabled him to compile editions known as "variorum editions" (because they incorporated the play's varied editorial and critical history). Pages 16 and 17 print just six lines from *The Tempest*'s opening scene to make room for the extensive commentary characteristic of a variorum edition.

American educators quickly enlisted Shakespeare as a moral and aesthetic exemplar. Thomas Jefferson had advised a friend in 1771 that sons and daughters could best learn "filial duty" by reading King Lear; *a year later, John Adams lauded Shakespeare as "that great master of every Affection of the Heart and every Sentiment of the Mind as well as all the Powers of Expression." Not surprisingly, quotations from Shakespeare appeared in American schoolbooks in the early nineteenth century and, for the same reasons, in equally "educational" but less didactic writings of the period.*

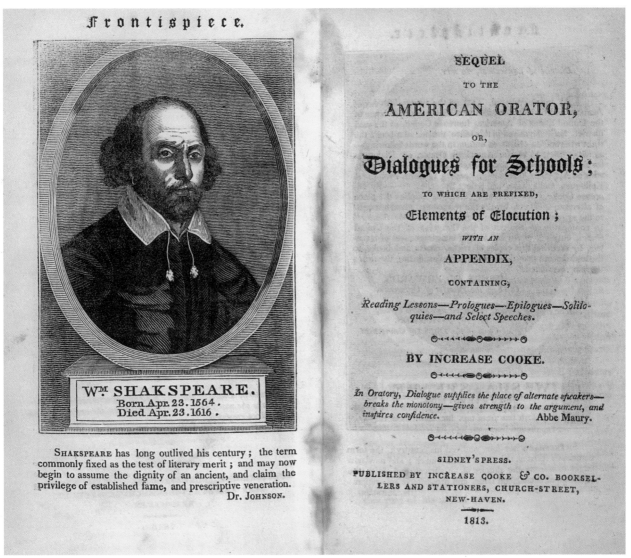

66.

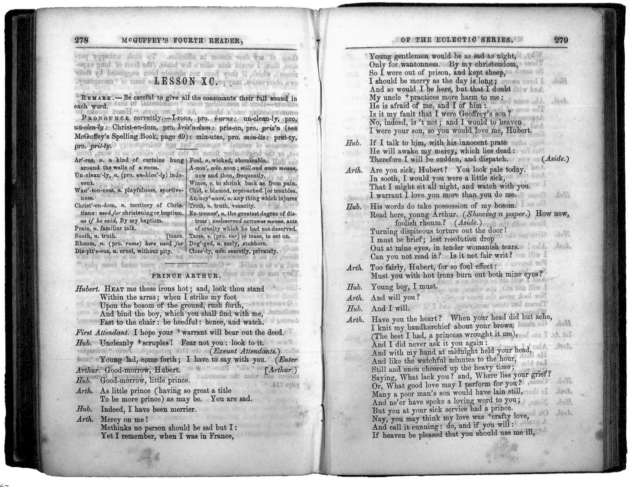

66

Increase Cooke (1773–1814)

Sequel to the American Orator, or, Dialogues for Schools

New York: Sidney's Press, 1813

Folger PN4201 C71

Title page

Early nineteenth-century educators believed that school-children should be skilled in oratory and declamation. Teachers often required students to learn passages from Shakespeare's plays by rote and to recite them effectively. This textbook by the leading compiler of oratory manuals of his era, Increase Cook, provides appropriate passages for such exercises.

67.

67

William H. McGuffey (1800–73)

McGuffey's Newly Revised Eclectic Fourth Reader,
Containing Elegant Extracts in Prose and Poetry.

Cincinnati, Ohio: Sargent, Wilson, & Hinkle, [1853]

Pp. 278–79: *King John*

Graciously lent by the American Antiquarian Society and
reproduced with the permission of the Society

As a youngster in Ohio, William H. McGuffey displayed
a prodigious memory, reciting whole books of the Bible,
as well as extensive secular texts. That skill served him well
in adulthood as preacher, teacher, and college president.
Beginning in 1836, his *Eclectic Readers* and *Eclectic Spellers*
provided generations of American youths with moral and
grammatical lessons, often with extracts from Shakespeare.
Total sales of the McGuffey books are estimated at 122
million copies.

68

Louisa May Alcott (1832–1888)

"Little Pyramus and Thisbe"

Autograph manuscript, ca. 1883

Folger MS N.a.32

P. 1

Alcott's retelling of the Pyramus and Thisbe episode from
A Midsummer Night's Dream, which Shakespeare had borrowed from Ovid's *Metamorphoses*, is a poignant romance
between a poor crippled Boston boy and a caring, wealthy
Italian girl. Their story owes little to Shakespeare's text but,
at the very least, it made young American readers aware
of Shakespeare's fairyland play. Alcott's story was published
in *St. Nicholas* children's magazine in two parts in 1883.

68.

69
Charles Alphonso Smith (1864–1924)
Why Young Men Should Study Shakespeare
New York: University Society, [1902]
Folger Sh.Misc. 1240
Pp. 4–5

Smith's pamphlet on why young men should study Shakespeare offers several answers, but two are central. Shakespeare, the author first proclaims, "completely individualized two hundred and forty-six" men and women. Since a knowledge of human character is essential to success in most vocations, "Shakespeare remains our supreme teacher." Second, Shakespeare teaches one to speak and write "clear and forceful prose."

70
Folger Shakespeare Library
Shakespeare Set Free; Teaching A Midsummer Night's Dream, Romeo and Juliet, *and* Macbeth. *An Innovative, Performance-Based Approach to Teaching Shakespeare.*
Peggy O'Brien, general editor
New York: Washington Square Press, 2006
Folger PR2987 S44 2006
Cover

The Folger Shakespeare Library's innovative performance-based teaching techniques and its *Shakespeare Set Free* publications have aided teachers throughout the United States. The content for *Shakespeare Set Free* comes primarily from the thirteen summer Teaching Shakespeare Institutes the Folger has offered for teachers. Additional curricula can be found on the Folger web site (www.folger.edu/lessonplans).

71
Elizabeth McKie
A Shakespearean Atlas; Containing the Locations of the Scenes from the Plays
Manuscript, ca. 1934
Folger MS W.b.638
Gift of Elizabeth McKie
Pp. 34–35

When Elizabeth McKie's father, a professor of literature, observed that there was no atlas in which to locate all of Shakespeare's settings, the young woman made one herself. This amateur, but comprehensive, colorful, and generally accurate compilation of maps and pictures appears to be a labor of love and was, presumably, useful to Elizabeth McKie's family and friends. On pages 34–35, McKie outlines the entire world of Shakespeare's imagination, including an inset replication of John Norwood's map of Bermuda (1626).

A MAP OF ITALY AND SICILY

Showing the location of certain scenes from All's Well That Ends Well, Coriolanus, Merchant of Venice, Much Ado About Nothing, Othello, Romeo and Juliet, Taming of the Shrew, Tempest, Two Gentlemen of Verona, and Winter's Tale.

Florence - All's Well That Ends Well - III - 1,5,7; IV - 1,2,3,4
Corioli - All's Well That Ends Well - I - 2,4,5,7; V - 6.
Antium - All's Well That Ends Well - IV - 4,5.
Venice - Merchant of Venice - I - 1,3; II - 2,3,4,5,6,8; III - 1,3; IV - 1,2
Othello - I - 1,2,3.
Belmont - Merchant of Venice - I - 2; II - 1,7,9; III - 2,4,5; V-1.
Messina - Much Ado About Nothing - entire.
Verona - Romeo and Juliet - entire, except for V-1.
Two Gentlemen of Verona - I - 1,2,3; II - 2,3,7.

Mantua - Romeo and Juliet - V-1. Two Gentlemen of Verona - IV - 1; V - 3,4.
Milan - Two Gentlemen of Verona - II - 1,4,5,6; III - 1,2; IV - 2, 3,4; V - 1,2.
Padua - Taming of the Shrew - entire except for IV - 1,3.
Petruchio's country house - location unknown - IV - 1,3.
An island in the sea - The Tempest - entire, see index.
Sicily - Winter's Tale - I - 1,2; II - 1,2,3; III - 1,2; V - 1,2,3.
Seacoast of Bohemia - Winter's Tale - III - 3; IV - 2,3,4.
See next map.

The Summer Ils
Sandys
Pembrok Cauendish Hamilton
Taken from Southampton
Stark: "A Bermuda Guide"   Warwick Padget   Smith
drawn by
J Norwood - a settler - 1618
"The still vexed Bermoothes"

71.

36

Alps
Bohemia (13th Century)
Lombardy
Milan
Seacoast
Verona
Mantua Padua
Venice
Genoa
Po R
Belmont
Adriatic Sea
Arno
Florence
Verona (Corioli, Antium)
(Porta Antica)
Antium Naples
Brundusium
Tarentum
Sardinia
Tyrrhenian Sea
An island in the sea
Messina
SICILY Etna
Carthage
Tunis
Syracuse
Hybla
Malta
Mediterranean
E. McKee

Beginning in New England in the late nineteenth century, the lyceum movement fostered Americans' desire for self-improvement. All across the nation, local clubs and societies offered lectures, discussions, readings, and other forms of popular education, often devoted to Shakespeare. The booklets in this case represent just a few of the numerous American Shakespeare societies, many of them active today. Some, such as the Shakespeare Club of Wheeling, West Virginia, were all male; others, like the Shakespeare Club of Pasadena, California, catered only to women. Whatever their constitution, the members of these societies did more than learn about the Bard; they also consumed a lot of food and drink and created entertaining traditions and rituals.

72
Shakespeare Club of New York
Constitution
New York, ca. 1854
Folger Sh.Misc. 614
Cover

Founded in 1854, the Shakespeare Club of New York was originally called the Garrick Club, presumably in honor of the famous English actor, David Garrick. This undated booklet contains their articles of association, dated December 1854.

73
The Shakespeare Society of New Orleans
Publications for the Year 1946, edited by
Edward Alexander Parsons, Master of the Rolls
New Orleans, Louisiana: By the Society, 1946
Folger Sh.Misc. 1634
Cover

This publication of the Shakespeare Society of New Orleans, a men-only club, includes an essay on *Macbeth* and three poems, all by members of the society. The pamphlet's title page quotes from *The Taming of the Shrew* (1.1.8–9):

Here let us breathe and haply institute
A course of learning and ingenious studies.

74
The Shakespeare Club, Wheeling, West Virginia
Proceedings . . . with the Address Delivered Friday Evening,
April 23d, 1875, by William Leighton, Jr.
Wheeling, West Virginia: Lewis Baker & Co., 1875
Folger Sh.Misc. 1678
Cover

The Wheeling Shakespeare Club was founded in 1874 when a group of gentlemen assembled to read *Julius Caesar* out loud. They agreed to meet weekly thereafter in hopes of becoming better acquainted with Shakespeare's plays and improving their elocutionary skills.

75
The Shakespeare Club, Pasadena, California
Shakespeare Club, Eighteenth Annual Announcement
Pasadena, California: 1906–7
Folger Sh.Misc. 1669
Title page

Founded in 1888, the Shakespeare Club of Pasadena, which restricted its membership to women, met at 2:30 on Saturdays from October to July at its own clubhouse. For their 23 April 1907 meeting, one hundred years ago, the Club's Dramatic Committee provided a program of "Songs and Scenes from Shakespeare."

76
The Shakespeare Society of Washington
"Meeting and Annual Election of Officers"
Typescript program for the 16 May 1959 meeting
Folger MS Add 1218

According to its letterhead, with the Droeshout engraving of Shakespeare from the First Folio of 1623, the Shakespeare Society of Washington was founded in 1916, the tercentenary of Shakespeare's death. Their program for 16 May 1959 included a lecture by Sydney Warren Murray, the Society's vice president, on "Shakespeare's Knowledge of French." Among the business to be conducted following the lecture was a vote on the removal of the Society's costumes from one member's residence to another's.

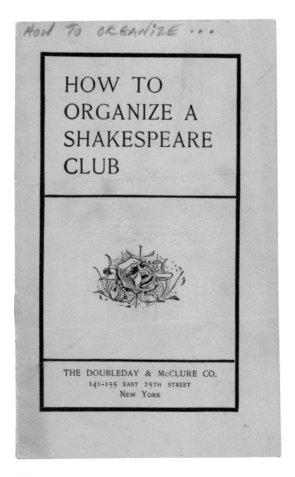

How to Organize... (handwritten)

HOW TO ORGANIZE A SHAKESPEARE CLUB

THE DOUBLEDAY & McCLURE CO.
141-155 EAST 25TH STREET
NEW YORK

77.

TWELFTH ANNUAL DINNER

OF THE

SHAKSPERE SOCIETY OF PHILADELPHIA

SHAKSPERE SOCIETY'S ROOMS No. 206 SOUTH FOURTH STREET

Lor. At dinner time
I pray you haue in minde where we must meete.—MERC. VEN., i., 1.

SATURDAY, APRIL 23, 1864
THE THREE HUNDREDTH BIRTH-DAY

——Feasts so solemne and so rare,
Since sildom comming in the long yeares set,
Like stones of worth they thinly placed are
Or captaine Iewells in the caronet.—SONNET 52.

Nor Mars his sword, nor warres quick fire shall burne
The liuing record of your memory.—SONNET 55.

1564, APRIL 26, GULIELMUS FILIUS, JOHANNES SHAKSPERE.
OBIIT ANO DOI 1616, ÆTATIS 53 DIE 23 AP.

Where euer the bright Sunne of Heauen shall shine,
His Honour and the greatnesse of his Name,
Shall be.—HEN. VIII., v., 4.

DINNER.

To. Does not our liues consist of the foure Elements?
And. Faith so they say, but I thinke it rather consists of eating and drinking.—TWELFE NIGHT, II., 3.
Sil. Ah sirra (quotha) we shall doe nothing but eate and make good cheere, and praise heauen.—II HENRY IV., v., 3.

AT 5 P. M.

Mar. By this, I thinke the Diall points at fiue.—COM. OF ERRORS, v., 1.
Keeper. Is our whole disembly appear'd?—MUCH ADOE, iv.
Lear. Let me not stay a iot for dinner.—LEAR, i., 4.

BILL OF FARE.

Which eyes not yet created shall ore-read.—SONNET 81.

OYSTERS ON THE HALF SHELL.

Cost. Easier swallowed than a flapdragon.—LOVES LAB., v., 1.
Brut. Kill him in the shell.—JULIUS CÆSAR, ii.

78.

77

How to Organize a Shakespeare Club
New York: Doubleday & McClure Co., 1898
Folger Sh.Misc. 859
Cover

"The pleasure and profit from the study of Literature increase if congenial persons meet to read together the same authors. The Shakespearean Drama especially encourages the formation of such clubs and classes by offering exceptional opportunities for instruction and entertainment." So begins Doubleday's pamphlet on how to organize a Shakespeare Club in any community. In "A Final Word," the authors urge those thinking of forming a club to write to them immediately. "The Morley Shakespearean Library with the first lessons will be delivered free." To keep the full eighteen-volume set, one could pay $8.00 (cloth binding) or $16.00 (flexible leather binding).

78
Shakspere Society of Philadelphia
Annual Dinners (scrapbook of menus)
Folger Sh.Misc. 372
No. 3: Twelfth Annual Dinner, 23 April 1864

Eating and drinking were important parts of the program
in most Shakespeare clubs across America, but nowhere
were refreshments more elaborately presented than in the
annual banquets of the Shakspere Society of Philadelphia.
This menu for the three-hundredth anniversary of
Shakespeare's birth offers an appropriate quotation for
every course.

79
The Grand Rapids [Michigan] Shakespeariana Society
Scrapbook, assembled in 1959
Folger Scrapbook 258624
Pp. 52–53

Founded in 1887 as an offshoot of the Ladies Literary Club,
the Shakespeariana Society of Grand Rapids met the second and fourth Wednesday of every month in members'
homes. This scrapbook, begun in 1959, commemorates the
society's history, as well as its members and their activities.

Jaques' explanation of the seven ages of man in As You Like It, *2.7.146–73, continues to be one of the most quoted Shakespeare passages. Two of the items collected here, an almanac and cards advertising Dobbins' Electric Soap, reference Jaques' well-known speech with visual images (reading clockwise) of the mewling infant, the boy "creeping like snail unwillingly to school," the lover, the soldier, the justice, the pantaloon, and finally, the aged figure of second childishness, "sans teeth, sans eyes, sans taste, sans everything." Calendars that provide a quotation from Shakespeare for every day of the year continue to sell today.*

83.

80
Thomas Nast (1840–1903)
Nast's Illustrated Almanac
New York: Harper & Brothers, 1872
Folger Art Vol. e106
Pp. 22–23

Thomas Nast, creator of the Democratic donkey and the
Republican elephant, often incorporated some element
from Shakespeare in his political cartoons. Here, in his
Illustrated Almanac for 1872, he draws on Jaques' seven ages
speech and shows the justice, "with good capon lined" and
the "lean and slippered pantaloon" *As You Like It*, 2.7.154, 158.

81
Edgar C. Abbott, compiler
The Bible-Shakespeare Calendar, 1916
Boston: Edgar C. Abbott, 1916
Folger Scrapbook E.4.1 pt. 1

Noting that Shakespeare took inspiration from the English
Bible, this calendar presents 365 parallel passages from the
Bible and Shakespeare's plays.

82
A Very Seasonable Kalendar for . . . 1897
Illustrations by Marie Danforth Page
Boston: Louella C. Poole and Andrea Jonsson, 1896
Folger Scrapbook E.4.1 pt. 1

Marie Danforth Page provided the illustrations for this
ornate Shakespeare calendar of 1897. The compilers
and publishers, Louella C. Poole and Andrea Jonsson,
designed the calendar "to bee used by ye manie lovers of
ye great poet."

83
Dobbins' Electric Soap
Advertising Cards: The Seven Ages of Man
Philadelphia: I. L. Craigin, undated
Folger Scrapbook E.5.1 (Advertisement Folder)

I. L. Craigin and Company offered seven collectible cards of
the "Seven Ages of Man" for customers who purchased
seven bars of Dobbins' Electric Soap (whatever that may
be!). Purchased individually, the cards cost $.25.

Despite the prejudice of their times, two courageous African-American actors performed Shakespearean roles to great acclaim before mostly white audiences. Ira Aldridge (1807–67), son of clergyman Daniel Aldridge, was raised in New York where he began acting at the African Theatre. After emigrating to England in 1824, Aldridge achieved great success as a Shakespearean actor in the provinces and throughout Europe, especially for his roles as Othello, Aaron, Shylock, and, later in his career, King Lear. Known as the "African Roscius," Aldridge received medals and honors in Prussia, Austria, Hungary, Scandinavia, and Russia. In 1863 he became a British citizen. Aldridge is buried in Lodz, Poland, where he died en route to a performance in St. Petersburg.

Paul Robeson (1898–1976) was also the son of a minister. Born in Princeton, New Jersey, Robeson attended Rutgers College, graduating as a junior Phi Beta Kappa, valedictorian of his class, and an All-American football player. After earning a law degree at Columbia University, he took up acting, appearing in two plays by Eugene O'Neill, The Emperor Jones *and* All God's Chillun Got Wings. *In 1930, his London appearance as Othello opposite Peggy Ashcroft's Desdemona shocked and excited audiences used to seeing blacked-up white actors in the Moor's role, but his finest acting came in 1943–45 in the Theatre Guild's* Othello, *directed by Margaret Webster. The production set the record of 296 performances for a Shakespearean drama on Broadway. For many, Paul Robeson was not simply the defining Othello for his generation, but for all time.*

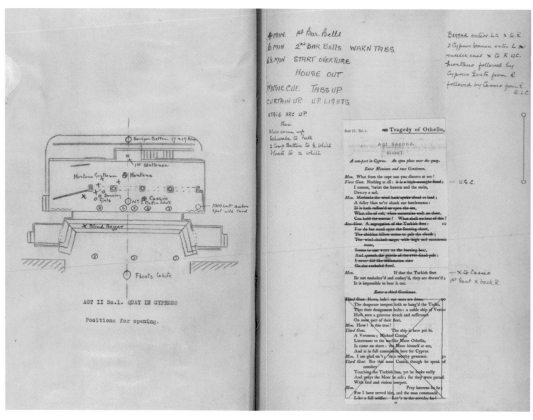

86.

84.

87.

84

"Mr. Ira Aldridge as Aaron"

London: London Printing and Publishing Co., ca. 1850

Plate from *Tallis's Drawing Room Table Book of Theatrical Portraits*

Folger Art File A365.5 no. 1 c.2

———————

85

Ira Frederick Aldridge (ca. 1805–67)

Autograph note, signed (his farewell to Dresden)

20 May 1853

Folger MS Y.c.1505 (1)

Although he was born in New York, some theatrical accounts claim Ira Aldridge came from Senegal in Africa, where he was the grandson of the Fulah tribal chieftain. In this handwritten note of 20 May 1853, Aldridge says farewell to the people of Dresden, signing his name as a "Native of Senegal, Western Africa." One of Aldridge's favorite roles was Aaron the Moor in Shakespeare's *Titus Andronicus*. As in the engraving presented here, the actor emphasizes the nobler aspects of Aaron's part—particularly his fierce determination to protect his child—and underplays the Moor's villainy. See p. 41.

86
William Shakespeare (1564–1616)
The Tragedy of Othello, the Moor of Venice
Souvenir promptbook, undated
Act 2, scene 1
Folger Prompt Oth. Fo.2

———————

87
Robert Edmond Jones (1887–1954)
Costume design for Paul Robeson as Othello
Ink and gouache, with fabric swatches, ca. 1943
Gift of James O. Belden in memory of Evelyn Berry Belden
Folger Art Box J79 no. 1

———————

88
The Theatre Guild
Souvenir Book: Paul Robeson in the Margaret Webster
production of *Othello*
New York, 1943
Folger Program Collection

———————

89
Carl Van Vechten (1880–1964)
Portrait photograph of Paul Robeson as Othello
Silver gelatin photographic print, 1944
Purchased as the gift of Virginia Mason Vaughan and
Alden T. Vaughan
Folger Art 251518

The promptbook for Maurice Browne's production of
Othello at London's Savoy Theatre in 1930 includes photographs of the seven elaborate sets. These plus the text,
marked for cuts, stage business, blocking, and cues, provide
a valuable record of what this ground breaking production
must have been like. The program for the 1943 Theatre
Guild production on Broadway also provides photographs
that suggest the visual impact of Robeson's Othello.
Robert Edmond Jones designed and lighted the production.
His sketch for Robeson's Moorish robe in the Theatre
Guild production, with "cloth slippers to match," contains
fabric swatches to show exactly what he wanted. Jones is
quoted in The Theatre Guild program commenting on the
importance of scene-designing, costuming, and lighting.
Their sole aim, he says, is "to enhance the natural powers of
the actor."

Carl Van Vechten, a cultural critic associated with several
African-American artists of the Harlem Renaissance,
turned to professional photography as a second career. This
formal portrait of Paul Robeson in costume for the Theatre
Guild production of *Othello* is a good example of his craft.

Following in the wake of Ira Aldridge and Paul Robeson, African-American actors such as Earle Hyman, James Earl Jones, and Denzel Washington have had great success in Shakespearean roles. In other arts—jazz, fiction, poetry—African-American artists have also incorporated Shakespeare into their repertoire. Here, we highlight just a few of the ways in which Shakespeare figures prominently on the African-American scene.

Office Phone - - HI. 7111
Box Office Phone HI. 7114

HOLLYWOOD THEATRE ALLIANCE INC.
(A NON-PROFIT CORPORATION)

H. T. A. MUSIC BOX THEATRE
HOLLYWOOD AT GOWER
HOLLYWOOD, CALIFORNIA

November 26, 1940.

Dear Dan,

Here I am down here helping to edit and arrange the Negro show that I wrote you about. Your swell jive Hamlet was received and very well liked by the committee---but you know show business. At the moment their feeling is that a Hollywood audience wouldn't understand jive well enough to really get it---unless it were accompanied by explanatory action---which it is impossible to devise for the solliquy. The feeling is now that if we just had the bed-room scene from OTHELLO done the same way--- the business about my love come to bed, etc., and where is the handkerchief?----that it could then be acted out. In other words jive in action---which would explain it for the uninitiated. And with a good comedian in Shakespearian costume ought to be very funny. The scene is the last one in the play, I think, Act 5, Scene 2---in case you'd like to try it. It should go perhaps up to the murder. Not more than three or four pages double spaced anyhow.....They have some pretty swell stuff for the show, music by Otis Renee, Elliott Carpenter, Will Grant Still among the Negro composers, and several white boys. Due to go in rehearsal next week, open New Year's Eve......Sorry to have been so long writing you, but was waiting for the more or less final skit line-up to evolve.

Current Productions

Sincerely

MEET THE PEOPLE - - - HOLLYWOOD
MEET THE PEOPLE - - - ROAD COMPANY
ZERO HOUR - - - - - MAYAN THEATRE

Langston

107

90.

90
Langston Hughes (1902–67)
Typed letter, signed, to Dan Burley
Hollywood, California, 26 November 1940
Folger MS Y.c.1745

In this letter to Dan Burley, a well-known musician and
theatre critic, Langston Hughes reports from Hollywood
that "your swell jive Hamlet was received and very well
liked by the committee," but they would probably prefer
"the bed-room scene from OTHELLO done the same way."

———————

91
Langston Hughes
Informal black-and-white photograph
Folger Art 261689.2

The poetry of Langston Hughes was heavily inflected with
the rhythms of jazz and blues. An important participant
in the Harlem Renaissance, Hughes captured in verse the
pain and the power of African-American music. Among
the many volumes of poetry he published was the blues-
inflected *Shakepeare in Harlem* (1942). See p. 76.

———————

92
The Federal Theatre Project
The Negro Unit in "Macbeth"
Program, 1936
Lent by the Library of Congress

In the 1930s, the Works Progress Administration's Federal
Theatre Project took major steps toward employing
African-American actors and making their performances
available to the general public. The most famous production by a Negro Unit was the so-called "Voodoo" *Macbeth*
directed by Orsen Welles and set in the West Indies. It

opened in 1936 at the Lafayette Theater in Harlem. The
managing producer was John Houseman.

———————

93
Duke Ellington and his Orchestra
Such Sweet Thunder (dedicated to the Shakespearean
Festival, Stratford, Ontario, Canada)
Reissue of the 1957 recording
Columbia Records, 1999
Lent by Rachel Doggett

Duke Ellington (1899–1974) is best known as a jazz musician and composer. He often based his compositions on
improvisations worked out in rehearsal. After a successful
concert at the Shakespeare Festival of Stratford, Ontario,
Canada, on 20 July 1956, Ellington, in collaboration with
Billy Strayhorn, composed *Such Sweet Thunder* (sometimes
called *The Shakespearian Suite*) for a follow-up performance at Stratford in September 1957. Although the juxtaposition of Ellington and Shakespeare may seem strange, both
were geniuses at performance, both took inspiration from
the artists who worked with them, and both created popular art forms that are now regarded as classics.

———————

94
Duke Ellington (1899–1974)
"Hamlet—Madness"
Facsimile of manuscript music in Ellington's hand
Courtesy of Duke Ellington Collection, Archives
Center, National Museum of American History,
Behring Center, Smithsonian Institution

Ellington's *Such Sweet Thunder* consisted of eleven sections,
each tied to a Shakespearean character. Among the best
known are "The Star-Crossed Lovers" (*Romeo and Juliet*),
"Sonnet to Hank Cinq" (*Henry V*), "Madness in Great Ones"

94.

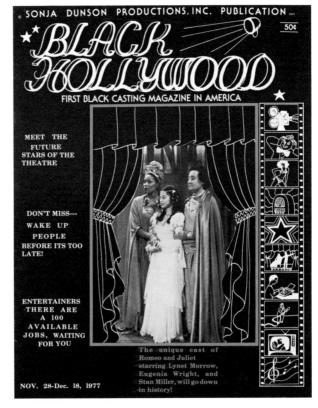

95.

(*Hamlet*), and "Lady Mac" (*Macbeth*). Ellington later added "Circle of Fourths," a number celebrating Shakespeare the artist. Because the entire piece is instrumental, Shakespeare's characters are conveyed through musical effects instead of language.

95
Black Hollywood, 28 November–18 December 1977
Hollywood, California: Sonja Dunson Productions, Inc., 1977
Folger Program Collection
Cover and p. 14

Black Hollywood casting magazine advertises opportunities for African-American actors. The cover highlights "the unique cast of *Romeo and Juliet*," Lynet Morrow, Eugenia Wright, and Stan Miller. Writing of this production at the Globe Playhouse in Los Angeles, director R. Thad Taylor notes, "William Shakespeare was the universal man who favored no race, creed, or color, but humanity as a whole, who introduced equal rights and opportunities. His theater was appropriately called The Globe."

96
Gloria Naylor
The Women of Brewster Place
New York: Penguin Books, 1983
Folger PS3564 A895 W6 1983
Pp. 102–3

Award-winning novelist Gloria Naylor (1950–) published
The Women of Brewster Place in 1981. Among the African-
American women of Brewster Place is Cora Lee, who takes
her children to see an all-black production of *A Midsummer
Night's Dream*. Enchanted by the performance, her son
asks, "Shakespeare's black?" Cora Lee replies, "Not yet."

97
Rita Dove
Selected Poems
New York: Vintage Books, 1993
Folger PS3554 O884 A6 1993
Pp. xii–xiii

Rita Dove (1952–) won the Pulitzer Prize for poetry in
1987 and served as U.S. Poet Laureate from 1993 to 1995.
"In the Old Neighborhood," which introduces her *Selected
Poems*, recalls her childhood. A voracious reader, the young
girl associates particular foods with Shakespeare's texts:
sardines with *Romeo and Juliet*, Fig Newtons with *King
Lear*, bitter lemon with *Othello*, and dry bread with *Macbeth*.

The musical comedy began in the 1930s as a uniquely American art form, and when composers and librettists decided to attach songs and dances to a recognizable narrative, they sometimes turned to Shakespeare's plays for a story line. Two of the most successful Shakespearean musicals were Kiss Me, Kate *(1948) and* West Side Story *(1957). Both adapted Shakespeare's original play—* The Taming of the Shrew *and* Romeo and Juliet, *respectively—to contemporary concerns. In* Kiss Me, Kate, *Cole Porter's feisty husband-and-wife team, Fred Graham and Lilli Vanessi, work out their marital discords while appearing in a performance of Shakespeare's farcical comedy. Leonard Bernstein's* West Side Story *moves the feud between the Montagues and the Capulets from the Verona of* Romeo and Juliet *to twentieth-century New York City, where youth gangs war over their turf and their women.*

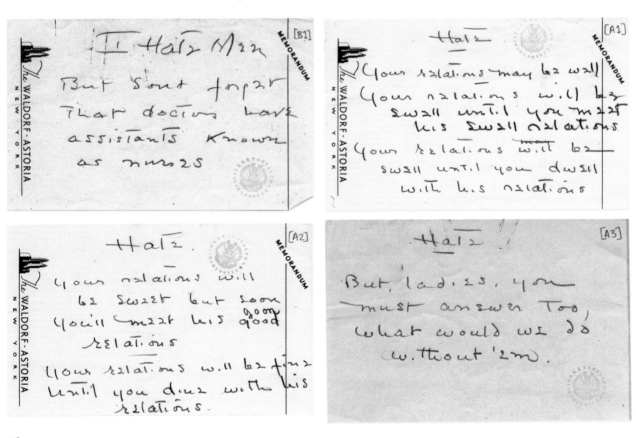

98.

98
Cole Porter (1891–1964)
Notes for "I Hate Men" from *Kiss Me, Kate*
Notepads from the Waldorf Astoria Hotel, ca. 1948
Lent by the Cole Porter Collection, Music Division, Library
of Congress

Cole Porter worked out the lyrics for "I Hate Men"—which
Lilli sings in a fit of anger at her ex-husband Fred—on
these notepads from the Waldorf Astoria Hotel, where he
was living at the time. The progression of rhymes and ideas
shows his creative process. See p. 65.

―――――――――

99
Cole Porter
List of words for Act I of *Kiss Me, Kate*
ca. 1948
Lent by the Cole Porter Collection, Music Division, Library
of Congress

This set of handwritten notes shows Porter experimenting
with different words as he works on catchy lyrics for the
first act finale of *Kiss Me, Kate.*

―――――――――

100
William Shakespeare (1564–1616)
The Tragedy of Romeo and Juliet . . . edited by George
Lyman Kittredge
Boston: Ginn and Co., [1940]
Leonard Bernstein's annotations
Facsimile copy supplied by the Leonard Bernstein
Collection, Library of Congress

101
Leonard Bernstein (1918–90)
Musical sequence outline for *West Side Story*
ca. 1954–55
Facsimile copy supplied by the Leonard Bernstein
Collection, Library of Congress

Leonard Bernstein's handwritten notes on this copy of
Romeo and Juliet indicate that he originally conceived his
musical as "East Side Story" and the feuding gangs as
composed of Jewish and Italian youths. Another document
in his hand shows how he worked out the sequence of
music—including songs and dances—for what became
West Side Story. See p. 66.

―――――――――

102
West Side Story
Souvenir program
New York: Program Publishing Co., 1961
Folger Art Vol. f182

―――――――――

103
West Side Story
Lobby card in Spanish
United Artists, 1961
Folger Art 252843

Three years after its success on Broadway, *West Side Story*
was made into a major motion picture. Natalie Wood
played Maria (Juliet) and Richard Beymer played Tony
(Romeo). Mirisch Pictures produced a wealth of publicity
materials, including souvenir programs and lobby cards
designed to reach a variety of audiences.

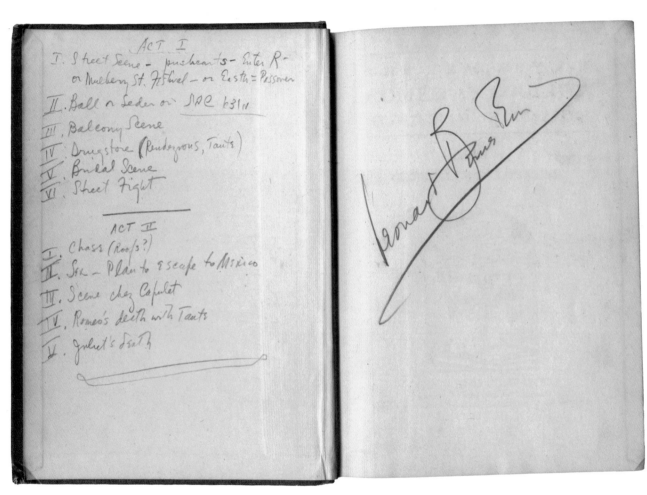

ACT I

I. Street Scene — pushcarts — Enter R—
on Mulberry St. Festival — or Easter = Passover

II. Ball or Seder on SAC b31N

III. Balcony Scene

IV. Drugstore (Rendezvous, Taunts)

V. Bridal Scene

VI. Street Fight

ACT II

I. Chase (Roofs?)

II. Sex — Plan to Escape to Mexico

III. Scene chez Capulet

IV. Romeo's death with Taunts

V. Juliet's death

Shakespeare in moving pictures, and subsequently on television, is almost as old as the media themselves. Extracts of ten to fifteen minutes from several Shakespearean plays appeared as early as 1905, and a full-length Richard III *appeared in 1912. Since then, American studios—and, of course, studios in other countries—have produced a variety of Shakespearean cinema, including filmed stage performances, made-for-television productions, and a wide range of films that borrow from Shakespeare's plots and sometimes his language. The first complete Shakespeare play to be televised nationwide was an Amherst College production of* Julius Caesar, *filmed in the Folger Shakespeare Library's Elizabethan Theatre in 1949.*

108.

104

A Midsummer Night's Dream
Typed screenplay for the 1935 film
Directed by Max Reinhardt and William Dieterle
Folger Ball Collection
Reproduced with the permission of the Max Reinhardt
Archive, Special Collections, Glenn G. Bartle Library,
Binghamton University, State University of New York
P. 17

The noted director Max Reinhardt emigrated to the United
States from Germany after Hitler rose to power. Soon after,
he joined with William Dieterle to direct *A Midsummer
Night's Dream*. This page from Reinhardt's bilingual screenplay is open to 2.2.79 where Puck applies the magic love-in-
idleness to Lysander's eyes.

———————

105
Mickey Rooney as Puck and Dick Powell as Lysander
Photographic still, 2.2.79
A Midsummer Night's Dream (1935)
Folger Ball Collection

———————

106
The Taming of the Shrew
Typed screenplay for the 1929 film
Adapted and directed by Sam Taylor
Starring Mary Pickford and Douglas Fairbanks
Folger Ball Collection

104.

107
Mary Pickford and Douglas Fairbanks
Photographic still, 2.1.183
Taming of the Shrew (1929)
Folger Ball Collection

The first American feature-length talking Shakespearean
film was *The Taming of the Shrew* (1929), starring Mary
Pickford as Katherina and Douglas Fairbanks as Petruchio.
In Act 2, scene 1, Kate and Petruchio meet for the first
time; each is brandishing a whip. The screenplay provides
directions for the humorous interaction between Petruchio,
whose whip is bigger, and Kate. See p. 52.

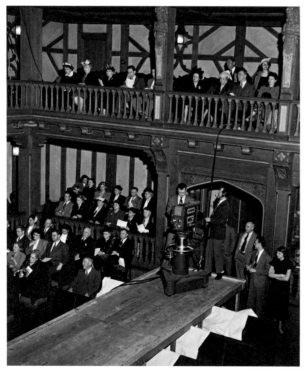

109.

108
The Amherst College "Masquers"
Julius Caesar in the Elizabethan Theatre
Folger Shakespeare Library, 1949
Photograph
Folger Archives

109
NBC films the Amherst College "Masquers" performing in
the Elizabethan Theatre
Folger Shakespeare Library, 1949
Photograph
Folger Archives

On 3 April 1949, a performance of *Julius Caesar* in the
Folger Theatre by the Amherst College Masquers was
broadcast by NBC. It was the first time that an entire
Shakespeare play had been televised. These photographs
document not only the performance but also the historic
filming of it. In order to make room for NBC's equipment,
numerous seats in the theater were covered by a platform,
seats that were given up by Folger staff members.

110
Julius Caesar
Promotional booklet
MGM, 1953
Folger Ball Collection

Joseph Mankiewicz's 1953 film of *Julius Caesar* brought
together English and American actors for a "classic
production." Seasoned veterans of the stage such as John
Gielgud (Cassius) and James Mason (Brutus) joined
Hollywood film actors Marlon Brando (Antony), Greer
Garson (Calphurnia), and Louis Calhern (Julius Caesar)
in a handsomely costumed period film.

Shakespeare mania is a nationwide phenomenon. In one of its major manifestations, the "festivals" located in small towns (e.g., those in Ashland, Oregon, and Staunton, Virginia) and in large cities (e.g., in San Diego, Chicago, and Washington DC) celebrate the Bard through frequent professional performances in more or less permanent facilities—some "in the park," some in custom-designed theaters. Ashland and San Diego launched the experiment in 1935; there are now more than two hundred annual Shakespeare festivals across the country, with a total attendance in the millions.

Shenandoah Shakespeare · Blackfriars Playhouse Staunton Virginia

121.

111

The Oregon Shakespearean Festival, Ashland, Oregon

The Oregon Shakespearean Festival Association presents . . . Twenty-third Season, 1963.

Souvenir program

Ashland: Oregon Shakespearean Festival, 1963

Folger Program Collection

See p. 91.

112

Virginia Shakespeare Festival, Williamsburg, Virginia

Shakespeare '82: Merry Wives of Windsor—Richard III–All's Well That Ends Well, July 15 to August 22, 1982

Williamsburg, Virginia, 1982

Folger Program Collection

113

Shakespeare by-the-Sea, Virginia Beach, Virginia

Poster, *Romeo and Juliet . . . Taming of the Shrew*

Virginia Beach Department of Parks and Recreation

August–September, 1982

Folger Program Collection

114

New York Shakespeare Festival

Delacorte Theatre in Central Park

Joseph Papp Presents Henry V . . . Measure for Measure

New York, 1976

Folger Program Collection

Joseph Papp founded the New York Shakespeare Festival in 1954. See p. 94.

115.

115

Shakespeare Festival of Dallas, Texas

Shakespeare Festival of Dallas Proudly Presents Richard III and Twelfth Night in Repertory . . . Fair Park Band Shell

Dallas, Texas, 1976

Folger Program Collection

Reproduced with the permission of the Shakespeare Festival of Dallas

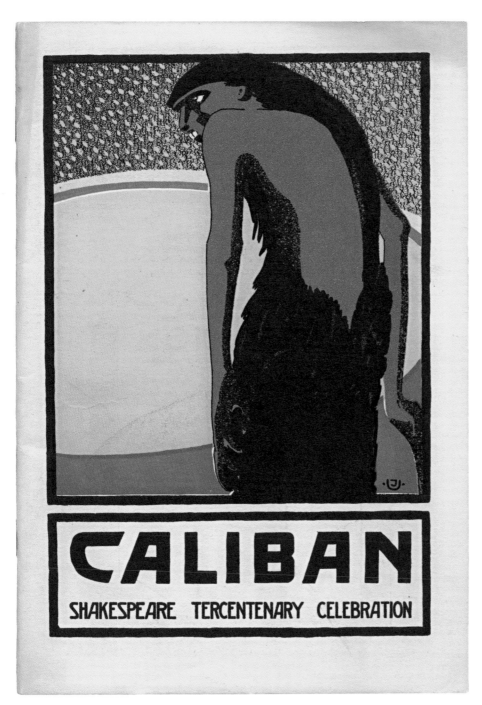

·118.

116
Shakespeare Society of America, Los Angeles, California
William Shakespeare's History of Troilus & Cressida
The Globe Playhouse
Los Angeles, California, 1977
Folger Program Collection

_____

117
The Alabama Shakespeare Festival, Anniston, Alabama
Get Thee to Alabama! Alabama Shakespeare Festival,
The State Theatre
Anniston, Alabama, 1983
Folger Program Collection

_____

118
New York City Shakespeare Tercentenary Celebration
Committee
Percy MacKaye, *Caliban by the Yellow Sands*
Lewisohn Stadium, New York City, 1916
Folger Program Collection

This special pageant brought together amateur actors from New York's varied ethnic groups for a celebration of the three-hundredth anniversary of Shakespeare's death.

119.

119
Folger Theatre, 2004
Photographic still, *The Two Gentlemen of Verona*
Directed by Aaron Posner
Brian Hamman as Valentine and Lucy Newman Williams
as the Duke
Winner of two Helen Hayes Awards
Washington, DC, Folger Theatre, 2004
Photograph by Carol Pratt

_____

120
The Shakespeare Theatre of Washington DC
Photographic still, *A Midsummer Night's Dream*
John Livingstone Rolle as Bottom; Lisa Tharps as Titania
Washington, DC, Shakespeare Free for All, 2005
Photograph by Scott Suchman
See p. 88.

_____

121
Shenandoah Shakespeare's American Shakespeare Center,
Staunton, Virginia
The Blackfriars Playhouse, Staunton, Virginia
Poster, undated
Lent by Alden T. Vaughan and Virginia Mason Vaughan

The Blackfriars is a reconstruction of the indoor theater Shakespeare's acting company used from 1608 to his death. The American Shakespeare Center features original staging practices.

By the end of the nineteenth century, Shakespeare's name and image were readily recognized across America. Entrepreneurs of every stripe counted on Americans' appreciation of Shakespeare's plays and his status as an icon of high culture to market goods and services. The items in this section demonstrate the creative ways Americans have exploited Shakespeare's name recognition in magazine articles, advertising, games, puzzles, and even food products, from the 1860s onward. The examples displayed here range from the artistic (a quilt crafted in homage to Shakespeare and his characters), to the clever ("Rosencrunch and Guildenpop"), to the mundane (Falstaff brussels sprouts or Hoff's malt extract).

122.

123. AND 125.

122
Patty Elwin Davis
Homage to Shakespeare "With wonder great as my content"
Quilt, signed and dated, 1986
Folger Art 254608

Patty Elwin Davis, whose hand-quilted and appliqued creations have been exhibited across the United States and in Japan, here pays homage to Shakespeare. Arranged around the centerpiece of Shakespeare himself, individual panels depict important characters from his plays.

123
Edward Arthur Wilson (1886–1970)
Titania, from *A Midsummer Night's Dream*
Color lithograph
John Morrell & Co., 1937
Folger Art 236215
Gift of Dorothy G. Edson

124
Edward Arthur Wilson
Calendar, "Scenes from Shakespeare. . . Titania"
Ottumwa, Iowa: John Morrell and Co., ca. 1937
Folger Art 261772
Gift of Alden T. Vaughan and Virginia Mason Vaughan

———————

125
Isabel Ayer after Edward Arthur Wilson
Jigsaw puzzle, "Ill met by moonlight, proud Titania"
Boston, undated
Courtesy of Bob Armstrong, www.oldpuzzles.com

Published by John Morrell and Company, Edward Arthur
Wilson's series of nine colorful lithographs of scenes from
Shakespeare's plays, taken from his original paintings,
circulated widely in the 1930s. They were also duplicated in
a 1939 calendar, and Isabel Ayer, one of Boston's premier
makers of hand-cut puzzles in the early decades of the
twentieth century, used "Titania" for one of her challenging
jigsaw puzzles.

———————

126
Isabel Ayer
Jigsaw puzzle, "Planting the Evidence"
Boston, ca. 1910
Courtesy of Bob Armstrong, www.oldpuzzles.com

Iago's theft of the handkerchief in Act 3, scene 3 of
Shakespeare's *Othello* is depicted in this early twentieth-
century puzzle. Recognizable Shakespearean scenes
were often used by jigsaw artists like Isabel Ayer in this
period because of their popular appeal. From 1908 into
the 1920s, Miss Ayer ran her own business in Boston
creating and selling intricately carved puzzles.

127
Frederick Heppenheimer
Advertising poster, "Falstaff Cigars"
New York, 1868
Graciously lent by the American Antiquarian Society

Defiance Cigars used this colorful image of Falstaff by
the American lithographer Frederick Heppenheimer to
advertise their cigars.

———————

128
Shakespeare Would Ride the Bicycle if Alive Today
Illustrated by F. Opper
Cleveland, Ohio: H. A. Lozier & Co., 1896
Folger Art Vol. e203
Gift of Twiss and Patrick Butler
Cover

This advertising booklet for the Cleveland line of bicycles
includes quotations from Shakespeare's plays paired with
humorous illustrations of his characters cycling.

———————

129
Johann Hoff's Malt Extract
*Shakespeare as They Are. Shakespeare's Seven
Ages of Man as They Might Have Been*
New York, undated
Folger Scrapbook E.5.1
Pp. 8–9: schoolboy

Shakespeare's "whining schoolboy" (*As You Like It*, 2.7.145)
goes happily off to school after having Johann Hoff's
malt extract.

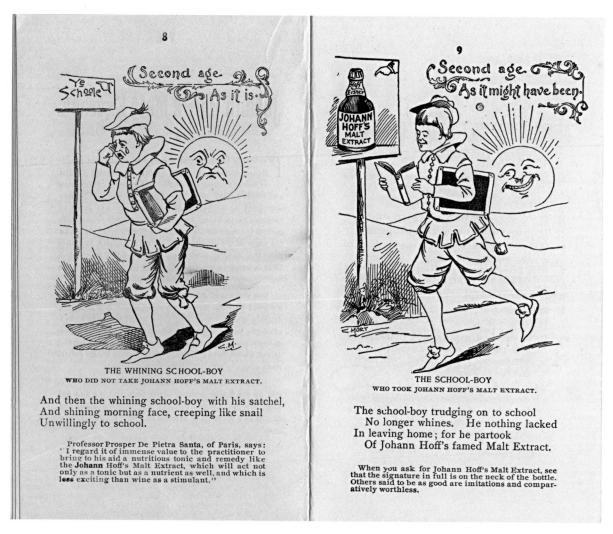

129.

130
Ray Bradbury
"Why Space . . . Why Shakespeare? Thoughts on visiting
the main rocket assembly building at Cape Canaveral for
the first time."
Friends ("distributed by your Chevy dealer")
34:4 (1977): 18–19
Folger Sh.Misc. 1880

131
Trader Joe's
Rosencrunch & Guildenpop Gourmet Sweet Popcorn,
Almond and Pecan Clusters
Needham Heights, Massachusetts: Sold exclusively by
Trader Joe's, undated

"To crunch or not to crunch?/ When that is the question, we have the answer. . . .share the sweet sensation with the people in your hamlet."

132

Falstaff Brand Fresh Brussels Sprouts

Santa Cruz, California: Packed and shipped by E. V. Moceo Co., Inc., 1928

133

Patti Hartigan

"Much Ado About Shakespeare"

Boston Globe Magazine, 26 February 2006

Lent by Alden T. Vaughan and Virginia Mason Vaughan

Pp. 26–27

"Two centuries after the morality police shut down a staging of *Romeo and Juliet* in Boston, William Shakespeare is everywhere," says Patti Hartigan at the beginning of her story. She goes on to report that during the past year there has been at least one Shakespeare production in the Boston area at any given time.

Writing of Henry Clay Folger after his death, Mrs. Folger said that he felt that "the poet [Shakespeare] is one of our best sources, one of the wells from which we Americans draw our national thought, our faith and our hope." The library the Folgers founded just one block from the U.S. Capitol continues to grow and to flourish, its collections shaped by that belief. The Folger Shakespeare Library celebrates its seventy-fifth anniversary by commemorating not only Shakespeare's pervasive presence in all aspects of American life but also the Library's presence and influence in the lives of scholars, students, performers, and visitors from across the country and around the world.

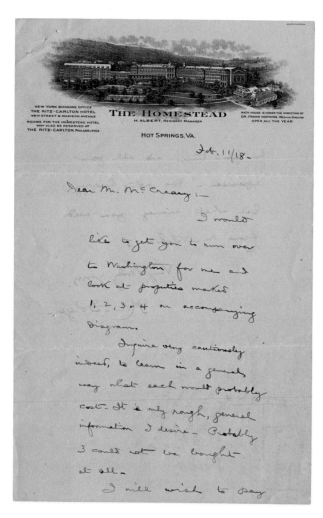

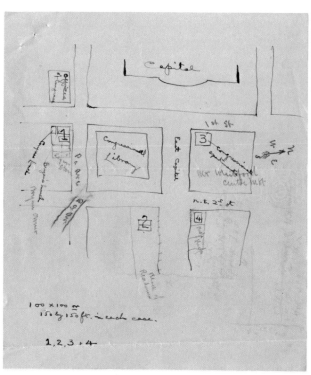

139.

134

William Shakespeare (1564–1616)

Complete Works . . . from the text of . . . George Steevens

Philadelphia: J. B. Lippincott & Co., 1875

Folger PR2752 1875k As.Col.

Title page

Henry Folger annotated this copy of Shakespeare given to him by his brother for Christmas in 1875, Henry's freshman year at Amherst. Many of the annotations are quotations about Shakespeare by Thomas Carlyle, Abraham Lincoln, Elizabeth Barrett Browning, and Ralph Waldo Emerson.

135

Ralph Waldo Emerson (1803–82)

Essays

Boston: Houghton, Osgood and Company, 1880

Folger Archives

Title page

On the title page of Emerson's *Essays*, Mr. Folger wrote, "Build therefore your own world," taken from the "Essay on Nature." Much of his early reading was on the development of moral character. Through his reading of Emerson, Carlyle, and others, Mr. Folger found in Shakespeare the values he thought fit well with American idealism.

136

Thomas Carlyle (1795–1881)

On Heroes, Hero-Worship, and the Heroic in History

London: Chapman and Hall, undated

Folger Archives

Title page

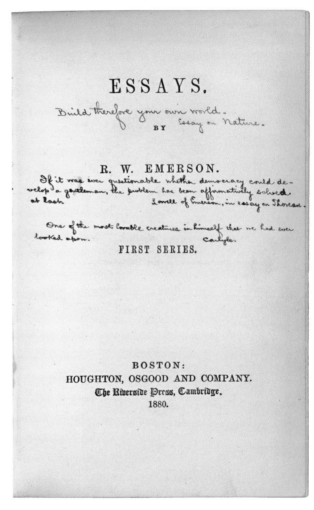

135.

Henry Folger purchased Carlyle's *On Heroes* six months after he graduated from Amherst. In Carlyle's essay "The Hero as Poet" he has twice underlined Carlyle's statement that Shakespeare is "the grandest thing we have yet done."

137
Horace Howard Furness (1833–1912)
Autograph letter, signed, to Mrs. Folger
Wallingford, Pennsylvania, 25 July 1874
Folger Archives Box 35
See p. 103.

138
Photograph of Horace Howard Furness
Folger Art File F988.5 no. 1 photo

When Emily Folger wrote to Furness asking him to set
her a reading list so that she could work towards a master's
degree in Shakespeare, he replied with some suggestions,
adding, "Take Booth's Reprint of the First Folio and read a
play every day consecutively. At the end of the thirty-seven
days you will be in a Shakespearian atmosphere that will
astonish you with its novelty and its pleasure, and its profit."
See p. 103.

139
Henry Clay Folger (1857–1930)
Autograph letter, signed, to Mr. McCreary, with diagram
The Homestead, Hot Springs, Virginia, 11 February 1918
Folger Archives Box 56

When Mr. and Mrs. Folger decided on Washington as the
location for their library, Mrs. Folger wrote, "That city is the
common capital of the whole United States; it belongs to all
the people." It took nine years to purchase the properties on
East Capitol Street and to obtain permission to use the land
for a private institution. In this 1918 letter to Mr. McCreary,
Mr. Folger writes, "I would like to get you to run over to
Washington for me and look at properties marked 1, 2, 3 & 4
on accompanying diagram. Inquire very cautiously indeed,
to learn in a general way what each would probably cost."

140
Photograph of the lot where the Folger Shakespeare
Library would be built (looking northeast)
Folger Archives Black Box 6

141
Henry Clay Folger (1857–1930)
Typed letter, signed, to Paul Philippe Cret
26 Broadway, New York, New York, 24 June 1929
Folger Archives Box 57

Mr. Folger writes to Cret about the name of the Library,
quoting from a letter he had just sent to consulting architect
Alexander Trowbridge: "We have never felt quite satisfied
that the name for our Washington venture has been the
best that could be thought of. . . . We have now come to the
conclusion that the simplest form will be the best. Let us,
then, put on the building 'FOLGER SHAKESPEARE LIBRARY.'
After all, our enterprise is primarily a Library, and all other
features are supplemental."

142
Photograph of Mrs. Folger in the Reading Room of the
Library, next to the portrait of Mr. Folger painted by
Frank O. Salisbury in 1927
Folger Archives Black Box 6

143
Photograph of the Exhibition Hall of the Library
Undated (early in the Library's history)
Folger Archives Black Box 7

144
Richard Eburne
A plain pathway to plantations (1624).
Edited by Louis B. Wright (Folger Documents of Tudor
and Stuart Civilization)
Ithaca, New York: for the Folger Shakespeare Library by
Cornell University Press, 1962
Folger JV1923 E2
Cover

Louis B. Wright, the Library's third director, established
several ambitious series of publications that included
"Folger Documents of Tudor and Stuart Civilization." These
documents comprised unpublished manuscripts and rare
books that shed light on the social and intellectual background of the period. Dr. Wright himself edited Richard
Eburne's important and scarce treatise on the colonization
of English America.

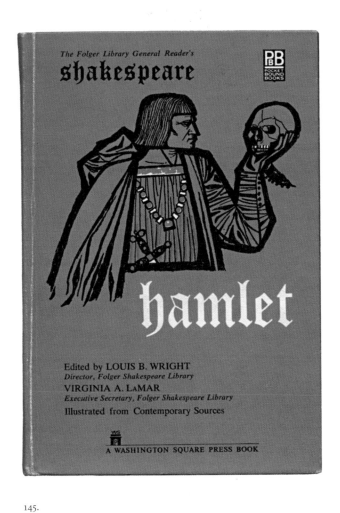

145.

146.

145
William Shakespeare (1564–1616)
The Tragedy of Hamlet, Prince of Denmark
Edited by Louis B. Wright and Virginia A. LaMar
New York: Washington Square Press, 1961
Folger PR2753 W8 1959 vol. 7
Cover

146
William Shakespeare (1564–1616)
The Tragedy of Hamlet, Prince of Denmark
Edited by Barbara A. Mowat and Paul Werstine
New York: Washington Square Press, 1992
Cover

Under Louis B. Wright, the Library began the Folger Library General Readers' Shakespeare series. These inexpensive editions of Shakespeare's plays were widely used and appreciated for their accessible introductions, notes, and illustrations from works in the Folger collection. In the 1990s, the New Folger Library Shakespeare was begun. This new treatment of the plays edited by Barbara Mowat and Paul Werstine continues the popular format of the original series. In both series, *Hamlet* was the first play to be published.

147
Virginia A. LaMar
English Dress in the Age of Shakespeare
(Folger Booklets on Tudor and Stuart Civilization)
Washington, DC: Folger Shakespeare Library, 1958
Folger DA312 F6 vol. 5

148.

148
International Shakespeare Association
Program, *Shakespeare in America*. The International Shakespeare Association Congress
Washington, DC, 19–25 April 1976
Folger Archives

In 1976, the International Shakespeare Association participated in celebrations of the bicentennial of the United States by holding its Congress in Washington, DC, hosted by the Shakespeare Association of America and the Folger Shakespeare Library. For that occasion, the Library mounted an exhibition entitled "Shakespeare in America" based on Charles Shattuck's book, *Shakespeare on the American Stage.*

149

Samuel Schoenbaum

Shakespeare: The Globe & the World

New York: Oxford University Press, 1979

Folger PR2933 F6 S3

In 1979, when the Library closed its Reading Room for renovations throughout the building, it mounted a large-scale traveling exhibition, *Shakespeare: The Globe & the World*, that traveled to six cities in the United States. The accompanying catalogue was written by the distinguished Shakespeare scholar Schoenbaum.

150

Fooles and Fricassees: Food in Shakespeare's England

Edited by Mary Anne Caton; with an essay by Joan Thirsk

Washington, DC: Folger Shakespeare Library, 1999

Folger TX717 F66 1999

Since the mid-1980s, the Folger Shakespeare Library has mounted increasingly ambitious exhibitions, many of them accompanied by scholarly catalogues. One of the most popular exhibitions was *Fooles and Fricassees*, put together by guest curator Mary Anne Caton. For the catalogue, distinguished food historian Joan Thirsk wrote a fascinating essay on food in Shakespeare's England.

151

Folger Consort

This England: A Season of English Music

Season brochure, 2006–7

Among the many programs for the public that take place at the Library are the concerts of the internationally acclaimed Folger Consort. To celebrate the Folger Shakespeare Library's 75th anniversary and its own 30th season, the Consort presents a season of English music from the medieval melodies of Chaucer's time to Renaissance holiday ballads and celebratory tributes to Shakespeare.

IRENE G. DASH is the author of *Wooing, Wedding, and Power: Women in Shakespeare's Plays* (New York: Columbia University Press, 1981), a feminist interpretation of Shakespeare, and the award-winning *Women's Worlds in Shakespeare's Plays* (Newark: University of Delaware Press, 1996). She has taught English for many years at Hunter College, CUNY, and is currently completing a book on *American Musical Shakespeare in the Twentieth Century*.

YU JIN KO is Associate Professor of English at Wellesley College. He is the author of *Mutability and Division on Shakespeare's Stage* (Newark: University of Delaware Press, 2004) and has also written numerous essays on Shakespeare as well as reviews of Shakespeare in performance. He is currently working on a book entitled *Shakespeare Across America*.

DOUGLAS M. LANIER is Associate Professor of English at the University of New Hampshire, where he teaches courses in Shakespeare, early modern British drama, film, performance, and cultural studies. He has published widely on early modern drama, Shakespeare, and Shakespearean adaptations in contemporary media. His book *Shakespeare and Modern Popular Culture* was published by Oxford University Press in 2002. In addition to essays on Shakespeare and popular culture for the SourceBooks editions of Shakespeare, he is currently working on a book about cultural stratification in early modern British drama.

LEIGH ANNE PALMER is the Research and Collection Development Librarian for English and American Literature at Johns Hopkins University.

KENNETH SPRAGUE ROTHWELL, Professor Emeritus at the University of Vermont, co-founded (with Bernice Kliman) the *Shakespeare on Film Newsletter*, 1976–1992; compiled (with Annabelle Melzer) *Shakespeare on Screen: An Inter-national Filmography and Videography*, 1990; and most recently published *A History of Shakespeare on Screen: A Century of Film and Television*, 2nd ed. (Cambridge: Cambridge University Press, 2004).

FRANCESCA T. ROYSTER is Associate Professor of English and Associate Dean for Undergraduate Studies at DePaul University in Chicago. She is the author of *Becoming Cleopatra: The Shifting Image of an Icon* (New York: Palgrave, 2003) as well as essays on Shakespeare, race, and culture in *Shakespeare Quarterly*, *Shakespeare Studies*, *Approaches to Teaching Shakespeare's* Othello (New York: Modern Language Association, 2005), *Colorblind Shakespeare* (New York: Routledge, 2006), and other journals and collections. She is currently completing a book project on sexuality in black popular performances in the "Post-Soul" era.

ALDEN T. VAUGHAN is professor emeritus of history at Columbia University, where he taught for several decades. His publications on Britain's American colonies include *American Genesis: Captain John Smith and the Founding of Virginia* (Boston: Little, Brown, 1975); *Roots of American Racism* (Oxford: Oxford University Press, 1995); and *Transatlantic Encounters: American Indians in Britain, 1500–1776* (Cambridge: Cambridge University Press, 2006). With Virginia Mason Vaughan he wrote *Shakespeare's Caliban: A Cultural History* (Cambridge: Cambridge University Press, 1991) and edited *The Tempest* (Third Arden Series, 1999).

VIRGINIA MASON VAUGHAN is professor and Chair of the English Department at Clark University. Her publications include *Othello: An Annotated Bibliography* (with Margaret Lael Mikesell; New York: Garland, 1990); *Othello: New Perspectives* (with Kent Cartwright; Rutherford: Fairleigh Dickinson University Press, 1991); *Othello: A Contextual History* (Cambridge: Cambridge University Press, 1994); and *Performing Blackness on English Stages, 1500–1800* (Cambridge: Cambridge University Press, 2005). She also co-wrote *Caliban: A Cultural History* (with Alden T. Vaughan, Cambridge, 1991) and co-edited *The Tempest* with Alden T. Vaughan for the Third Arden Series (1999).

GEORGIANNA ZIEGLER is Louis B. Thalheimer Head of Reference at the Folger Library and president of the Shakespeare Association of America (2006–2007). She has curated several exhibitions for the Folger, including ones on Shakespeare's heroines and Shakespeare for children, and has been a consultant on the radio programs and web site accompanying the exhibition *Shakespeare in American Life*. She is author of exhibition catalogues: *Shakespeare's Unruly Women* (Folger, 1997) and *Elizabeth I Then and Now* (Folger, 2003), and has published essays on Louis Carroll and Shakespeare and on the reception of Lady Macbeth and Catherine of Aragon in the Victorian period. Currently she is working on a book about Shakespeare and women in the nineteenth century.

Design:
Studio A, Alexandria, Virginia
www.thestudioa.com

Printing:
HBP, Inc., Hagerstown, Maryland
www.hbp.com

Paper:
Mohawk Options, True White, Smooth, 70 text
Lustro Dull, White, 100 cover with matte lamination

Type:
Benton Sans
Minion